ERK

FOOTBALL, FANS & FRIENDS

Best Wishes
To Kenan Kern
Erk Russell
12/24/91

THE AUTOBIOGRAPHY OF A LEGENDARY FOOTBALL COACH.

ERK

FOOTBALL, FANS & FRIENDS

ERSKINE RUSSELL
WITH RIC MANDES

SOUTHEASTERN
SPORTS MARKETING
Statesboro, Georgia

Distributed by
LONGSTREET PRESS

Published by
SOUTHEASTERN SPORTS MARKETING
P.O. Box 851
Statesboro, Georgia 30458

Distributed by
LONGSTREET PRESS, INC.
2150 Newmarket Parkway
Suite 102
Marietta, Georgia 30067

Printed in the United States of America

1st Printing, 1991

Library of Congress Catalog Number 91-61832

ISBN 1-56352-019-2

This book was printed by Arcata Graphics, Martinsburg, West Virginia. The text was set in ITC Goudy Old Style by Typo-Repro Service, Inc., Atlanta, Georgia

Photo Credits:
Jean Russell   - pages 1, 2, 3, 4, 5, 20
Clate Sanders - page 7
Claude Felton - pages 6, 7, 8, 9, 10, 11
Frank Fortune - pages 12, 13, 14, 15, 16, 17, 18, 19
Peri Parks   - inside back cover

Dedicated to all assistant football coaches throughout America.

FOREWORD

Nineteen-sixty-four was a banner year of Georgia. Vince Dooley, Erskine Russell, and I — two great coaches and one great fan — all arrived in Athens in the fall of that year.

I remember the first time I laid eyes on that fabled chrome dome. I was in the press box in Tuscaloosa for Georgia's opening game of the '64 season, having been invited by Ed Thilenius to be the spotter for Georgia's opposing teams. I was watching the pre-game drills and noticed that some strange man in a Georgia coach's outfit was butting heads with the defensive squad. Let me clarify that — he was butting his bare, bald head against their helmeted ones, and damned if you couldn't see the blood running down his forehead.

"Who is that lunatic?" I wondered.

I found out. Everybody found out. It was Erk Russell, the defensive coach whom Vince Dooley called "the cornerstone of our staff for 17 years."

What an amazing man! Great on-field coaching was only part of what he brought to Georgia. His ability to instill team spirit, to create that special magic that turned individuals into a team, was legendary.

In 1965, Georgia was losing to Tech at the half, and Erk saw some equipment in the visitors' looker room stenciled with G.T.A.A. (Georgia Tech Athletic Association). Erk shifted one of the A's, and the team had a new slogan: GATA — "get after their asses." Georgia dominated the second half and won the game, and GATA became a team symbol for years afterward.

It was Erk who came up with the Junkyard Dog theme of 1975 and '76. It was Erk who, during the national championship season of 1980, produced team shirts with the word "TEAM" in big letters on top and the word "me" in little letters underneath. It may not have been those shirts that enabled Buck Belue to throw that pass to Lindsay Scott in the Florida game, but they sure didn't hurt.

Erk loved to complain to Vince that he had kept all the talent for the offense and given Erk "the neck of the chicken," but Erk really didn't mind. He relished the underdog role, and he loved a defense that would scrap and fight. Twenty-eight times during his tenure at Georgia, the Bulldogs came back from a halftime deficit to win the ball game.

Every Georgia fan hated to see Erk leave the Bulldogs, but it's hard to hold it against him in retrospect. All he's done at Georgia Southern is create one of the greatest success stories in the annuals of college football. Starting from nothing — less than nothing — he somehow produced three national champions in nine short years.

Only Erk could transform a rainwater gulley alongside Georgia Southern's practice field into the "miracle water of Eagle Creek," and only Erk could have transformed a dormant program into a national championship.

Erk's got some fascinating memories — many glorious ones, not a few painful ones — and we're mighty lucky that he has decided to share them.

Lewis Grizzard
1991

INTRODUCTION

My story.

It's not a great story, but it's a good, positive story. You don't read much positive stuff about football nowadays. Shucks, the fact that I coached 40 years without getting fired is a story good enough to tell.

Sports has been my life for as long as I can remember. First as an athlete (and I use the term loosely), and then as a coach. I loved playing. I loved coaching. That somebody paid me for 40 years to coach is unbelievable. On the other hand, the way I coached during some of those years was unbelievable too.

Others have said it before and it is true. Competitive athletics are like life. You get out of them just about what you put into them. I never fully realized this as a player, but it struck me early during my coaching career. The longer I coached, the more I became aware that those who really worked at it were those who were winning. Great victories on Saturdays are most often the result of great practice sessions on Tuesdays and Wednesdays.

As a reminder of this, a sign hung inside my locker for the last 25 years I coached. It read, "As you practice, so shall you play." I also found that I was coaching the intangible qualities of "trying hard" and "wanting to" as much as I was coaching the basic physical fundamentals like blocking and tackling, because they are just as important.

Trying to tell the story of my great love for football and what is has meant to me has been a real challenge. I thought it would be easy until the time came to write about it. There have been so many great people, places and experiences. From the early years with my parents and all they taught me, until the last game was over, as my players carried me from the field that final contest. We were National Champions for the third time in five years. There have been some very special memories.

I'm thankful for those of you who led me, or let me lead, including the coaches, players, fans and most of all, my family. I'm going to do my best to remember right. Forgive me for those special moments we've shared that slip by this time around, but I still remember them all somewhere inside.

This book is like the game we're talking about. It has four quarters: The Early Years, The Georgia Years, The Southern Years and a section my co-writer would not let me see. It's called "From The Sidelines." We'll all find out together.

The pros, (you know, the people who are helping me with this book), are asking me to hurry so that we can get this to press. And I would like to finish before I enter the fourth stage of senility. In case you are not aware of the four stages of senility — first, you forget names; second, you forget faces; third, you forget to zip your fly up; and fourth, you forget to zip it down.

TABLE OF CONTENTS

1 *GETTING STARTED*

From where I sit, my life has been pretty simple. From the time I was 5 or 6, I loved to play games. That's about when Frank Hawkins, the kid who lived behind us, taught me to shoot marbles. Frank was good and it didn't take me long to learn I didn't want to play "keeps" with him. He went on to become the marble shooting champion of the United States. How about that? I played with a champion right in my own back yard. That was my first experience with competition, and Frank sparked it. It was here to stay for the next 60 years.

I've seen the will to win, (later to be called "a bad case of the wants"), turn an average player, or an indifferent player, into a "difference maker." A winner. "Wanting to" makes us try harder. It's simple, and to try hard is all I could ever ask of my players.

I'm not smart enough to escape the simplicity. So simply stated, I was born on July 23, 1926, in the TCI Hospital in Fairfield, Alabama. TCI is short for Tennessee Coal, Iron and Railroad Company. Just about everybody in Fairfield and the western suburbs of Birmingham depended on the TCI for a living.

We lived at 1704 Jefferson Avenue in Ensley when Frank showed me how to shoot marbles. Later we moved to 28th Street. Our house was next to "The Hollow," a small public park complete with a kids' swimming pool where I learned to swim, three red clay tennis courts and a baseball field which became a football field in fall and winter. This was just about as good as a young boy could have it. There was always something going on, but if there wasn't, all you had to do was head to the middle of the field, yell and throw a ball in the air. In no time, a game would be going.

ERK

I came home from elementary school every day, changed my clothes (we had play clothes and school clothes), and headed for "The Hollow" to play — whatever game was in season. Or whatever somebody wanted to play.

Organized sports really didn't exist at "The Hollow" for kids age 10 to 12. Most of the activities were dominated by older guys and the young'uns did the blocking for the big guys in football. The 10s and 11s didn't get to catch or throw many passes, but that ain't all bad. When you finally got your chance, you really wanted to make the most of the opportunity.

I can't tell you how many hours I shagged fly balls for the big guys just to get five cuts at the baseball. I loved it. Of course, one day I'd be one of the big guys.

I'd stay and play until dark or until Mama stepped out to the back yard and called me. Sometimes I'd acknowledge, "I'm coming," but would keep on playing. When Pop came out and "whistled" me in, I stopped whatever I was doing and ran home.

Living there with a tremendous playground as my back yard helped get me started on a lifelong love of sports and competition. This is a great example of the good fortune I have always enjoyed. I was at the right place at the right time. The time was circa 1936, and the place was "The Hollow."

The best Christmas I can ever remember was while we were living by "The Hollow." I got a J.C. Higgins baseball glove, a J.C. Higgins football helmet and an Acme tennis racquet. They all came from Sears and each item cost $2.98. Pop let me pick them out. This was good stuff. I already had a bike. Now I had just about everything a boy needed. I felt like the luckiest kid in the world.

Several years later as a high school sophomore, I went out for football for the first time. Football shoes were furnished for the top 22 players, but others had to provide their own. I was far from being in the top 22, or even the top 52, so I had to find some football shoes. Pop said new shoes were out of the question.

Billy Stewart was a senior and had a pair of shoes he had used (for about a hundred years). They were a couple of sizes too big and Billy was an inside-out walker, while I walked outside-in. He was pigeon-toed and I was slew-footed. I've never seen a good slew-footed athlete. Have you?

Some of the nails came up through the bottom, but inner soles would help. Trouble was, I didn't know inner soles existed so I used several layers of cardboard. That helped with the nails and served as a filler for the oversized shoes.

That was the bad news. The good news was two-fold. First, the shoes only cost two dollars and second, they provided one hell of an incentive for me to make the roster of 22 players the next season. (I made it, by the way.)

When I was 12, my folks moved to 1617 27th Street. It was only six blocks away. I hated to leave "The Hollow," but fortune seemed to smile on me again. Our new house was just a block from the Ensley YMCA, and that was to become my second home (or first, if measured by time spent there).

The "Y" building was an old National Guard Armory. The basketball court was pretty small which made it easy to play a zone defense at our place. Our zone wasn't nearly as effective on a regular size court.

The ceiling was extremely low. That's why my two-hand set shot had such a low trajectory, even when I moved into the high school gym and on to college.

A.J. Killebrew, a math teacher at Ensley High School, was also the head man at our "Y" and he coached the guys my age. In the summer, it was baseball. And in the winter, it was basketball. At the "Y" we became a part of a team and we had a coach. This was a new and thrilling dimension in sports for me because I really had someone to tell me how to play. And Killebrew, as we all called him, was perfect for working with kids. He was patient and gentle, with just enough steel in his makeup that we all listened and did as he told us. He was a competitor and he insisted we do as he said. He liked to win, but taught the "do rights" of things as well as the technical aspects of the games. Today, we refer to guys like him as role models. He was a great one for all of us. We loved him.

Killebrew was responsible for getting me to come to the "Y" and introducing me to basketball. What a great experience to be exposed to a new game and grow to love it as much as I loved football and baseball.

I'll never forget my first athletic uniform of any kind. It was my Ensley Y basketball uniform — plain black shorts, plain white shirt with the letters "E Y" on the front and a number on the back. I was number three and we were the Ensley Y Team and we played pretty good.

We practiced every day at our place and went to Central "Y" in downtown Birmingham on Saturdays to play league games against teams from other parts of town. I couldn't believe the excitement of team sports and my first taste of the thrill of victory and the agony of defeat. I loved it, and we thrilled more than we agonized.

Places are important and I feel so lucky to have lived by "The Hollow" and the Ensley "Y" and to have been coached by a man like Killebrew. Later, my boys Rusty and Jay would have the same kind of experiences at the Athens "Y" with one of America's truly great men, Cobern Kelly, as their mentor.

2 *MAMA, POP AND NANNY*

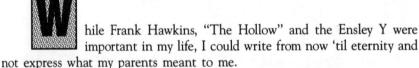

hile Frank Hawkins, "The Hollow" and the Ensley Y were important in my life, I could write from now 'til eternity and not express what my parents meant to me.

Even during the Depression, I can't remember lacking for much of anything. Oh, I can recall eating mayonnaise sandwiches for lunch, but heck, I still get the desire to have one of those every now and then. We did eat lots and lots of grits. It's been said that people in Ensley ate so many grits during the 1930s that it was common for a whisk broom to hang next to the toilet paper in the bathroom.

There was a stretch of time when Pop was cut back to three days a week at the TCI, but things got better and he returned to a five or six day week. We didn't have a car much of the time, but a lot of people didn't have one and most everything I wanted was within walking distance anyhow.

Both my parents were completely supportive of my sports activities. I guess they reasoned, just as today's parents should reason, that a kid who is involved in athletics can't get in too much trouble. So they let me play. Yet, Mama was always afraid I'd get hurt, especially when I started playing on the high school level. I suppose that's pretty normal for a mother.

I don't mean to suggest my parents never had anything more to worry about than a boy who couldn't stop playing. I'm sure times were rough for them when they experienced the worst that can happen to parents. My sister, Carolyn, died when she was 3 — a victim of spinal meningitis. I was 6 then. They clearly knew my games weren't the most important thing in the world. I'm just thankful they understood how important they were to me.

Pop loved sports. He rarely missed a game I played if he could get to it.

After I got to high school, he kind of made this his hobby. Probably because he really didn't have many hobbies as I remember.

His entire adult life, Pop smoked at least three packs of Camel cigarettes a day. He would sit for hours on our front porch in his rocking chair, feet on the banister, smoking those cigarettes and flipping the butts in the front yard. About once a month I'd rake up a bucket full. He would rock, and think, and feed the squirrels in between reading the Birmingham News from front to back. He was very much aware of the economic and political health of the world. One of his theories was that socialized medicine would someday replace our present medical system. Do you suppose he was right on course? His greatest fear was that a prolonged illness would drain all he had been able to save.

Pop had a great sense of humor. It was a quiet, subtle kind, and if you didn't listen closely, you'd miss some of it. He loved a good story. We had an icebox, as opposed to an electric refrigerator, until I was about 12 years old. The ice man came every day and brought a dime's worth. One time, a refrigerator salesman was trying to convince Pop that if he bought a new refrigerator, he could save one-third of his present food bill. Pop thought about it for a minute and then told the salesman he would take three and save the entire food bill. He did buy one new refrigerator.

Pop grew up in Morris, Alabama. Population about 100. As one of four children, how about these family names: Erskine; his brother, Tellis; and two sisters, Berlie and Eva. His father was Rufus. What a great name! I always wanted to name one of our boys Rufus, but Jean wouldn't let me. Pop's favorite cousins were Roscoe and Mally. His Uncle Eli ran the general store at Morris. Veenie and Viney were twin aunts.

Pop mostly called me "boy." When it wasn't boy it was "Bozo." He never called me by any other name — ever. He expected me to say "yes, sir" and "no, sir" when I answered adults. Once when I was 14, I forgot and answered him with a "yeah" instead of the accepted "yes, sir." The next thing I knew I was picking myself up out of the yard. He said, "Boy, you say yes, sir."

Now I'm not suggesting that as an everyday method of discipline, but it sure was a great example of communication. Communication, you see, is the most important technique in coaching, teaching and everyday living. When you show people what you are trying to get across to them it is so much more effective than when you simply attempt to tell them.

Pop was a cane pole fisherman and when he let me go with him, I was elated. I'd just about rather go fishing with him than anything else. If I knew we were going ahead of time, I'd ride my bike down to Village Creek and dig the worms. Most of the time he'd come home and just say, "Boy, let's go" and our first stop would be at the worm man's house. For a quarter, you could buy enough red wigglers to last a week. I don't believe we ever ran out. We'd usually go to Warrior River or to Turkey Creek. If we went to the river, we'd rent a boat for a dollar a day. If we went to the creek, we'd fish from the bank. I didn't care where we went, I just wanted to go.

We always stopped at a little country store on the way to pick up something to eat. Something to eat for one of Pop's fishing trips included a box of crackers, two or three cans of Vienna sausage (pronounced - Vie ee' nah) and a pound of New York State extra strong cheese. You know the kind they cut from a big round chunk. He always got a Coca-Cola, which he called "dope," and I got a "big orange" or a "big grape."

A real fishing treat was to spend the night on the banks of Turkey Creek. Pop would "swim out" a trot line, then he'd run it before dark and early in the morning. We caught lots of catfish, the biggest eel I ever saw and even an occasional bass. Those were good times.

Pop never gave me any bad advice. One bit he emphasized over and over to me made a great impression. "Boy, do something for a living that you really enjoy doing. Do something you like to do." I did.

At age 59, Pop died of cancer of the esophagus and other organs, the result of all the Camel cigarettes and a lot of straight bourbon whiskey. He didn't linger too long. The prolonged illness he worried about - draining his assets didn't happen. Yet his assets were minimal. He gripped my hand and it was as strong as ever as he labored for his last few breaths and his final words to me or to anybody were, "Boy, take care of your Ma." Then he died.

Looking back, I'm not sure he ever told me he loved me, unless it was in a letter while I was in the Navy. But, you know, I never even thought about it. There was never any doubt.

Pop took me fishing, hit me fly balls and took me to see the Birmingham Barons play at Rickwood Park ... all those good things a boy loves to do.

But it was Mama who was always there to do those everyday things a mother has to do when raising a son. When I was 4 or 5, I can remember her scrubbing my ears until I thought they'd fall off. Then she was still reminding me to do it when I was in high school. Mama had a thing about clean ears and cleanliness in general. I was well-scrubbed, which may explain why I lost all my hair at such an early age.

She's the one who got up in the middle of the night to take care of sore throats and earaches and toothaches and to see that I got off to school with a good breakfast and to make sure I had my lunch money. At Minor Elementary School, we could get a plate lunch which consisted of a meat, two vegetables, bread and a half-pint of milk, for a dime.

She'd be there when I got home, first to make sure I got home, and then to do whatever I had to do before going to "The Hollow" or the "Y." I never had an abundance of chores to perform in those early years and that gave me plenty of time to play. Thank goodness.

She always fixed a good supper for Pop and me and it was around the supper table that my parents discussed their game plan for me and made sure

I was following it. In other words, this was the time that we talked about things that I was supposed to do or be doing. It was always about suppertime that Lum and Abner came on the radio and we'd listen to each exciting daily episode on the old Grunow. The dialogue and characters reminded Pop of those he grew up around in Morris, Alabama.

A radio was big for kids in those days, maybe not as big as TV is for them today. During the warm months, I'd take the radio out on the front porch after supper and the neighborhood kids would gather to listen to "Gang Busters" or "The Shadow." Nobody would say a word except during commercials and we watched it on the radio with great excitement and anticipation.

My favorite radio program of all was Bull Connor's re-creation of the Birmingham Barons' out-of-town baseball games. I don't know how much information was coming over the ticker you could hear in the background. Probably very little. But old Bull would make up and improvise and bring the game to you in a way that made you feel as though you were watching it live and in color. I lived and died with the Barons. Unless you were there, you can't believe the importance of a series between the Barons and the Atlanta Crackers. Too bad old Bull Conner threw away such a great career in broadcasting to enter politics.

Mama made certain I was in Sunday School and church at the Ensley Highlands Methodist Church just about every time the doors opened. If Pop happened to be going fishing and the choice was Sunday School or fishing, Mama chose Sunday School for me. Later it was Epworth League at church on Sunday nights too. I didn't realize it then, but I do now. Those aren't bad places for a growing boy to be, and besides that, there were some mighty good looking girls at those league meetings.

Sunday lunch was one of Mama's strong suits. She'd usually get up early on Sunday morning and prepare lunch so when we got home from church, all she'd have to do was shove the rolls or biscuits in the oven and we'd be ready to eat. It was fried chicken at least three-to-one over any other entree. She always cooked one chicken unless we had a bunch of special company, then it was two. I got a drumstick, sometimes two. Mama chose the wings and I thought she was making a great sacrifice until many years later when I discovered the wings were the best part of the chicken. Just look at all they're doing with wings nowadays — buffalo wings, drumettes, hot wings and a whole host of chicken wing delights.

My grandmother, whom we called "Nanny," took the neck, back, gizzard and liver when she ate with us and that left the choice pieces for Pop and any company we had.

Mama's other Sunday specialty was beef pot roast and she could do one up right. Then she'd bring on the fried okra, fresh string beans, corn on the cob, hot rolls and butter (oleo) with iced tea. You know, it just didn't get any better in 1940 on a Sunday in Birmingham, Alabama.

Mama made me take piano lessons for at least two or three years, but I could never concentrate on piano lessons because the thought of playing some kind of game or ball wouldn't allow me to concentrate. Although I took piano lessons, the piano lessons didn't take on me.

I suppose the greatest heritage my mother left me was a solid foundation of "Do Right." She worked at it daily and as best I could tell, lived it herself. Don't get me wrong, there are many things I haven't done right, but it certainly wasn't because I didn't know. Mama made sure of that. She is 88 now and lives nearby. I'm 65. I see her once or twice a week and I never leave her company that she doesn't remind me in some way to "Do Right."

She's in good health, although a little hard of hearing and she has to hold on to my arm when we walk. She's still got a grip like a gorilla, and she's just a little woman. There are times when she gets up right close to me and I'll swear I believe she's checking my ears to see if they're clean.

My maternal grandmother, "Nanny," lived with us from time to time as I was growing up and I would, indeed, be remiss if I did not acknowledge the impact this great lady had on my life. She was stout and looked a little like Aunt Bea on those Andy Griffith reruns.

Her gift to me, other than the fact I knew she loved me dearly, was the example set forth in her work ethic. As a little kid I can remember when things were pretty tight and she would get up before daylight and go to Ishkooda or Bayview, or Number Seven Mines or to any of the commissaries or company stores.

She "demonstrated" any of several products like flour or coffee. It was tough for her to stand up all day, meet and greet people, then sell them something. But she was good at it and she worked hard at it. It might not have been what she really wanted to do, but that's what was available for her in the 1930s. Hers was the perfect example of "you gotta do what you gotta do," regardless of what it is, how tired you are or how badly you feel. She was a real competitor in her own way, with her tireless, energetic, "never say it can't be done" attitude. "Can't" simply wasn't in her vocabulary.

"Nanny" later became a dietician for the Birmingham School System and served there until retirement. She bought me my first suit of clothes and my first wristwatch, but her greatest gift to me was the living example of hard work and determination.

These three people had more to do with shaping my life and my future than anybody else, at least in terms of passing on to me the ideals and values necessary to get along. I felt well-schooled in that respect. Pop with his humor and philosophy about people. He was a good judge of character. Mama making certain, as best she could, that I was at the right place with the right people doing the right things. And Nanny, who believed she could do anything she had to do, just one more time.

There's no telling how many times during a 40-year coaching career that something these people "ground" into me, or maybe just whispered, helped me over the hump when the going was tough and I needed a lift. It might have been in the fourth quarter when we needed extra effort to survive. It might have been at the funeral of a player who was killed in a tragic accident when I had to stand and speak and somehow get it out. It might have been the day after a disappointing loss when we had to stop moping and get on with the next game. It could have been when I needed to provoke a few smiles with some laughter and a good story, hopefully to forget what happened last Saturday so we could dedicate ourselves to what would happen next Saturday.

My folks didn't give me just a few cards from which to draw. They gave me a whole deck. Everything was there that I needed. When I screwed up, it was my fault.

3 | *ENSLEY HIGH - "COME ON 10!"*

I was 14 when I entered Ensley High School. That was in January, 1941. It took me four-and-a-half years to get out because I flunked Geometry I and Geometry II along the way. I was an average student because my "academic attitude" was average. Mostly, I did what I had to do to stay eligible for whatever sport was in season. That and my parents' insistence that I must "apply myself." I made a whole bunch of C's and an occasional B or D along the way. I made A's when I repeated Geometry.

We were offered a good education at Ensley High thanks to our good teachers. There were two courses of study. College Preparatory for those who thought they might move on to college and Commercial for those who didn't plan to attend. I took the College Prep curriculum hoping I'd get to play football at Alabama. Pop told me when I was a senior in high school, I'd better get a scholarship because he couldn't afford to send me. He probably would have found a way, but fortunately, I landed a scholarship.

Our system of education comes under criticism nowadays because it is not getting the job done. They say some of our young people can't read or write beyond the fourth grade when they graduate from high school. As I look back, I seem to recall those fourth graders who did not read at that level, stayed in the fourth grade until they learned to read at that level. I guess we can't do that today for "social reasons," whatever that is. For most of the kids I knew and grew up with, when we messed up at school, that was just the beginning of our problems. If the principal had to take his paddle to me (yes, that was a form of discipline back then), I got it again when I got home. That was real communication. The teacher was right. Always do it his way. We were in school to do what they told us to do. Do it! Once this attitude prevailed, learning had a chance to take place. There are parents' responsibilities and there are teachers' responsibilities. Today many parents want to turn their responsibilities over to the school to perform. Do you reckon our educational system has slipped so badly, or has our parental system?

I didn't mean to get off on a tangent, I simply wanted to make the point that those who came through the Birmingham Public Schools in the late '30s and early '40s had a chance for an outstanding education. I guess you could say we had three choices. We could go to school and do what was required, go to work at the steel plant or join the Army. How 'bout them choices?

I walked into the boys' bathroom one day at school. It was during sixth period, the last period of the day. I was a junior, age 16. Right there, before my very eyes was an old fashioned crap game going on. There were six or seven boys standing in a semi-circle. The shooter was down on his knees rolling the dice against the wall. No roll unless both dice hit the wall. I got in line and waited my turn. When it came, I assumed the shooter's position (down on my knees), and pulled out the only dime I had. That was quickly covered by two guys for a nickel each. I rolled a 10. Tough point to make. With every roll I was yelling, "Come on 10." I must have worked at that 10 for at least seven or eight rolls, each time yelling, "Come on 10."

All of a sudden, after I rolled and said, "Come on ten," I felt a tap on my shoulder and a voice said, "Come on Russell." Mr. Sparks, the shop teacher, was standing over me. All of the other participants had gone. Just him and me. I'll never forget those dice. They were red with white dots. I had the bones in my hand. I was literally caught red-handed.

We went to the principal's office and it didn't take long. I was "out of here" for three days or until one of my parents brought me back with the full knowledge of everything that had happened. I don't remember anything being so difficult to explain to my folks. I just told it like it was and begged for mercy. Needless to say, they were disappointed. My real punishment was the look on their faces and Mama's utter disbelief that I could have done such a thing. I think Pop could visualize the same thing happening to him.

Mama came to school with me the next day. Mr. Sechrist, the principal, and I got it straight that there would never be any further participation in crap games for as long as I was at Ensley High. I never did that again, but I've always wondered if I could have made that 10, and I still don't know what happened to the twenty cents I was shooting for.

You know how things spread around the school. For weeks as I walked down the halls, some "buddy" of mine would say, "Come on 10," or "Come on Russell." Marvin Kallman still reminds me.

Sports have always been big in Birmingham and Ensley High always competed well in all of them. We just never, while I was there, quite got over the hump and won the championships. The "Big Five" was a tough league and when we weren't playing one another, we were playing the best from all parts of the South.

In 1942, we made a football trip to Miami by train to play Miami Senior High in the Orange Bowl. They were beating everybody in those years and although national rankings weren't in existence to my knowledge, they were considered one of the best teams in the United States.

We dressed out 25 or 30 players for the game. We were already out warming up, when their team took the field. They came on in single file and they kept coming and coming. Must have been a hundred of them. That's not so unusual now, but in 1942, that was a bunch. We stopped our pre-game warmup to watch. They were the largest, best-dressed squad I had ever seen. Even the colleges didn't dress out that good. They went through their paces like a drill team. Perfect precision and execution. To top it off, all their backs had on low-cut football shoes. None of us had ever seen low-cuts. Some even had single digit numbers and that was really different.

The precision and execution by Miami continued throughout the game to the tune of, 42-6, and we had the 6. Old timers may remember Arnold Tucker and Bruce Smith. Both played that night for Miami and both later starred as All-Americans with Army and Minnesota, respectively.

We closed out that season with Jordan High of Columbus, Georgia. They had a great back by the name of Chase Riddle. He was like everybody's All-State candidate. We had a third-team back, Hugo Linton, who weighed 130 pounds and didn't play much. During pre-game drills, their man, Riddle, and our man, Hugo, ran together as each was looking over his shoulder to catch a pass. Hugo got up and their guy didn't. Their star couldn't play and we won. There are all kinds of ways to win a football game. Hugo Linton, now a Birmingham physician, didn't play but he won the game for us.

I wonder how many accidents like that have occurred in pre-game warm-ups? I'll bet you there have been many.

Coach Claude McLain was my high school baseball and basketball coach, and Coach Buddy DeYampert was the head football coach. Both were outstanding men and successful coaches.

Coach McLain, in today's vernacular was "laid back." He never got overly angry or excited, regardless of the situation. He was extremely patient. He wouldn't say SH— if he had a mouthful, and I thought that was great. He was tall and lanky. His hands hung almost to his knees when he walked and he would cross his legs when he sat and have both feet flat on the floor. He was a wonderful person and a very good, positive influence on the young men he coached. Besides that, he was one of the most successful basketball and baseball coaches in Alabama history.

Coach DeYampert was a small, wiry guy and much more excitable than Coach "Mac." He wore very thick glasses and sometimes had trouble seeing players' numbers on the field. The story goes that somebody made an outstanding tackle during a game and Coach De couldn't make out who it was.

He asked, "Who made that tackle?" Roy Winton, a sub who was standing next to the coach said, "That was Roy Winton." The coach shouted, "That's the way to go, Roy. Great tackle." From that point on, Roy got to play a lot more!

Bernard Paxton, now a doctor in Miami, was my good friend and teammate. He was a devout Catholic and our pre-game meal always consisted of roast beef, a baked potato and English peas. That was it, no exceptions, no substitutes. Paxton wouldn't dare touch a piece of meat on Friday and we always played Friday night games. Early on, I made a deal with him, my baked potato for his roast beef. What a swap! I could get a potato at home. He was a year behind me and there were guys waiting for me to graduate so they could trade with Paxton for his roast beef.

The first game of the season in 1942, I got my first opportunity to play with the varsity. I was standing next to Coach DeYampert, remembering the Roy Winton story and hoping to capitalize, when we came up with a fourth down punting situation around mid-field. All of a sudden Coach yelled, "Russell go in there and punt." Now, I had worked with the punters, but I had no idea I would be called on at this stage of the game.

The adrenaline was flowing. The snap was really high and I made a helluva catch just to bring it down, then punted the ball in a perfect spiral, out of bounds at the 5-yard line. I was the punter until I graduated, but I never kicked one that good again.

My first real job was on Saturdays at the Sanitary Market in downtown Birmingham. I could make 25 cents an hour in Ensley at the A&P, sacking and carrying out groceries, but Sanitary paid 30 cents an hour and that was great pay in the early '40s. I went to work at 7 a.m. and got off at midnight. I got 30 minutes for lunch and 30 minutes for supper, but that didn't count as pay time.

We closed the doors at 11 p.m. and started cleaning the place, and I mean we cleaned it good. It was inspected and approved or we did it again. The final touch was putting new sawdust on the floor. The boss man would then pass out the little brown envelopes with our money enclosed. For a full day's work of 14 hours, I made four dollars and a little change, cash money. I'll swear they took out either three or four cents for Social Security. The last monthly payment I made to Social Security before I retired was $532.70.

I recently drew my very first Social Security check and my thoughts went back to the Sanitary Market. I'll guarantee you, I'll spend that money very carefully, because it wasn't easy to come by.

My buddy, Marvin Kallman, had a job at a clothing store, We got off from work at about the same time, so we'd meet and ride the street car back to Ensley. One night as I left the market, I wrapped up two huge cow leg bones and was carrying them home for my dog. The package must have weighed 10 pounds. The car that went from Birmingham to Ensley Saturday at midnight could well have been called, "Street Car Named Fatigue."

Just about everybody was asleep or nodding in anticipation of his stop coming up. I got off first. Marvin had another couple of miles to go. As I waited for the street car to pull off, I noticed he was leaning against the window with his eyes closed. I was going to tap on the window with my shank bones and wake him up. When I did, the whole damn window came out with the crash of breaking glass that fell all over Marvin. That woke him up.

I took off up 27th Street and set a new half-mile record to my house. I looked back once and saw the street car had stopped.

Marvin phoned as soon as he got home to call me an S.O.B. and to ask what I had done. I explained and fortunately, he wasn't hurt. The conductor had asked who broke the window and Marvin said he was asleep. He didn't see anything. The conductor asked who was sitting with him on the street car and Marvin told him it was Billy Campbell. Somehow, anytime that anybody in our group needed to come up with a fictitious name on the spur of the moment, it was always "Billy Campbell." Billy lived down the street from me and was a really nice guy. He just got blamed for a lot of stuff. No telling how much time Billy spent at the principal's office explaining things he didn't do.

Marvin was our football manager. He took care of the equipment and issued new socks, jocks, shoulder pads and all that good stuff to the players. If you could pick a good friend to have, the manager was the one you wanted. Marvin saw that I had the best equipment available. He and I always had new white sweat socks to wear to school. I wore mine to dances and to church too.

Fraternities were also taboo at Ensley High School, so as juniors and seniors we formed our own social group, The Esquires.

There were other groups like us, but with all the modesty I can muster, I'll have to say ours was best. All were athletes of some description but that really wasn't our common ground. If I had to pick one common ground, it would be girls. All Esquires were pretty good students. Some were outstanding. We were representatives in student government, the band, ROTC and in all areas of school and community life. Best of all, we were good friends and we had fun together.

We didn't have any smokers or drinkers. Those were the two biggest "no-nos" during that era. Then, it was so much easier to "do right" than it is today.

When there wasn't a basketball or football game going on, we'd get together on Friday or Saturday nights and do something. The war dissolved the Esquires as a social group but fond memories and the friendships go on.

Who were the Esquires and what happened to them? They were Guy Elmore, a retired insurance executive; John D. Stewart; retired from U.S. Steel; Marvin Kallman, insurance executive; Joe Stammer, pharmacist; Doug Stevens, Blue Cross-Blue Shield; Jimmy Velotos, sales executive; Rush Lester, attorney (deceased); Jack Tate, management (deceased); Bernard Paxton, physician; Elmore Scott, investments; Reginald Edwards, sales; and Erk Russell, coach.

All good people and good friends who shared some good times together.

4 | *ALABAMA OR AUBURN?*

My senior year at Ensley High School was one of the best years of my life. It was 1943-44, and many of my buddies were in or going into the military. It was a time when you thought about the war every day and knew your time was coming. Maybe we tried to squeeze in as much fun as we could, knowing we had only a year of freedom before we got drafted or volunteered.

We had good teams in football, basketball and baseball. Won a lot of games. You may remember Harry Gilmer, an All-American at Alabama and, later, an All-Pro with the Detroit Lions. Harry was a single wing tailback at Woodlawn High and his patented play called for him to run to his right and keep the ball on a sweep or jump and pass the ball downfield as he reached the corner. He did it in high school, college and in the pros, and that became his trademark.

My dream as a defensive end was to catch him in mid-air as he was passing and eliminate him from the contest. I did catch him in mid air. I did drive him to the turf at Birmingham's Legion Field, but it was always just after he had released the ball, usually completing the pass. It was Harry who would help me up and say, "Nice tackle," and go back and do it again. There were 19,000 in attendance when Woodlawn beat Ensley for the city championship in 1943. A dozen players from that one game went on to play for Alabama or Auburn. In between games there was always something going on with the Esquires. One of the best and least expensive things a group of guys and their dates could do was pitch in a couple of dollars each, rent a truck, fill the truck bed with hay and have a hayride. We'd go somewhere out of town and cook hamburgers or hotdogs. This was an especially popular activity during the winter, because the girls would have to sit real close to keep warm. Marvin, the football manager, was able to get his hands on several of those big "storm jackets" or "hoods" the team used for foul weather. Those things were big enough for both you and your date to squeeze into and that made it nice. The truck driver had instructions to go real slow, especially coming home. Oh, why was I so shy when I was 17?

I almost forgot. We had to have chaperones for such activities. When you got a date to go on a hayride, every girl's mother wanted to know who would chaperone the outing. Same for a dance or just about any function. It was always like somebody's uncle or cousin. The younger, the better, and the best situation possible was to have them drive the truck, so they wouldn't put a damper on things that were going on in the back.

As a senior, I received the annual Kiwanis Club Award as the outstanding student-athlete at Ensley High School and I still consider it one of the best honors, ever. I was a member of the chorus of "H.M.S. Pinafore," a Gilbert and Sullivan operetta, and actually had a "part" in another one. I can't remember the name.

I was voted "King of the May" and I don't remember what that meant, but the picture is in the back, somewhere.

The senior Yearbook carried this thumbnail sketch: ERKSINE RUS-SELL, JR. - (Erk)

Ambition: To succeed Coach DeYampert. Tennis team '41-'43, Baseball '42, alternate captain '43, Basketball '42-'43, Football '42. alternate captain '43, Kiwanis Medal '43, Hi-Y National Congress, "H.M.S. Pinafore," "A Waltz Dream," Acappella choir, "E" Club, "Tin Can Alley."

High School years were great years. Good friends. Good times. My dad didn't have a car, but two or three of the Esquires did. Gasoline was rationed and if you could get your hands on a few gas stamps, you could always get a ride for you and your date.

Of course, there was no TV and the only air-conditioning was in a downtown theater or the large department stores. As I look back, I wonder how one got dressed in his "finest" to go somewhere during those hot summer months. I can't even remember what there was before Right Guard.

I graduated without honors, but as I mentioned earlier, received a good high school education in spite of my "average attitude" toward the books. I thank the teachers and my parents who "made" me do it.

The war in Europe was winding down in 1944, but they were still drafting and I would turn 18 years old in July. Most of my friends were already in the service and I knew they'd get me eventually. However, I could possibly start college, get into a military program at school or even get a college deferment. Sometimes that happened.

I could go ahead and volunteer and select my own branch of the military. I decided I would start college in May (summer session), and see what happened.

The University of Alabama sent four of us from Ensley High bus tickets to Tuscaloosa. When we arrived, we were joined by several other high school "prospects." The Alabama coaches issued equipment and we proceeded to block and tackle and to catch passes. After a rather lengthy workout, Coach Malcolm Laney called me into his office and told me I had a scholarship to Alabama and I should plan to start school summer semester. For as long as I could remember I had dreamed of playing for Alabama. I couldn't believe this was happening to me.

My folks were happy, to say the least, and I'm sure Pop would have turned a flip if he could have.

Two days later, Coach Jeff Beard, a track coach at Auburn came by my house and asked me to come take a look at Auburn. I told him about the Alabama thing, but like any good recruiter, he came back with "Plan B." He was going to take two of my Ensley teammates, Russell Inman and James McDaniel, to Auburn for a visit and why didn't I come along just to see what it was like? In those days, enrollment in school was your final commitment to that college. There was no signing of a binding grant-in-aid like there is today.

I told Coach Beard I'd go for the heck of it, just for the trip. We left and drove straight to Auburn. We stopped long enough for the coach to pick up some clothes and we were off to Gulf Shores, Alabama, to do some fishing. For two days we fished and sailed around Mobile Bay, and then drove back to Auburn.

I enrolled at Alabama Polytechnic Institute (now Auburn University) in May, 1944. I started classes and began practicing football. We would wait and see what would happen in the war and with the military.

Somehow, I just didn't feel right about myself in that situation. Here I was going to school, practicing football and most all my buddies were somewhere in a military uniform. Sometime in early June, I left the Auburn campus without telling anybody, hitch-hiked to Birmingham and joined the Navy.

I was off to boot camp on June 16, 1944.

I spent two years, almost to the day, in the Navy. For me it was a series of schools. Radio school, radar school, advanced communications, gunnery, counter measures and others. The war in the Pacific ended and I spent the remaining few months flying around San Diego and Jacksonville, as part of a PBY crew. I was too big for the dive bombers, TBMs.

I really don't feel I benefitted a great deal from those two years in the Navy. I did learn there are good people from all parts of the United States. Indeed, there are some good Yankees, even though they had a hard time adjusting to grits. I wonder whatever happened to George Rusetski.

I was discharged from the Navy on June 6, 1946, and within a week, I was on "The Rolling Plains of Dixie," (Auburn) practicing football with about a hundred others recently released from the military. Some had played at Auburn in 1941 or 1942 and had been waiting to get back to the game they loved so much. From ex-colonels to buck privates and everything in between. They were there, going through the rigors of two-a-day practices and the first game was three months away.

I am certain that the same scenario was being played out on every college campus throughout this great land of ours. I don't know if all were about practicing twice a day for the next three months like we did, but everywhere the veterans were coming back to college and giving it "the old college try."

Folks, it is hot, real hot in Auburn during June, July and August, and everybody suffered. There were some guys in their late 20s who hadn't played football in four or five years. They really suffered. I was amazed at the number who stuck it out. Physically, it was grueling, but some of these guys had dodged flak over Berlin or the Japanese on some South Pacific island. By comparison, two-a-days in Auburn were a piece of cake .

Football has really changed from the 40s to the game we know today.

One of the greatest changes in football training philosophy was the introduction of the "water break" in practice. I really don't know how those of us survived, who practiced under the old belief that drinking water (or anything) during practice was a blatant abuse of training rules. The coaching staff was much smaller then and the practice sessions were often twice as long as today's. One could develop a tremendous thirst in three-and-a-half-hours of football in 95 degree weather. Fortunately, we didn't lose any players from dehydration during the late 40s, but I don't know why we didn't. On any number of occasions I can remember going straight to the shower after practice, lying down on the floor, shoes, uniform and all and letting the water hit me in the face while I drank all I could hold. Upon reviving, I'd take off my uniform and take a regular shower while consuming another gallon. Whoever invented the water break during football practice should be awarded America's highest honor for service to mankind.

Coca-Cola or any related beverage was considered to be bad for an athlete, and peanuts would definitely "cut your wind." Today, every coach will schedule two drink breaks into each practice session, sometimes three. Trainers constantly roll their drink carts to areas where players can have water at any time. The dreaded Coca Cola or such products, can be found in all dressing rooms at halftime.

Another big change is the philosophy of weight training. When I was in college, we were told, "Don't lift weights because they make you too tight." The term used was "musclebound." This theory among coaches and trainers slowly began to change during the early '50s, but weights were strictly forbidden at Auburn in the '40s. Swimming, they said, made you too loose, so we were discouraged from that activity also.

Today, we spend as much or more time in strength training activities as we do practicing the football fundamentals of blocking and tackling. Weight training has brought the game to a different level. Millions of dollars have been spent in an attempt to develop the biggest, strongest and fastest players through strength programs. I've heard many coaches say their strength coach might be the most important member of the staff, and I agree. However, the strength coach and all football coaches must be on the same page and hold the same belief that the end result of all their labor is to win games.

As I mentioned earlier, our practice sessions were long. The addition of face masks to the helmet has changed the basic techniques of blocking and tackling to some extent, but those two fundamentals haven't changed all that much. The changes which now allow the use of hands in blocking has led to a different technique more than anything else. Today, the best blockers are the best "holders."

I can remember a tackling drill which must have lasted 45 minutes that called for the squad to line up in two long lines, regardless of position. There was a line of runners facing a line of tacklers. Billy Ball, 160 pounds, would be tackling Denvard Snell, 275 pounds, if they happened to come up against one another. You could see guys way back in the tackling line counting the runners and saying, "Oh hell, I gotta tackle him." Then you'd see some jockeying for position going on so he wouldn't have to tackle that big lineman or that shifty runner. The same thing was happening in the runners' line.

Today with a different practice organization and a larger coaching staff, we can get just about all the tackling we can stand in 10 minutes. The present movement toward reducing the size of the college coaching staff is a serious mistake for a number of reasons, but I'll just give you one: the safety of the players.

Take some of your old football programs or media guides from the '50s, '60s, '70s and '80s and compare the heights and weights. You will find with each decade comes a bigger, stronger and faster group of athletes. People have asked me if the players of the '40s and '50s could compete in today's game.

Some of them could, because the size of the heart and the attitude of some player hasn't changed like height, weight and speed.

5 | *TEN LETTERS AND A BRIDE*

I played football for Auburn from 1946 through 1949. I really wasn't a very good player, but I started most of the games during that period and I played in every game for four years. It wasn't that I was all that durable, I was just good at avoiding contact.

I played end, just plain old end. We didn't have tight ends or split ends, so I was an end. In those days we played both offense and defense. Specialization hadn't arrived. If there was one particular skill I possessed, it was an ability to catch the football. Only thing was we didn't throw the ball much. I did catch 25 passes during a nine game schedule in 1949 when I was a senior. This established an Auburn pass receiving record but it didn't stand very long. Today, a fair receiver catches twice that many passes in an average year.

I guess another thing of note was my contribution to the firing of two head coaches during my football career at Auburn. Carl Voyles was the head man in 1946-47. We didn't win many games, so he was replaced by Earl Brown, who coached the team in 1948-49. We didn't win many games those two years either, so they let him go after an 0-10 season in 1950. Coach "Shug" Jordan came on in 1951 and had a long and very successful career. I would later join his staff in 1958.

I always felt we had some pretty good players on hand, but for some reason, we couldn't put together anything that resembled a winning football team. Travis Tidwell, a Birmingham Woodlawn High product, was our single wing tailback in 1946. A freshman, he led the nation in total yardage that season. Tidwell was as good a competitor and football player as I've ever been around, but he broke his ankle sliding into second base against Georgia Tech during a baseball game the following spring. Tidwell was talented enough to have been the difference between good Auburn teams and average teams. He was that good before his injury, but he limped through the next three years and so did our football team.

In 1948, the intra-state rivalry between Auburn and Alabama which had laid dormant for many years was resumed. What happened years before was that the two schools had to cease hostilities because fans were fighting in the stands and hurting each other more than the players on the field were. The state legislature passed a law that said y'all (Auburn and Alabama) will play each other again, so we did. Well, Alabama commenced to beat up on us to the tune of 55-0. The next year Alabama came into the game heavily favored, anticipating a bowl bid. We had a record of 1-4-3, so everybody expected something like the '48 fiasco to happen again. We won the game, 14-13, in one of the all-time great upsets in Southeastern Conference history. What a super way to end a not-too-illustrious football career. We finished our season with a 2-4-3 record. I'll always remember the headlines following the Alabama game in '49: "Tie Tired Tigers Trip Timid Tide, 14-13."

By the way, our other victory in 1949, was over Mississippi State. They had a tackle by the name of Jerry Clower who became one of America's funniest country comedians. I blocked Jerry pretty good that day, but I can't prove it. You'll just have to ask him.

I'm not going to tell you the overall record of the Auburn teams during my four years with the Tigers. Suffice it to say we lost more than our share. On a positive note, however, I can say that I found losing to be most distasteful and uncomfortable. I honestly believe this experience made me try harder not to lose during my future coaching endeavors. I had lost enough as a player. A good example of, "If life deals you lemons, turn them into lemonade."

I played basketball during my freshman and sophomore years. I was good enough to be a starter, but I was far from being good enough to help us win many games. We finished last in the Southeastern Conference my first year and as a result, drew Kentucky in the first round of the tournament which was always held in Louisville. Coached by the legendary Adolph Rupp, Kentucky was a powerhouse. Groza Beard, Rollins and Wah Wah Jones are names all true basketball fans will remember. They may have been national champions that year.

Realistically, we knew we couldn't win that game so our objective was to hold them under 100 points. I brought the ball up the court and the coach instructed me to use the full 10 seconds to get the ball across the center line. Then we'd pass it around in front court until they made us do something with it. We accomplished our goal. They only scored 89. I think we got 40.

The next year, we had a much better team, but still nothing to write home about. We made a trip up north to play Southern Illinois and St. Louis University. I'll never forget Southern Illinois because with 40 seconds remaining in the game, I made two long two-handed set shots. They would've been three point shots today, but they counted only two back then. That was my production for the evening, but it was enough to win the game for us. The coach congratulated me afterward for my clutch shooting. I told him that was the least I could do, since the man I was guarding had scored 20 points.

Baseball season followed basketball and I was there for a two-year diamond career. I would have been a decent baseball player if opposing pitchers hadn't been allowed to throw curve balls. I was an outfielder my first year and played first base the following season. I was captain of the '48 team, which was a weak-hitting squad. Like the good captain I was, I led the Tigers in weak hitting.

For two years I had gone from football to basketball to baseball and I loved every minute of it. I have made some tongue-in-cheek remarks regarding my playing of those sports, but this was a wonderful experience for me. I had the opportunity to play with and against some great athletes in three sports. I played in some kind of athletic event on just about every campus in the Southeast, and I got to visit places and see things I couldn't have if it weren't for the games. I thrived on the competition.

Then I made the best play I ever attempted. I talked Jean Farmer, an Auburn co-ed, into marrying me. She had grown up about four blocks away in virtually the same neighborhood. Although she was a couple of years younger than I was (now she's quite a bit younger), I knew Jean and her sister, Ann, from Ensley High School. Her brother, Jimmy, was in my class.

After I was released from the Navy, I dated Ann a couple of times. Once when I went by the house to pick up Ann, Jean was waiting for her date. She looked really good and she always had great legs. So in a few days, I called Jean for a date. She accepted, and that started it all. Her folks liked me and her dad even let me borrow their car since I didn't have one.

Jean and I were married on Christmas Day in 1948. I can't think of a better day. I can assure you I have never even come close to forgetting our anniversary. How many people do you know who can say that? Sometimes I have even made one gift fit both occasions, like a pair of shoes, one shoe for Christmas and one shoe for our anniversary.

If I make it through this damn book, and right now that looks extremely doubtful, we'll celebrate our 43rd anniversary this Christmas. I've got my eye on a nice pair of gloves for her. During winter quarter in 1949, we set up housekeeping at Graves Center, the complex which accommodated Auburn's athletes. The rent was $15 a month with all utilities furnished. My G.I. check increased from $90 to $120 a month, and Jean took a part-time job with the college making 50 cents an hour. Heck, we went to the Tiger Theater every time the movie changed. Financially, we might have been better off then than at anytime over the next 43 years.

When Jean and I decided to get married, I thought it might be time to think about calling it a career for basketball and baseball. Both sports required considerable travel and three sports called for year-around practice sessions. Here I had this good-looking bride with the great legs, so I decided to stay with football and drop the others. I did sneak in another year with the tennis team. I had lettered in tennis as a freshman.

I became a better student after marriage and I wrapped up my under-graduate work in just 10 quarters, which is the same good number of varsity letters I achieved in collegiate sports at Auburn.

6 | COACHING AND FAMILY LIFE BEGIN

W hen I completed my undergraduate program from Auburn in the fall of 1949, I went right into graduate school the winter, spring and summer quarters of 1950.

It was while I was doing my graduate work that Mr. Sid Scarbrough, director of athletics for the Atlanta Public Schools and an Auburn graduate, assured me he would have a job for me that September.

Sid invited me and Red Emmert, an Auburn teammate, to have lunch with him at the Ansley Country Club. He offered Red a job at Roosevelt High and me a place at Grady. As we were leaving, I put a quarter in the slot machine, pulled the lever and hit three plums. That paid 14 quarters. I had a good feeling about coming to Atlanta.

The summer of '52 when I returned to Auburn to finish graduate work, I roomed with Red. We were back in Graves Center again.

Red smoked Tampa Nugget cigars all the time, except when he was asleep. In self-defense, I fired one up and haven't stopped since, especially in the glow of victory. Also, during that summer Red and I would go to the gym and play half-court basketball after classes. That's where I first ran into this kind of short-stocky guy with a long nose. He was quick and could really handle a basketball. It was Vince Dooley. He was Auburn's quarterback then.

At the end of the summer session of 1950, Jean and I moved to Atlanta into the Hilltop Apartments for $59.95 per month. I went to work at Grady High School as an assistant football coach, head basketball coach and a member of the faculty teaching three classes of world history and two classes in citizenship or as some folks called it, civics.

And, I coached tennis in the spring.

With my tennis program, I had the pleasure of working with a young man by the name of Crawford Henry who won the Georgia singles championship four straight years and went on to Tulane on a full tennis scholarship.

Later he became one of Atlanta's best teaching professionals. I want you to know I didn't mess with Crawford's game while I was tennis coach, but he helped me a lot with mine.

Spec Landrum was head football coach when I got to Grady. He was a good person to work with and to learn from. We had a three-man varsity staff and I was the line coach.

After the 1951 season, Spec moved onto the University of Georgia, and ultimately to Georgia Tech. I became head football coach at Grady in 1952 and installed the "Notre Dame Box" offense, just like we did back at Ensley High. The system was so old and outdated nobody knew how to defense it. We began to win pretty good.

Two great events took place during 1953. Rusty, my first son, was born. And that fall as head coach of Grady's football program, we won the state championship by defeating Lanier High of Macon, 9-6, in my second year at the helm.

In that contest we scored first and then I'll bet we quick-kicked the ball 10 times. That's the truth and we kicked some on first down too.

I'll never forget the torrential rain. It was beautiful and we won. I was really proud of that team as I was all the teams I coached from 1950-57.

I believe our record while I was head coach for those six seasons was 42 wins, 14 defeats and three ties.

I remember that championship game for another good reason: our kicker and fullback, Wilbur Lofton, forgot his shoes and had to borrow a pair from my assistant. We didn't take too much time reasoning out why he forgot his cleats, and the assistant coach was proud his shoes had done such a great job of kicking.

Don't forget, I was about 25 years old when I got that head coaching job. So there was a lot of learning for me to do. When you are young, you just do things that look tough or daring or mighty. Shoot, what I did at Grady I did because I loved the game and the players and the time it took me to get things done.

It might be interesting to note when I was assistant coach and head coach at Grady High School, there were no special privileges offered to those positions.

I still taught a full load of classes in addition to directing the sports program. Not only that, but outside of Grady, I kept pretty busy trying to earn an extra dollar.

For instance, I officiated basketball games through the YMCA on Saturdays. I would call games two nights a week for the city recreation department down near the State Capitol. That section of town wasn't a desirable place to be even in 1955.

In an old gym down there on Tuesdays and Thursdays, I'd "ref" two games each night, sometimes three, for two dollars a contest. This was an adult basketball league, and was a pretty good job for one official to handle especially when the Syrians and the Greeks played.

It was just downright mayhem. They'd get after one another something fierce. I learned to throw the ball up to start the game, back off and let them have at it.

Two dollars a game, two games a night wasn't very much money. But it was something. I thought that was pretty good at that time

By the way, while we're going through all the things I was involved in back at Grady, I recall vividly the first month's paycheck I ever received from the Atlanta School System. It was $188.50.

That was when Jean and I lived in those Hilltop Apartments and it was just the two of us.

Later on in 1953 when Rusty was born, we bought our first house. We paid $13,200. Our payments were a little more than $59.95, which was what our rent was each month. Interest at that time was four percent and we had 30 years to pay for it.

Of course, those were the days when Jean and I could go to the grocery store and buy $10 worth of goods and have to make two trips to the car to get all the packages. Going to the movie cost a quarter. A soft drink was a nickel. Gas was about 35 cents a gallon.

But still it took my working some of those extra jobs to keep things going, particularly after we started our family.

As I have mentioned, being head coach or a winning coach of a good high school didn't offer any privileges. I didn't think anything about those extra jobs on the side. I still don't. I was happy with everything except losing a ball game. I had a great wife, I was involved in a good sports program and that's what I wanted.

I guess the best way to say it is that I loved what I was doing. It was exactly what I wanted to do and I just couldn't believe someone would pay me for that.

Grady was the top academic high school in Atlanta. It was a first-class operation. First there was R.W. Stephens as principal, then Roger Derthick. Both were top-notch educators, so both realized the importance of a good athletic program.

All in all those were good days when I was at Grady.

Let me stop right here, while I talk about those days and say how much my wife Jean has meant to me first as a fine person, but also as someone who just understood what coaching is all about. From the very beginning she made it possible for me to put coaching first. And my success in this profession can be attributed to her being a great coach's wife.

There are the practices, watching game films, having meetings, teaching classes and going back at night and thinking about the forthcoming contest. When you play on Friday night, you scout on Thursdays and Saturdays.

Jean always understood those things. And my success as a coach is shared with her. I never left for a game or to go on the road without knowing things were right at home in her role as a wife and mother.

She let me decide when I wanted to make a career move. Of course, we would talk it over. She always said, "You're the one who's doing the work. And if you're happy, I'll be happy."

It was in 1957, that I coached my last football season at Grady. We had an undefeated regular season. The next year I was at Auburn University as varsity coach for baseball and head coach for the freshmen football team. In those times the freshmen couldn't play varsity ball. They had their own three-game schedule. The freshmen team put on the picture for the varsity, like the scout team does today.

In June, 1958, Jean and I and our two sons, Rusty and Don, moved to Auburn at the invitation of Jeff Beard who had recruited me from Ensley High School. Coach Beard was now athletic director.

There I was back at my alma mater, involved with a major football program at the university level. I had a great wife and a fine family and another boy, Jay, was born in Auburn in 1959.

I mentioned earlier, that Rusty was born in 1953. Don was born in 1956 and then Jay in '59.

In 1960, the toughest experience that has ever taken place in my life right up to this moment happened when Jean and I lost our middle son Don in a tragic accident. He was 3.

Rusty and I had gone fishing. It was the week before Easter Sunday.

There were a couple of small ponds located on a golf course there in Auburn and the fish bit pretty good. Like my dad had taken me fishing many times, I began sharing that same experience with Rusty.

Don stayed home with Jean and Jay. Jay was small, just beginning to walk. In fact he and his mother were in the front yard that afternoon letting Jay do the things little kids do.

Our backyard was sort of a playground for the boys. We had an old tire swing they liked a lot. It had provided so many rides, the tire was dragging the ground. So I cut off the tire and tied the rope over the tree branch which had served as the axle for those many good trips in the air.

Jean went to check on Don and found him hanging from the rope. By the time Jean got to Don, it was too late. His little blue car which he had used to reach up for what had been planned as a fun swing, was still sitting there.

How our son got tangled up in the rope so quickly, we'll never know.

Hal Herring, defensive coordinator at Auburn and a good friend of mine, came out to where I was fishing with Rusty and said, "Erk, something bad has happened." I asked him how bad. And all he could say, was "Real bad, Erk. Real bad."

I drove straight to the hospital. There in the emergency room, I said goodbye to Don.

I still don't know and I don't think anybody knows how you get through a situation like that. And I'll be the first to admit that for a period of time I wandered in the wilderness. But I had a job I had to do and that kept me busy.

Coaching was something I loved to do, plus a good wife and two other sons. Those things were my salvation in terms of being able to get over the hump.

It was tough.

So many good friends helped, too. John Moulton, an former Auburn teammate, was there when I needed him. I appreciated that.

There was a period of time when I wondered, "What's this all about?"

We always ask why? Why Don? Which is not a good thing to do. It's something you have to fight your way through.

And then time. Thank God for time. Time seemed to be the great healer.

Jean and I worked together on this. It was 10 years from that tough experience. We had just lost to Tech for the first time since we'd been at Georgia. It was a hard loss, 6-0.

That evening the Georgia coaches and others were sitting around not happy at all, like there would be no tomorrows, when my wife said, "Y'all shouldn't act this way about losing a football game. This is not the worst thing that can happen. I lost a son."

This seemed to put the Georgia Tech loss in its proper perspective for all who were present!

7 DEFENSE: MY SIDE OF THE BALL

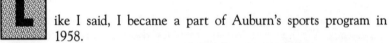

Like I said, I became a part of Auburn's sports program in 1958.

Just the year before, the Tigers had whipped everybody and won a national championship. They were tough and on a roll. Football — I mean the kind fans liked to watch — was being played at Auburn.

That same year on the other side of the state, the University of Alabama hired a new coach. His name was Paul "Bear" Bryant. He had been brought in to try to even things out as far as football was concerned. "The Bear" went to Alabama the same year I went to Auburn. Which school do you think got the "impact coach?"

In '57, Auburn cleaned every team's platter, including the University of Alabama's. In 1958, Auburn went nine wins and one tie and with just one year at the University of Alabama helm, "the Bear" gave us fits. It was a sign of the Tide beginning to turn.

In 1958, Auburn was put on a five-year probation keeping us out of post-season play.

From the fall of 1958 to 1962, I was varsity baseball coach. Additionally, I was freshman football coach three of those years and was promoted to defensive end coach for the varsity my final two years.

In 1961 Joel Eaves, who had been coaching the defensive ends and scouting, decided to devote his full-time duties to Auburn basketball. That was when Coach Shug Jordan asked me to take over Eaves' duties and Dooley, who was the quarterback coach at that time, became freshmen coach.

I suppose I might say this was the real beginning of my working primarily with the defensive side of the ball. The rest of my career as an assistant coach was on defense — stopping the opponent.

Auburn was the second stop in my coaching career and those five years I spent there provided great learning experiences. A major college position, a fine staff led by Coach "Shug" Jordan, an opportunity to work with great athletes and a winning tradition.

Every day I felt like I learned something new. One such experience took place in 1959 in Athens, Georgia.

We were playing the Bulldogs. We score. Making it Auburn 12, Georgia 7. We're in the fourth quarter.

When we went in for that touchdown, our coach on the sidelines threw down his headset and ran toward the end zone where the action had taken place.

I was doing all I could to talk to somebody down there telling them to go for two. "Go for two." Twelve is just as good as 13.

But I was talking to nobody. We lined up to kick the extra point.

As luck would have it, Georgia jumped off sides. Now the ball was on the one and a half yard line. Surely we would go for two now.

We kicked the extra point.

Now the score was us 13, them seven.

With just a few minutes left to play. We fumbled, they recovered. This kid by the name of Fran Tarkenton from Georgia threw a pass to Bill Herron for six. They kicked the extra point and go on to win the game, 14-13, and the Southeastern Conference Championship.

This was a learning experience. I learned there is no purpose in having a couple of coaches in the pressbox if there is no one on the sidelines listening to them. That Southeastern Conference Championship might have been Auburn's, instead of one of Georgia's finest hours.

Another learning experience at Auburn was when haircuts went up to a dollar. The barber spent more time trimming the hair in my nose and ears than he did in cutting the hair on my head. It was at this time I decided a dollar was too much to pay for this service. So, I purchased some barber shears and from that point on I began styling my own hair.

I was in the Atlanta airport in 1963 headed for the American Football Coaches annual meeting in Dallas, when I was paged. I had a phone call. It was Jack Green who had recently become the new head football coach at Vanderbilt. He wanted me to come to Nashville and discuss the possibility of becoming his defensive coordinator.

Right there, I got on an airplane to Nashville and in two days, I was the defensive coordinator at Vanderbilt.

That year was as long a season as I've ever spent, because we had a 1-7-2 record. On the flip side of that coin, the good thing was I had a job of coordinating the defense at Vandy and the opportunity to work with a great group of kids. All of them made over a thousand on the Scholastic Aptitude

Test and were in the top half of their high school classes. These were Vanderbilt's requirements at that time.

Talk about effort. Those guys gave it to us. They just couldn't run and jump good enough to win many games. We played a lot of people close. But we weren't good enough to get over the hump and win.

Jack Green was one of the nicest guys I've ever had the pleasure of being around. He certainly deserved a better record than we were able to achieve.

Recruiting at Vanderbilt means recruiting the world because of those high entrance requirements.

"Baby" Ray, head recruiter and long-time great center for the Green Bay Packers, called me in and said, "Russell, you are going to Cincinnati." So I flew to Cincinnati to visit a number of high schools.

When I landed it was snowing.

I rented a car and started driving. The further I went the harder it snowed. I have never seen so much snow in all my life.

Sometimes a person just has to take a situation into his hands. And I did. I pulled into the first decent looking motel I could find and parked that car. For the next three days I didn't move.

I had never driven in snow and I was scared to death.

My motel was right next door to a Fritch's Big Boy Restaurant. During those 72 hours, I never ate so many Big Boy hamburgers in all my life. But I wasn't about to venture out into strange country in all that snow. When the snow melted I left the motel in search of football talent.

It was during this talent search that I visited Moeller High School coached by Jerry Faust, who would later become head coach at Notre Dame. This was new and different but a very valuable recruiting experience for me, although I still prefer not to drive in the snow.

On the day President Kennedy was assassinated, Jack Green and I were on a recruiting trip to the Atlanta area, more specifically to go to Cedartown High School to see if an outstanding tackle, Edgar Chandler, might be interested in Vanderbilt. Cedartown was coached by "Doc" Ayers, who was a very successful high school coach and one whom I had known for years.

We came back from seeing "Doc" and our next game was with George Washington University, Jackie Kennedy's alma mater. There was a good possibility the game would be cancelled because of this connection.

Fortunately for us, the game went on and it was our only victory of the season.

The next month Jack and I revisited "Doc" and Cedartown High School, still thinking about Edgar Chandler. When we walked into "Doc's" office he asked us if we had heard that the University of Georgia had a new head football coach. We told him we had not. Who was it?

"Doc" said he didn't know the guy. Only thing he knew was whoever he was, he had been coaching the freshmen at Auburn.

I said, "Vince Dooley."

And old "Doc" said, "That's the guy."

Just a couple of weeks later, "Doc" took a job at the University of Georgia as freshmen coach. Needless to say, Edgar Chandler also signed with Georgia.

In the meantime, I couldn't wait to get back to Nashville to call Vince and say for the first of many times, "Hey Vince, how about a job?"

My persistence finally paid off because he offered me the job as defensive coordinator at Georgia in January, 1964.

8 ON BECOMING A DAWG

t was early February, 1964. Rusty had just turned 11. Jay would soon be 5. Jean was still in her 20s. Thank God for her energy and patience in situations like this. I was 36.

The movers had loaded up our furniture and were on their way. So the four of us left Nashville to meet them at our house in Athens the next day. I led the way in a '55 Chevy I had bought from a "shade-tree mechanic" in Nashville for $150. Not really knowing if the heap would make it to Athens, Jean and the boys followed in the "good" car.

Things went well until I began to go 65 through those Tennessee hills. All of a sudden, she began to smoke like a furnace. I had anticipated that, because I knew she used a little oil. So I stopped and poured several quarts into the engine from my supply in the trunk and we were off again. In a few miles she began to "clang" pretty good up under the hood and wouldn't go over 20. We limped to the outskirts of Chattanooga with stops every few miles to add more oil.

I pulled into the first used car lot I saw and asked the man if he wanted to buy a good "used" car. He asked what was wrong with it and I told him I didn't know. He got in, cranked it up, listened, turned it off and said he'd give me $40. I took it.

When I had visited Vince in Athens a couple of weeks earlier to finalize the coaching job, I had gone alone and had Jean's permission to secure a house if I found one I liked. How many wives would give their husbands such latitude as to pick out a house without the wife even seeing it? I'm not much of a shopper. I liked the first one I was shown. I just wanted to get settled and start living in Athens, Georgia.

Only one thing bothered me. The rate of interest was an outrageously high 6¼%, but I couldn't beat that anywhere. So I signed. We had a house and it turned out good. We lived there for 17 years.

Everybody has heard how Dr. O.C. Aderhold, then president of the University of Georgia, was weary from all the problems experienced by the athletic department for several years. So he hired Joel Eaves, the successful basketball coach at Auburn, as his athletic director. The story goes that Dr. Aderhold told Coach Eaves, "This is your athletic department. Go get yourself a football coach. I'm going to get a drink."

With that, Coach Eaves hired Vince. No search committee, no interviews. No suggestions from alumni. Vince, at 32, became the youngest major college coach in the country. Very little coaching experience, an unknown. Folks, if you don't mind my saying so, Joel's making that decision took balls. I've told Coach Eaves that more than once. He would simply smile and say he was fully confident that Vince would be a successful head coach.

It still took guts.

I hope Georgia people appreciate what Joel Eaves did for the University. He was responsible for turning the Georgia Athletic Department around and making it one of the best in the country. He hired Vince who became one of the most successful coaches in college football. That's history now and it all happened because Dr. Aderhold was "tired and thirsty."

Vince used very good judgement in hiring his first coaching staff. This was in keeping with everything else he did. He put great thought into his decisions, never doing anything impulsively. He returned some coaches from the previous staff and brought in five new ones. All good coaches. All good people. I was the last one hired for the new staff. I think Vince took me so I'd quit calling him. I later told him on many occasions the two smartest things he ever did was to hire me and marry Barbara. He accepted that.

I spent 17 great years as an assistant coach at Georgia. Some years were better than others, but collectively, they were great years. However, these were Vince's years and those were his teams. He and others have already written volumes on Georgia football during this era. I'm just going to try to remember some of the things from my time at Georgia as seen through the eyes of a career assistant football coach. After all, I was a "working coach" in the Southeastern Conference for 23 years and that's a career for some folks. I may have been a varsity assistant at Georgia longer than anybody else.

From the beginning, Vince and Coach Eaves were very "image" conscious. Georgia had experienced some tough years, not only on the scoreboard and in the win column. Media-wise, the Dogs had come by more than their share of negatives. Georgia Tech was winning and the media loved Coach Dodd. So Georgia had some ground to make up. This was the first order of business in 1964. We figured the best way to get people to change their opinions, was to win lots of football games. This was the objective as we met our squad and began spring football practice in '64.

Vince knew what he wanted to do on offense and defense from the outset and that was to be a ball control team, emphasizing a power running game and utilizing an eight-man front on defense. His years with Coach Jordan at Auburn had taught him this combination, along with a strong kicking game, could be successful. I'm sure you've heard that a coach's team on the field is a projection of the coach himself. If you had ever seen Vince throw the football as a player or later in drills as a coach, you'd understand why he didn't want his quarterbacks to put the ball in the air.

Seriously, Vince was greatly influenced by Coach Jordan. His basic philosophy of football and recruiting, along with some of his mannerisms, all came from Coach Jordan. As the years passed, however, you could see him "borrowing" from other successful coaches. This was wise. A new play here or there, or a different way to block an old play. A new punt return. The game changes and a certain amount of change on a coach's part is sometimes necessary to keep up. However, Vince's basic philosophy of "grind" on offense and play solid defense rarely changed. The result: 201 victories for Georgia over the next 25 years. He believed, "If it ain't broke, don't fix it." I do too.

There were times when things weren't going so well and Vince's offense was described as "run it up the middle twice, throw it in the hedges and punt." This was a bad rap, but you know how football fans are. It's easy to call plays on Monday, but it's tough as hell on Saturday afternoon if your right tackle won't block. Sometimes that happens, you know.

Vince was also frugal. I can remember taking him home after practice one evening when we were coaching at Auburn. He and Barbara were newlyweds and I knew he was looking forward to getting home and relaxing with his new bride after a hard day's work. As we drove up to the apartment, he exclaimed, "Just look at that. Barbara has every damn light in the house on."

We traveled together quite a bit in those early years and Vince always carried a $50 bill. We'd stop for a sandwich and a Coke, or whatever, and he'd pull out the fifty and say, "How about taking care of the check. All I have is this fifty." Later, after Oklahoma stirred things up by offering Vince a job, we won a couple of Southeastern Conference Championships and he began using a $100 bill.

Vince was an organizer. One of the best. He was great for details, small details. Very thorough. I used virtually the same practice schedule when I went to Georgia Southern. I cut my practices by about 30 minutes a day because I felt that fit our situation better. For the most part, I used Vince's practice schedule and copied many of his meeting and organizational methods.

Players sometimes complained that Vince didn't care about them, that he was aloof and hard to get to know. He was aloof and he was hard for some people to get to know, but I don't believe he tried to be that way. That was his nature and he never made any great effort to be something or somebody he wasn't.

I'm sure many of those same players look back now and re-evaluate their assessment of Vince's feelings toward them. He did what he did best — plan and organize. His mentor, Coach Eaves, had taught him well in this area. One of his strongest points was his ability (and this is an ability) to allow his coaches to coach. I don't mean to imply that he backed off and turned it all over to his assistants. But as long as he felt his coaches were getting the job done, he let them do it. I always appreciated his approach because it is so important to the morale of the staff. Coaches work harder when the responsibility is theirs.

I never really liked the name "Dooley's Dawgs" because that implied they were Dooley's and I felt they were mine too. I made an absolute 100% investment in the Dawgs. I thought Georgia football was the most important thing in the world. So did some of our other assistant coaches. Aw, I know that Vince was the head man and Dooley started with a D and Dawgs started with a D and put together, "Dooley's Dawgs" were naturals. I didn't like it years later when people referred to our Georgia Southern team as "Erk's Eagles." Makes it seem like a one-man endeavor. Nothing could be further from the truth. Whether Dogs or Eagles, football is the greatest "team" game in athletics.

I may as well go ahead and get this off my chest too. After we began having some success at Georgia, I was agitated when people began naming their babies after Vince and their dogs after me. That is, it bothered me until I moved to south Georgia and discovered how much people really love their dogs. To any of you who ever named a dog "Erk," I am honored and I thank you.

I'm sitting on the beach recalling 1964, our first year at Georgia and the series of events that occurred to get that staff together. Joel Eaves, Vince, my going to Georgia. I wonder what would have happened to me if I hadn't gone to Georgia? Without this link, how about Georgia Southern? Talk about a game of inches and decisions.

I just got word that Coach Eaves passed away today. He was 77. Jean and I will be driving from Fernandina Beach, Florida, to Athens to pay our last respects to a great coach and friend. I feel like he started it all at Georgia.

As we met our troops for the first time during spring practice in 1964, it was obvious there were some good players "on board." But the thing that really jumped out at me was they really wanted to play. Although Georgia hadn't enjoyed great success the past two or three years, these guys seemed ready and more than willing to do what we wanted them to do. When you begin with a new group like this, the first task is to find out who wants to play. Actually, those who lacked in desire soon departed, because that first series of practices were "slobber-knockers." I was impressed that those players already knew what those helmets were for. I should have known that. I had played against Georgia four years and had coached against them for six. Georgia was always a physically tough team. Now, I was just hoping I wouldn't do anything to disturb that tradition.

I really wondered about our future when Alabama clobbered us, 31-3, in Tuscaloosa on Saturday night, September 19, 1964. In spite of the one-sidedness of the game (and they did beat the slop out of us), our guys played hard. They didn't quit! They fought for 60 minutes and we thought because of that attitude, there was hope. Anytime you have a group of players who care and are willing to pay the price for success, you know good things are going to happen. It turned out that Alabama was a pretty good football team and with Joe Namath at quarterback, they won the national championship that year.

We went home and made several personnel changes. Vince moved me from linebacker coach to line coach and Jim Pyburn from line coach to linebacker coach. That had to be a tough decision for him to make after only one game. It might have been the quickest decision he ever made, but it proved to be a good one. I spent the next 17 years in the trenches with the defensive linemen and I loved every day of it (except when we lost).

We beat Vandy at their place, 7-0. It was a tough contest, but it went under the "W" and we were 1-1.

In Columbia the next week, we let South Carolina off the hook with a 7-7 tie. They only had about 40 yards rushing and we had a chance late in the game, but dropped the ball on their 25-yard line going in. We're all even now at 1-1-1 after three games on the road.

Clemson, with the legendary Frank Howard as coach, came to Athens for our season's home debut. We won, 19-7, on an interception, a punt return and a safety. It was great to finally play between the hedges and even greater to win there.

Thirty-seven years later the Touchdown Club of Atlanta would be roasting me as part of their annual jamboree. I had just hung it up as coach of Georgia Southern and we had finished the 1989 season by winning our third National Championship in five years. Coach Frank Howard, now 80 years old, walked into the banquet room and I went over to say hello. As we visited, a photographer asked if we would pose for a picture. That had happened before at such occasions since Frank and I wear a similar hair style. They call it the "absent look." As the photographer finished, I asked if he would send me one of those pictures. He said he would. What was my address? Since Statesboro, Georgia, ain't no big place I simply said, "Send it to Erk Russell, Statesboro, Georgia." Frank spoke up and said, "Send mine to Frank Howard, U.S.A."

Frank loved to harass, taunt and embarrass his coaching associates at every opportunity, and preferably in front of an audience. He always called Vince "Young Genius," and referred to Bill Dooley, Vince's brother, as "Little Brother." After Bill left Georgia, he was head coach at North Carolina for several years and apparently fished with Frank on occasion. One of Frank's favorite lines to me was, "I don't like that 'Young Genius' too much, but I really like 'Little Brother.' He beats me at fishin' and I beat him at football." You know, I don't believe Frank ever beat "Young Genius."

Years later after he had retired from coaching, Frank and I were chatting at a cocktail party. He handed me a piece of paper and said, "Now that I ain't coachin' no more, how 'bout drawing that screwed-up defensive front y'all used on me. Me and my coaches could never figger that damn thing out." He could have fooled me, because Clemson used to run for miles up the middle against Georgia. They just didn't score much.

It's October 17, 1964, and the Florida State Seminoles are in Athens. They bring to town the best passing attack in the country and feature quarterback Steve Tensi and wide receiver Fred Bilitnikoff, now a member of the professional football Hall of Fame. They had an offensive line that took great pride in protecting their quarterback. They shaved their heads and called themselves, "The Magnificent Seven" after Yul Brenner and the movie of the same name. We had one idiot on our side who shaved his head and he was supposed to call the defenses against one of the best offenses in the business. We really didn't have much of a chance. But we did, because our guys cared so much and wanted to win so badly. They almost overcame their coaching. Preston Ridlehuber scored on a punt return right at the end, and we would have won the game. But clipping was called and we lost, 17-14.

To be 2-2-1 at the halfway point of the season might not be encouraging in most situations. But to a new coaching staff, we knew we could compete with the best. If we could just help our guys a little more, we really had a chance. Just as important was the coming together of Georgia fans during the FSU game. It was almost like the crowd awakened during the game and said, "Hey, that's our team out there. They're trying like hell. Let's do all we can to help 'em." They helped. Georgia people were pulling together again. We were all on the same Georgia team.

We had Kentucky in town for homecoming the next week and they were strong. They were so strong they took the opening kick-off and kept the ball for most of the first quarter. They would run for six, four, seven, three, five, four, eight. We couldn't stop them. When they finally scored after about 10 minutes and led, 7-0, our crazy fans stood and cheered as our defensive troops trudged from the field. A standing ovation for a bunch that had just let a team drive 66 yards for a touchdown. I couldn't believe it! The team couldn't believe it!

Folks, that's motivation. Kentucky didn't cross the 50-yard line the rest of the game. I wish I could tell you I got my guys off on the sideline and made adjustments to stop Kentucky. But I'm not that good. The Georgia fans on that day made the mental adjustment for us and that was the difference. Leroy Dukes, a middle-aged linebacker on that team, told me recently that incident was the beginning of a great defensive tradition at Georgia. We beat

Kentucky, 21-7, and it was homecoming and the Bud never tasted better after the game.

North Carolina had one of its better teams in recent years led by Ken Willard, their All-American fullback. During our film study we saw that on Willard's best play, a quick trap up the middle, the center always blocked back on our defensive guard so the trapping guard could pull. We told middle linebacker John Glass to see the center and when that happened, to simply step forward and tackle Willard. It worked. Willard wasn't a factor and Glass must have made 15 individual tackles. On that day he was the All-American. We won, 24-8.

The 1964 Florida game was my first exposure to the great Georgia-Florida series as a participant. I had scouted the game when I coached at Auburn. But you can't really get the true feeling of that contest and the atmosphere surrounding it until you're a part of it, as a player or a coach.

There were always two things I wanted to do before I shuffled off this mortal life. One was to watch a Georgia game from the railroad tracks in Athens, and the other was to go to a Georgia-Florida football game as a fan. Now, they've enclosed Sanford Stadium and the view from the tracks is no more. And I still haven't had an opportunity to see a Florida game since I've always had Georgia Southern business to take care of. But I'm still planning to go one of these days if I can get a ticket.

The air in Jacksonville was full of electricity and all the people were wired. From the time our plane landed Friday afternoon, there seemed to be but one thing going on in the world, and that was this game. Georgia people feel that Jacksonville is a part of south Georgia and, of course, Florida people call Jacksonville their territory. In this setting, some mighty battles with most unusual and strange outcomes have taken place.

In the beginning, I thought Florida had a great home field advantage and Coach Eaves threatened to move the series to home-and-home because the Gators were allotted more tickets. When that was evened out, I was convinced Jacksonville was the place for the game and the series should remain there. I still feel that way.

The carnival atmosphere always added to the excitement and tradition of the contest. Usually, the weather was beautiful and a great stadium on the banks of the St. Johns River was always packed with fanatics. Looking back, all the screwy things that happened over the years made the Georgia-Florida series very special to me. They tell me that it's not quite as wild now as it used to be when the game was billed as, "The world's largest outdoor cocktail party." But during my 17 years it was my favorite game, my favorite series. We were 11-5-1 during that stretch. In spite of our success against Florida during that time, I always thought the Florida job might be the best coaching job in the country. I still do. Don't forget you read it here first.

Well, it's 4:30 p.m. on November 17, 1964, and Georgia is playing Florida in the Gator Bowl. We're in the fourth quarter and the score is tied

7-7. Bobby Etter is back to attempt a field goal. The line of scrimmage is the 5-yard line and we get a bad snap. Barry Wilson, the holder, deflects the ball to Etter, a math major who quickly calculates the shortest distance to the Gators' goal line is around left end. He runs the ball in, assisted by a great block from Wilson at about the 3-yard line. We win the game, 14-7.

One of the most enthusiastic post-game celebrations I've ever seen took place in our dressing room, because Georgia wasn't supposed to do that to Florida on this particular day. The Gators had won the last four games and had a hell of a team, but our guys just wouldn't let them prevail. After the celebrating died down somewhat, I happened to look over in the corner and there stood President Aderhold, who was grinning real big and had his hands thrust deep into his pants pockets. He was rocking back and forth from his toes to his heels, as was characteristic. I walked over, stuck out my hand and said, "Congratulations, Dr. Aderhold." He smiled even bigger and then I said, "Dr. Aderhold, how about a raise?" He busted out laughing and rocked real hard back and forth and said, "If y'all keep winning like this, we'll get a raise." The president was happy and Georgia people around the world were happy.

There ain't nothing like being a Bulldog on Saturday night after whipping Florida.

Auburn was also good that year. Some of the experts had picked them to win the National Championship. They didn't. But they beat us, 14-7, and we were 5-3-1 with Georgia Tech coming up after a week off.

I had played and coached at Auburn and I knew the intensity of their rivalry with Alabama. It didn't take but one year at Vanderbilt to catch the feeling of the bitterness of the Vandy-Tennessee series. Now I'm coaching at Georgia and all of a sudden it is obvious to me that the Georgia-Georgia Tech contest is the granddaddy of intra-state rivalries. I mean, there was considerable dislike on the part of the Bulldog loyalty toward the Yellow Jackets, and vice versa. Nobody tried to hide it either. This game was big.

Tech had withdrawn from the Southeastern Conference in 1963. In time, the series, in my opinion, would lose some of its importance and intensity. The strongest of feelings, however, were still there throughout the '60s. As we prepared for the '64 contest, Tech had won the last three games and 11 of the last 14 including a streak of eight straight, commonly referred to by Georgia people as "The Drought." It was "The Drought" that really grated upon the Georgia people and magnified good, old-fashioned hate into something stronger.

Tech was going to a big bowl. If we won, we would go to the Sun Bowl. The grass had turned brown in Sanford Stadium, as it does in November. But it was a perfect Saturday afternoon for football and tickets were $5.50. As far as I was concerned, this was the opportunity of a lifetime. Evidently, our guys thought so too. We hit them and they hit us. This game was as physically tough as any I've ever seen. Wayne Swinford (Georgia) and Johnny Gresham

(Tech) had one of football's hardest collisions and knocked one another out. Both refused assistance in getting off the field after being revived and each returned to the game after catching his breath.

That was the kind of game it was. Leroy Dukes, our middle-aged linebacker, said our defense was able to pre-call every Tech play except two, which were called at the line by their quarterback. I can't confirm that, but our guys did good. We got a fumble at Tech's 22 and scored late in the third quarter and led, 7-0. Tech came back and put on a drive late in the fourth quarter. They had 4th-and-1 at about our 20-yard line. I called a blitz, which sent all linemen and linebackers through their respective gaps. George Patton, at that time the world's skinniest defensive tackle, shot through his gap and stopped the play at the line of scrimmage and we won the game. Great play. Great game. We had snapped a three-game losing streak to Tech and were going to the Sun Bowl. The regular season was over and I thought it would be appropriate to pass out cigars to the players after the game. I had bought a box of Tampa Nuggets, two for 15 cents, and we all lit up. We were 6-3-1. All of us felt good. The Tampa Nuggets were delicious. November 28, 1964 — life was delicious.

El Paso, Texas, was too far to drive my family. And Jean had not found out that vodka eases the pain of flying, so I took Rusty on the team charter.

We played on December 26, so we missed Christmas at home, but we had our own Bulldog Christmas Party at our team's headquarters on Christmas Day. Somehow, I drew the job of playing Santa Claus and it was my duty to pass out the gifts that had been worked up by our players' parents and some of the team's supporters who made the long trip. If this was a violation of NCAA rules, nobody thought about it and we did it innocently. The guys preferred gag gifts anyhow. For most of our team, this was their first Christmas away from home and although we went traveling 11 more times, we were never away on Christmas Day. Our team's Christmas parties became a tradition and a great time was always had by all. I improved my Santa Claus act as I gained experience.

I enjoyed that first Sun Bowl as much as I enjoyed any of the 11 bowls that followed. We wanted to go to the Sun Bowl and they wanted us. They entertained us well. One of the highlights was a Texas-style breakfast put on by a group called The Sheriff's Posse. The Sheriff's Posse was a service organization like Rotary or Lions or Optimist, and their president was called The Sheriff. Hence the name. This was an all-male organization. But as the present sheriff explained to us several years before, they had a woman sheriff and while she was sheriff the membership grew at a tremendous pace. "As a matter of fact," he said, "while she was sheriff, she had the biggest 'posse' in 'El Puso.'"

In spite of trips across the border to Juarez, Mexico, some authorized and some not, our guys got themselves ready to play. They had to play a great game because our opponent, Texas Tech, was the best offensive team in the

Southwest Conference. They had a great tailback named Donnie Anderson, who later played a long time for the Green Bay Packers and others.

Defensively, our philosophy was to take away the things they did best so the end result would be a good chance for us to win. That day we did just that. Texas Tech only managed 40 yards rushing and our offense kept the ball most of the game.

They had a chance late in the game, but somebody deflected their pass and Vance "Blinko" Evans, our defensive tackle, caught the ball in mid-air and squatted on it. It was one of the most beautiful plays I've ever seen. We won, 7-0, and our season was complete with a bowl victory. Now our guys could go to Juarez legally and celebrate with clear consciences..

The Sun Bowl people were gracious. They had provided our coaches with courtesy cars to serve as transportation while we were in El Paso. Each car was decorated with huge banners attached to both sides of the automobile. Mine read, "Coach Erk Russell, University of Georgia, Sun Bowl." Joel Darden, a senior defensive guard on the team, approached me after the game and asked if he could borrow my car to show his bride the town. Although I knew better, I'll do just about anything while savoring the thrill of victory, I told him he could use the car if he wouldn't have anything to drink ... and above all, if he wouldn't take the car across the border to Juarez because the insurance was no good in Mexico. Naturally, he promised to behave and, no sir, he wouldn't think of crossing the border in my car. I gave him the keys.

Later that evening the coaches, wives and the official party went to Juarez for dinner on a courtesy bus. Would you believe right there, big as life, was my car, (signs and all) parked on the main street of beautiful downtown Juarez, Mexico.

Fortunately, nothing happened to the car, or the occupants. Later when I questioned Darden about his actions he said several teammates who accompanied him made him do it and besides, his wife drove and, "She ain't ever had a drink in her whole life."

All's well that ends well and the football season of 1964 had ended well. Actually, it was great, and for several reasons. Vince and his staff had proven they could coach, at least for a year. The Georgia fans pulled together for the first time in several years, all cheering for the same folks to do good. I think the Florida State game was when it seemed to happen. And the Kentucky game, as Leroy pointed out, was the beginning of a great defensive tradition at Georgia. This group allowed an average of only 9.8 points a game and had Georgia's best rushing defense in almost 20 years.

We beat Georgia Tech and won a bowl game. So 1964 was important because it was the "first" year and we needed to be good, so bad.

I have used this particular team many times as an example of what can be accomplished by players and coaches with "a bad case of the wants." We had some players with great ability. Don't get me wrong, not many teams can line up any better at tackle than Rismiller and Wilson.

But as a team, this group had a superior desire to excel. Attitude, balls and communication, the ABCs of football, were in abundance on the '64 team.

9 | *GATA AND MAMBO GOOK*

This was the summer I started out the first issue of what I called the "Friendly Reminder Calendar" to all our team members back home. Not just to the defense, but to all the players. I filled it up with some humor and some serious stuff. I wanted them to know their coaches were thinking about them and wanted them to begin getting in good shape and to be prepared when they returned to practice.

Nowadays, most big schools keep their players on campus during the summer so coaches can make sure the guys stay in shape. Back then, they left after spring quarter and you saw them in late August.

The calendar caught on. It was an effort to wake up the players. It said, among other things, "Get your butts out of bed and start running." The guys liked it. So for the remainder of my years at Georgia, I'd put out an annual edition of the "Friendly Reminder Calendar."

We returned a good nucleus from the '64 team. We lost some mighty good players but there seemed to be some good help coming up from the freshman and "B" teams. The prognosticators picked us to finish 8th or 9th in the Southeastern Conference.

We wanted to prove we could pick up where we left off. To show that '64 wasn't just a "one-year splash." Our schedule was somewhat less than ideal to prove that point. We had four home games and six on the road. We replaced South Carolina with Michigan at Ann Arbor — a terrible swap. Alabama came to Athens on September 18th, 1965, to open the season. They were defending National Champions and figured to be very good again. It was to be nationally televised.

Our guys were in a strong, competitive mood, remembering the 31-3 score of '64.

We led, 3-0, in the second quarter when Jiggy Smaha, our defensive right tackle, hit Bama's quarterback, Steve Sloan, just as he released a pass. The ball fluttered to George Patton, our defensive left tackle, who had a great knack for being where the football was. Patton caught it and ran 55 yards for a touchdown. It happened right in front of our bench. I could see it coming and I ran with him down the sideline to about the 10 where I was sure he would make it without my help. Our photographer filmed Patton's run with me running right along side of him.

Two weeks later at Ann Arbor while we were in pre-game warm-ups, Tony Mason, Michigan's offensive coordinator, walked over to me and allowed he was glad their staff didn't have to play our staff because we had the fastest coaches he had ever seen. He had reviewed the film of the Alabama game. Mason said, "I knew you were fast when you passed that little black coach like he was standing still."

That little black coach was Squab Jones, our all-purpose manager, trainer and "jack of all trades" who always tried to retrieve the ball from the "touchdown maker" in the end zone. Squab must have been 65 years old then. The last time I saw him alive, which was about a year before he died in 1989, he wore his National Championship ring along with Southeastern Conference Championship rings on every finger, both hands. He was one more proud Bulldog.

Back to the Alabama game. We led, 10-0, after Patton's interception, but the Tide scored 17 unanswered points with the last touchdown coming with less than three minutes remaining in the game. They led, 17-10. We got the ball for the last time and on 3rd and long from our 27-yard line, Kirby Moore fired a 10-yard pass to Pat Hodgson, "hooking." Pat flipped it back to Bob Taylor, our tailback, who ran down the far sideline in front of Bama's bench for 73 yards and a touchdown.

This was the famous "Flea-Flicker" play. Sanford Stadium exploded. I mean exploded!

Pictures show that Hodgson's knees "might" have been on the ground as he lateraled the ball to Taylor. Actually I'm looking at a picture right now and you got to be a real Dawg fan to say that Pat's knees aren't touching the ground.

The "Flea-Flicker" only gave us a chance, because we were still behind, 17-16. Now it's "real decision" time. We could tie the game. Bobby Etter was virtually automatic on extra points. Coach Bryant had once said, "Tying a game is like kissing your sister." Tying Alabama, the defending National Champions, in this first game of the season on national television might have been better than that. But not under the circumstances. Not when you've got a chance to win. Vince turned and said, "We got to go for two." I doubt if anybody in the house disagreed.

The two-point play was called. It was a sprint pass to the right. Moore would run if the opportunity was there or if the receivers were covered. Well, the Alabama defensive end got upfield and made Kirby pull up quicker than planned. Our receivers were well covered and they had to start bouncing out of their original routes. Hodgson found an empty spot right in the back of the end zone and Kirby skipping around back there under pressure, found him and threw it through a small hole in the defense. Pat caught the ball and held on. Two great individual efforts gave us two points and we were ahead, 18-17.

'Bama still had a minute and they got a shot at a real long field goal, but it wasn't close. On national television, Georgia beat Alabama. And national TV was really special back then. What a way to begin the season. There weren't too many people winning football games from Alabama in those days. I want to remind you just one more time, "There ain't nothing like being a Bulldog on Saturday night after beating Alabama."

A player who really impressed me on the '65 team was Tommy Lawhorne from Sylvester, Georgia. Tommy was a pre-med major. During Tommy's four years at Georgia, he made two A's. The rest were A+'s. The reason he made the two A's? His teachers in those courses didn't believe in giving anyone an A+.

He was a Rhodes Scholar candidate. Why he wasn't selected, I'll never know. Maybe because of all those A+'s, and being a good football player, he was over qualified.

But there was Tommy. A good player. Not a great player. But a guy you could go over the scouting report and the hit chart one time, then he had it implanted in his mind.

He could stand on the other side of the ball and read formations and boil things down to one or two plays which would be forthcoming. He'd find the ball.

Tommy is now a physician in Columbus, Georgia. Like the linebacker he was for the Dogs, he's still making good calls when folks come into his office.

He was a special young man. He was the epitome of what one person could do as a football player and as a student when it came to calling on every ounce of potential.

Tommy got his chance to play when a regular linebacker got hurt. He had practiced at the position for a total of eight days before the '65 Alabama game. He remained a first team player for the next three years.

Tommy reminded me recently that following our pre-game meal prior to the Alabama game in '65, that I walked over, put my arm around him, blew cigar smoke in his face and said, "I'd rather have you playing linebacker for Georgia today than anybody I know." According to Tommy, "The most amazing thing was I believed you." Believing is the first step on the road to success in any endeavor.

After the Alabama victory, we were due to be flat when Vanderbilt came to town. We were flat, but for the second week in a row, a defensive lineman scored on an interception. Vance Evans hit Vandy's quarterback from the blind side and Dickie Phillips caught the ball and ran 45 yards for the go-ahead touchdown. Football teams go for years without scoring in this manner and we had done it on consecutive Saturdays. Maybe this was our year.

On Friday, October 1, 1965, the Georgia team boarded two Southern Airlines DC-3s and flew to Ann Arbor, Michigan. And in the words of the one and only Dan Magill, "On October 2, 1965, at Ann Arbor before 59,470, the University of Georgia won its most notable intersectional regular season game in over three decades. The magnificent 15-7 triumph over previously unbeaten Michigan, 1964 Big Ten and Rose Bowl champion, also was the first Georgia victory over a Western Conference team in three attempts."

We had gone into Michigan's "Big House" and before the biggest crowd most of us had ever seen, beat them, 15-7.

The DC-3s brought the team back to Athens and the flight home was quick and easy. As we approached the airport, the pilot come on and announced that a huge crowd was waiting to meet the team. We looked out the windows and saw what looked like thousands of people on the ground and miles of automobile lights as far as we could see. It was the biggest crowd and the biggest traffic jam in the history of Athens, Georgia. People had driven from Atlanta and Augusta and Macon, probably farther, to meet and greet the Georgia team upon its arrival. Right there on the front row by the fence stood Jean, Rusty and Jay. Like the man in the Old Milwaukee commercial says, "It just doesn't get any better than this."

I had a dream back in July that year (honest) that we were in our pre-game warm-up before the Clemson game and had won our first three games. I tried to remember to tell Jean before breakfast so it would come true. I don't know if I did, but I told the staff later at a meeting. I got the usual retorts like, "I'll settle for 2-1," or, "I'll settle for 1-2 with this schedule," or, "You must have been dreaming."

Now we were playing Clemson and we were 3-0. Clemson led, 9-6, at half time and gave every indication that they intended to win the game.

In the third quarter, their punter stood at about his own 35-yard line and punted the ball. "Spade" Cooley got loose up the middle, stuck up his huge rubber padded arm broken in the Michigan game and blocked the kick. The ball hit the rubber and literally "sprung" some 35 yards backward to the 2-yard line where Larry Kohn finally caught up with it and fell into the end zone for a touchdown. We won the game, 23-9. Maybe this was to be the year Georgia people had waited for.

"Your highest highs are never as high as your lowest lows are low." Whoever said that first must have been on our plane as we returned to Athens from Tallahassee, Florida, after our game with Florida State.

We led, 3-0, going into the fourth quarter. Bob Taylor, our best runner, had broken his leg and was through for the year. Joe Burson and Doug McFalls, two-thirds of our secondary, were out. And Lawhorne was hurt.

The Seminole team was relentless. They didn't let up. They scored 10 points in the fourth quarter and beat us, 10-3.

What a difference two weeks can make. As we landed in Athens the throng that had invaded the airport after the Michigan game was missing. Only a few loyal "regulars" cheered and cried as they carried Bob Taylor from the plane on a stretcher. There was no traffic jam. It wasn't fun being a Bulldog on that Saturday night.

The next week, it was a cold and windy night in Lexington, Kentucky, and the Wildcats beat Georgia, 24-10. We were banged up and played with a patchwork lineup. It didn't get any better when they broke Kirby Moore's nose and we lost him for the next game or two.

Lynn Hughes was just about the only "whole" player we had left. Thank goodness for him. He would fill in at quarterback for a while and then move over and do his usual outstanding job at safety.

We were rapidly going from the penthouse to the outhouse. We had lost two consecutive games for the first time since coming to Georgia.

Somehow we got enough people together the next week to go to Chapel Hill, North Carolina, and out-score the Tarheels, 47-35.

With five minutes left in the game we pulled within one point at 34-35. Then Billy Cloer, at 150 pounds soaking wet, recovered the ensuing on-side kick and gave us the chance we needed. We scored 13 points in the time remaining.

We went to Jacksonville the very next week. With some of our regulars back who had been injured, we played better against a much better team. We had Florida, 10-7, with four minutes remaining in the game when Steve Spurrier, the Gator quarterback, completed back-to-back passes for 45 and 32 yards, the second for a touchdown. They beat us, 14-10.

The night before the Florida game, Bill Dooley, our offensive coordinator, and I were rooming together. There we were just settling in for what we had hoped would be a good night's sleep, when the phone rang. It was midnight.

I answered it and this guy plainly said, "You better come take care of your players before I kill them. They got our girlfriends in their room."

"By the way," he added before hanging up, "our women are driving a gold Barracuda and it's parked in front of their room."

Anyway, I told Bill what the guy had said. So we put on our clothes to go down to see what was happening. Both players were defensive players — one a senior, the other a sophomore. By the time we got to their room it was all clear, and our guys were just sitting there.

From all indications there had been some activity in their room a few minutes before we arrived. But they had done a pretty good job of cleaning up. They were the picture of innocence.

Bill and I talked to them at length and tried to make sure the girls weren't going to come back, so neither would the boyfriends. We told them what the guy had said about killing them, which really got their attention.

We left it at that. But they knew they were in real trouble — caught doing something they weren't supposed to be doing.

When we got back to our room, I asked Bill what he thought. And he said, "Well, I've always believed any S.O.B. that won't f—k, won't fight." We didn't do anything. But we let those guys know they owed us one. You know how word gets around. Before long every player on the team knew about the incident. They all referred to it as "The Gold Baccaruda Story." I told you earlier that a lot of screwy things happened in the Georgia-Florida series.

That Florida contest was our first experience at losing a game right at the end, but it wouldn't be our last. It didn't take long to get a "double dose" of heartbreak because the very next Saturday against Auburn, we fumbled and they recovered at their 1-yard line, going in. We were behind, 19-21, with a minute left to play in the game. That's how it ended.

What started out as a "dream" season had turned into a nightmare. We had been 4-0 with a high national ranking and now we were 5-4 with "Georgie" Tech coming up and they were good again. I always referred to them as "Georgie" Tech because that's the way Coach Dodd said it and I figured he had been there long enough to know.

We had two weeks to prepare for the Yellow Britches and we needed to prepare well. Tech was going to a bowl. Georgia wasn't. It was our last chance to prevent a break-even season and salvage a winning one. I even went back and pulled "Mambo Gook" out one more time. Usually, I just told it before the season began, but we needed something extra.

On defense, each player has a primary area of responsibility. For example, the defensive end's first responsibility was the "eight hole." The linebacker had the "four hole." We expressed areas of responsibilities for every position in terms of "hole numbers." There was rarely a time during the next 17 years that someone did not write in big letters on the blackboard prior to the game, "Mambo Gook."

The "Mambo Gook" story goes like this: A young Georgia Tech engineering graduate had been working in the oil fields of Saudi Arabia for around six months. He was about to go stark raving mad because the only women that he had seen in Arabia were those who were dressed in the long gowns with veils covering their faces. The women were not very friendly at all. As a matter of fact, he hadn't spoken to one since he had been working there.

He had been used to the feminine pulchritude of Peachtree Street in Atlanta and missed that scenery and his feminine companionship more than anything else. As he was sitting in the little bar at the golf course there in Saudi Arabia, he happened to be seated next to one of the local sheiks.

This particular sheik had spent some time in the United States and conversed with the young engineer as best he could with the little English he could speak. As they sipped on their drinks the young engineer expressed to the sheik that he liked everything fine, except he really missed the feminine companionship that he once enjoyed back in Atlanta. The sheik could get enough out of that conversation to understand what the young man meant. He promised the engineer that he would have, from his harem, one of his wives waiting for him when he got off from work the following afternoon.

Well, the young engineer hustled and worked through the day. He could hardly wait until quitting time. As he approached his tent, he saw this woman standing out front with her long gowns and veil. He figured that she knew why she was there and he surely knew why she was there, so he wouldn't waste any time. He picked her up right there at the tent flap, rushed her inside, threw her down on the cot and commenced to making wild, passionate love to the woman. Immediately she began to shout, "Mambo Gook," "Mambo Gook." She repeated that over and over and over again. The young engineer figured this was an Arabian, expression of ecstasy.

Well, it didn't take too long for the young man to finish the first round and as soon as he relaxed his grasp, the woman still screaming, "Mambo Gook," ran through the tent flap and disappeared across the desert, continuing to scream, "Mambo Gook."

The next day the young engineer and the local sheik had made arrangements to play golf and the young engineer wanted a chance to thank the sheik for his courtesy of having the woman there. As they played the first hole, the sheik hit a magnificent shot, straight to the green, the ball hit, bounced and rolled right into the cup. It was a great golf shot and the young engineer wanted to express the greatness of that shot with something more than the usual, "Nice shot," or, "Great shot." The thought of the Arabian expression of ecstasy occurred to him, and he said, "Mambo Gook, sheik, Mambo Gook.".

The sheik turned to him, looked at him with amazement and said, "What do you mean, wrong hole?"

The point of this story was that as you line up to play defense you're thinking to the opposition, "If you think you're coming my way, that's the wrong hole brother, because you ain't gonna make nothin' here."

So here we were — the last game of the season. We were playing Georgia Tech at Grant Field.

At halftime, we were winning 10 to nothing. Our guys were playing great. The meeting room provided by Tech was a classroom, and all over the walls were signs with big letters, GTAA. I assumed that meant the Georgia Tech Athletic Association. Somehow I got the bright idea we could take that T and move it over between those two A's and make it GATA. I grabbed one of the signs and showed the squad the new arrangement of letters. The idea was that GATA was what we had to continue to do to win the game. Those letters meant, "Get After Their Ass." Our guys did GATA. Georgia beat Tech, 17-7.

That was the first of GATA and it stuck. Every week somebody would write it on the blackboard or a fan in the stands would hold up a GATA sign. Even when we went on road trips, the motel marquees would read, "Welcome Dogs, GATA."

Like GATA, the best way to teach anybody anything is to show them. You can talk until you're blue in the face and never get your point across, but one good picture might get it done. That's how it is with coaching, and coaching the proper tackling techniques in particular.

We used a drill every day in which we emphasized the most important elements of tackling. They are: (1) Eyes on the target; (2) Leg extension and drive; and (3) Wrap up with the arms. At a party one night, a friend of mine happened to overhear me discussing those points and thought I was talking about making love.

In demonstrating to my players these important points, without a helmet, I would occasionally bump into a sharp ridge of a shoulder pad or perhaps get scraped on an abrasive surface of a uniform. Sometimes this would lead to a nick or cut on my forehead or nose. These little nicks would sometimes become larger scrapes with repeated demonstration and sometimes my head or nose would bleed profusely.

Somewhere along the way I began to participate in that drill with our players before our games. Maybe it originally began because my adrenaline was flowing and I just wanted to hit somebody. Whatever the reason, it became somewhat of a tradition that I would do before games. My head would bleed and it seemed to get our player's attention and it sure as hell got mine.

I really went through this ritual and hoped it would be symbolic of the fact that football was a tough game and one might even have to shed a little blood to get the job done. It was worth it. People have asked repeatedly, "Doesn't that hurt?" I'm going to be honest about it. Sometimes it hurt like hell.

My wife has told me on at least a hundred occasions if I came home with my head beat up like that again, she would leave me. I did and she didn't and that's how all this "head butting" came about.

10 | GENERAL PATTON, "STAND STILL" AND MILLIE

In 1966, the experts still didn't believe the Bulldogs were going to be contenders for the Southeastern Conference Championship. We were picked anywhere from fourth to seventh. Again, I reminded everyone on our squad what dogs did to polls.

We finished that season winning the Southeastern Conference Championship. Seems as if the pollsters would have gotten the message about what dogs do freely and easily ...

We won some close ones that season beating Mississippi State, 20-17; South Carolina, 7-0; Ole Miss, 9-3. The Dogs clinched the Southeastern Conference crown at Auburn. The contest was played on a soggy field and found us behind at the half, 13-0. But our fullback, Brad Johnson, put it "in gear" the second half, running the ball and leading us to 21 points. The defense "shored up," lighting the board at the end of the game. Dogs 21, Tigers 13.

We beat Georgia Tech, 23-14, in Athens. We got off to a great start when Kent Lawrence returned the Jackets' first punt 70 yards for a touchdown. Kent Lawrence, I have always said, is probably the fastest white boy in Georgia history.

Well, Kent does his thing and it is time for Etter to go in and kick the extra point. Just as Etter brings back his foot to kick the ball, our cheerleaders fire off a newly acquired cannon. The noise nearly knocked him down. He missed the extra point and Vince was livid.

It was the first time the Georgia cheerleaders used the cannon. And the last. It's sort of funny now, but back then, there was no laughing as little Etter trotted off the field with that cannon's roar still ringing in his ears.

We were invited to play Southern Methodist University in the Cotton Bowl, allowing us the chance to face SMU's All-American receiver, Jerry Levias.

In preparation for that contest, we called on one of our players, David Cooper, to impersonate Levias in practice ... do the things Levias would do, giving us a chance to sharpen our skills. By the way, Levias was black.

One of the coaches talked to Cooper about the idea and Cooper responded to the challenge, so much so that as we walked onto the field that first day of preparing ourselves for the Cotton Bowl, here came Cooper, covered in black shoe polish — legs, arms, hands and face.

"Hey," he responded, "if you want Levias, you got him."

We beat Southern Methodist, 24-9, and ended the season ranked fourth in both AP and UPI polls.

After the Cotton Bowl victory, our dressing room was full of everybody rejoicing, especially the seniors, who had just played their last game for Georgia. Guys walked up and told me how much they enjoyed playing and how much they were going to miss it.

Frank Richter came by and said about the same stuff, but he added, "Coach, there's one thing I'm not going to miss."

"What's that Frank?" I responded.

"I'm not going to miss hiding in the bathroom at the Rockwood Inn until you leave." The Rockwood Inn was my watering hole for a few minutes on my way home from practice every day." I thought word had gotten out Rockwood was my place.

George Patton, a senior and our captain, was an All-American that year. I remember Vince putting him in during the last series of the Cotton Bowl in the shotgun and telling George to "gun it." The guy could throw it a mile. I believe he did. Five years earlier, Patton had come to Georgia with the understanding he would play quarterback, and instead, he wound up playing defensive tackle. I never heard him complain about making the switch.

For the last three years, "General Patton" was roaming all over the place making big plays, one after another, and helping us win football games. He had definitely over-come his coaching. There have been others over the years who have been big play-makers. But Patton, former quarterback, made more than his share and really helped us in those early years to get off on the right track.

And one of the nicest individuals you'd ever hope to meet. Being an All-American never phased him. He was pleasant. Spoke to everyone. My kind of guy. And my kind of football player.

We finished the '66 season 10-1, losing to Miami, 7-6. We had an opportunity to kick a winning field goal, but we couldn't handle the operation. This was a talented team that had a darn good chance to go undefeated.

This same season, we became aware of a sophomore by the name of Bill Stanfill, who for the next three years would be a major force in Georgia football at defensive tackle.

I remember Stanfill had sustained a neck injury the week of the Florida game and it was doubtful as to whether he would play. However, Dr. Hubert, our team physician, performed some of his magic and Stanfill was in the lineup and stayed in Steve Spurrier's (Florida's quarterback) jock all afternoon. Spurrier by the way, would win the Heisman Trophy that year. But not on his performance that game - thanks to one Bill Stanfill.

This story goes that a few weeks later. Spurrier was being measured for a new suit, obviously provided by a Florida alumnus, to wear to New York to receive the Heisman award. As he stood on the box, while the tailor measured his trouser length, it seems Spurrier was fidgeting, moving around and the tailor said, "Stand still!"

Steve thought he said, "Stanfill," and fell off the box and sprained his ankle. Ironically, I referred to Bill on many occasions as "Standstill." So did his teammates. You see, he wasn't the most energetic player in the world during practice sessions. He turned it all the way up for games, though.

Throughout my 17 years at Georgia, my Friday routine was to leave Athens after our brief workout in Sanford and drive into the Atlanta area to see a high school football game. Sometimes I was able to catch two games.

Then I would find a place to eat a late supper. I had heard about this seafood place called The Crossroads, where you could get all the shrimp you could eat for $3.50. Since the game I saw this night was close by, I decided to make this my stop. I was seated and my waitress introduced herself as Millie. I had intended to get the shrimp, but decided on soft shell crabs instead. Later when she brought my order, she said that another waitress had told her I was a football coach at Georgia.

She asked if this was correct. I told her it was. She then proceeded to tell me not to worry about tomorrow's game, because Georgia was going to win. When I asked her how she knew, she informed me she was psychic and she got "feelings" about things like that.

The next day we won.

For about the next 10 years whenever I could get to The Crossroads on Friday night, she was there. I had to get there. I always ordered the same thing — soft shell crabs. Sometimes they were great. A lot of times they were awful. I really didn't care. All I wanted to hear was how Millie felt about tomorrow's game.

Most of the time she was right, and she didn't always pick us to win. She would say things like, "Watch out for that red-headed player on their team." Or, "They have a left-handed boy who could be dangerous."

I was convinced that Millie and those soft shell crabs had as much to do with our winning games as any of the good athletes we had. If Millie wasn't there on those Fridays, she always left "word" with the waitress who had her station. I stayed with Millie until she retired.

Coaches are not superstitious. But there's no point in taking chances.

11 | *THE COLOR PINK*

I n 1967, we went 7-3 during the regular season. Kirby Moore was our captain. He was one of the most versatile players Georgia ever had. He could run it, throw it and was our regular punter at one time. That made him a triple-threat player and this kind of player is an endangered species.

We started off 3-0. Went to Ole Miss and Archie Manning made it 3-1.

We went to Houston and took on Paul Gipson and the veer offense in the Astrodome. It was the first time the Dogs played football indoors. By the way, Houston had the best rushing team in the country at that time. In this contest, Gipson ran for about 200 yards and we got beat, 15-14.

When I left the dome that night, I made a promise to myself that Gipson would not run for 200 yards the next year. No way. I was right. The next time we met him, he ran for 230 yards in Athens, and later that year was the Atlanta Falcons' number one draft pick.

There's no telling how many opposing running backs got big pro contracts because of my coaching.

But with all their great running, all Houston's touchdowns came on passes. In fact, the three times they scored on the Dogs in our two contests, all three were on long passes. We led them in this game, 14-0, going into the fourth quarter. They came back to beat us — passing.

By the way, this is the game we had to leave Jake Scott and Mark Stewart at home. Coach Dooley had bumped into them at the Waffle House in the early hours. That's two-thirds of our secondary we played without.

Remember Tommy Lawhorne, the bright young doctor-to-be linebacker?

Well, when Houston scored that second touchdown, we could see right away they were not going to be satisfied with a tie. The score read, Dogs 14, Cougars 13. So they lined up to go for two. We figured they are going to run their option play, because that's what they did best. We had practiced all week against this play in the two-point situation and our plan was for our linebacker to call any color if he (the linebacker) was going take the quarterback. No color call at all told the end to take the quarterback and the linebacker to take the pitch. Houston ran the option and two Dogs knocked the crap out of the quarterback. Nobody took the pitch. And of course, the pitch man virtually walked in for the two points.

After the game, I asked Tommy if he had called a color on the two-point play. He said he had. And I asked him what color he used. And he looked at me and said, "Pink." I glared at him and said, "Hell, Tommy, anybody that calls pink ought to get beat."

Another game I remember really well that season was our Florida outing. They beat us on national television, 17-16.

Our kicker, Jim McCullough, missed an extra point that could have given us a tie game. It was a heartbreaker. On the plane trip back from Jacksonville, we passed out the box lunches. Billy Kinard, our secondary coach, who also coached our place kickers at that time, went back to McCullough and took away his box lunch. He told McCullough he didn't deserve to have anything to eat after missing that extra point.

The life of a kicker can be pretty tough. But wait until '68. Kinard and McCullough became friends again.

We shut out Auburn, 17-0, and Jake Scott returned punts all over the place and played centerfield like an All-American. After that we put away Georgie Tech, 21-14. This was the first year I looked across the field and didn't see that bow-legged walk of Coach Bobby Dodd's. He had retired. What a great coach and person he was. I was privileged to be associated with him.

Our record was 7-3, and we were invited to the Liberty Bowl to play North Carolina State. We got beat, 14-7, in Memphis. We had two punts blocked and it was a frustrating day.

I cannot close out this year without mentioning Steve Greer, a 200-pound defensive guard who, pound-for-pound. might have been the best football player I've ever seen. He was forever running around people, jumping over blockers doing his thing in much the same manner as George Patton had the three years previously. Whatever it took to get the job done, he would do it.

In 1980, when I left the University of Georgia to go to Georgia Southern, I passed all my gear on to Steve, including my red rubber jacket that had GATA on the front and "Tuck Fech" on the back. Steve was the Dogs' defensive line coach and I knew he would carry on the tradition.

12 | *SUGAR NOT SWEET FOR CHAMPS*

T he '68 team was one of the best we ever had in terms of sheer football ability. We finished the regular season 8-0-2. We were tied by Tennessee and Houston.

We were to open against Tennessee. Their field was Tartan Turf, an artificial surface. In fact, this was to be the first outdoor football game ever played on an artificial surface. How about that? Well, old Vince, back during the summer, got to thinking about this game. He wondered what would be the best shoes for this surface.

Always the stickler for small details, he insisted that we go check things out. So a group of us coaches flew in a small plane to Minneapolis to visit the 3M plant that produced Tartan. We wanted to test the different types of shoes we might use when we went to play Tennessee.

It was a one-day trip. We left Athens early one morning, got there, had lunch, went into the plant and tried out various assortments of footwear.

The 3M people were great hosts. When we left to come home on that small aircraft, they gave us a case of beer — a local brand. All passengers (except the pilot) found the beer very much to our liking. Consequently, it wasn't long before we felt the extreme necessity to land that plane so we could relieve ourselves.

The pilot got down and started looking for any old landing strip. I'll always remember that as one of the most welcome relief stops I've ever had, and I've had some pretty enjoyable ones over the years.

So, what with that trip up north and running on the sample Tartan Turf and sipping the "nectar of the gods" in that small plane with no restroom, Vince and the rest of us came to the conclusion that plain old basketball shoes were just as good as any of the specialized footwear we could find for the Tennessee game.

What a bitter disappointment in terms of a contest you should have won ... but let get away. Tennessee scored with no time left. We now led, 17-15. With the game over, they lined up and went for two and made it. Final score, 17-17. I still wake up nights thinking about a couple of bad, bad defensive calls I made in that game.

One of our Dogs did find that artificial stuff to his liking. Jake Scott, our safety, with good footing returned a punt 90 yards for a touchdown. During his run, he came steaming by our bench. With our players jumping up and down, somehow one of our guys lost his helmet and it rolled onto the field right in Jake's path. Scott came within an inch or two of stepping into the helmet.

I can't remember who was responsible for that moment of anxiety, but we all thought right at that time the guy who belonged to that helmet sitting out there on the field was a prime candidate for castration at sunrise had it stopped Jake's momentum.

That other tie this season was with Houston and the veer and Gipson, leading the group with the best rushing stats in the country, again. Well, I'm proud to say our defense held them to 10 points, but they wore out our grass between the 20s. And with just 12 seconds left on the clock, remember that kicker, McCullough (from last year who didn't get a box lunch on the plane trip home from Florida)? Well, all he did was kick a 38-yard field goal, allowing us to tie this bunch of Texans, 10-10.

Guess who was the first one on the field meeting McCullough halfway to the sidelines hugging the kid's neck? You're right! Kinard! Last year, no box lunch. This year, a hero and an invitation to the Last Supper if McCullough wanted it.

Later we went to Jacksonville for the outdoor party with Florida. Things hadn't been going too good for the Gators. For this contest, Coach Ray Graves, in a drastic move to turn his team around, put his offensive staff on defense and his defensive staff on offense. It didn't work.

In the world's worst downpour, I mean in a real "frog strangler," we beat the Gators, 51-0. I've got the game ball on my shelf at home. It still feels damp.

We beat Auburn, 17-3, at their house and sewed up the Southeastern Conference Championship. I remember this being another great occasion on which I treated the troops to a cigar. This time they were two-for-a-quarter jobs and they smoked good.

As you read this and question my giving out cigars to the team, just remember my rule: "When it comes to smoking being harmful to one's health ... cigars don't count."

Everybody felt good about being Southeastern Conference Champs and about being undefeated (we were 7-0-2). Bowl bids were forthcoming on this very weekend and we would get a good one. The Georgia players wanted to go to the Orange Bowl. The Orange was a little more prestigious at that time.

The Orange Bowl people wanted us if we beat Auburn. The Sugar Bowl folks said they'd take us win or lose if we'd make a deal before the Auburn game.

Auburn never is easy and I'm sure Vince thought a "sure thing" in New Orleans was better than a "maybe" in Miami. If he waited and we lost, we might miss out on both. Now that is a tough call. What would you have done?

Georgia made a deal with the Sugar. We would go to New Orleans, win or lose.

Coach Dooley announced to the team on Sunday we had accepted a bid to the Sugar Bowl. This news went over like a turd in a punch bowl. They wanted Miami, thought they would get Miami and were disappointed to say the least.

Their disappointment stemmed from their feeling they should have had an opportunity to let their choice of bowls be known.

This decision didn't seem to have a negative effect on the team when they beat Tech in the final game of the season, 47-8.

The players' displeasure over the bowl choice has been mentioned as the reason Arkansas beat us in the Sugar Bowl, 16-2. Plus the scuttlebutt had our guys going out on the town nightly during our stay in New Orleans.

I don't buy either of the "alibis." The truth is, Arkansas was a good team. They played just about as well as they could play, and we didn't.

The Sugar Bowl put a dull finish to an otherwise bright season. The '68 team was an outstanding group and could have gone undefeated.

I'll remember 1968 because it was Jake's last year, as it was Stanfill's. Both made All-American and both went on to play in the National Football League. They played with the Miami Dolphins, won two Super Bowl rings and were both All-Pro. They gave us good years. Shucks, they gave us great years.

As one career ends, another begins. Mike Cavan had a terrific year as our sophomore quarterback. A quality player all the way. I regret to say, the first time I ever heard our fans offer the ugly sound of "boos" directed to a Georgia player was two years later, with a different supporting cast. Mike did not have the great success of 1968. But he handled it like the quality player he was.

Mike is now the head coach at Valdosta State and is doing a fine job.

Another player I want to mention is Billy Payne, the guy responsible for the 1996 Olympics coming to Atlanta. Payne had been a tight end in 1966 and 1967, and he was a good one. With Dennis Hughes and Billy Brice coming on strong at that position, Vince and the offensive coaches asked if

ERK

we would like to have Payne on defense. We said, "Yes we'll take him. He's a winner." We didn't get many like Billy in deals with the offense.

All he did in that one season was to become one of the best defensive players we ever had and was named All-Southeastern Conference Defensive End.

13 | ***THE WHEELS COME OFF***

n 1969, the Dogs started out, 35-0, against Tulane; 30-0 against Clemson; 41-16 against South Carolina. We got beat by Ole Miss at Oxford. But then we came back to defeat Vanderbilt and Kentucky. Then the wheels came off. We lost to Tennessee, tied Florida, lost to Auburn and lost to Georgia Tech.

About that Florida contest, with just less than a minute left in the first half, we were ahead of Florida, 10-7. Florida had the ball on our 20-yard line. It's fourth down. They lined up to kick a field goal. But they faked it. The holder got up and threw the ball to one of the upbacks.

Incomplete.

But from the end zone, an official came in waving his arms saying, "No play." His message was the Florida band had moved into the end zone and he had called a timeout.

This gave Florida another chance. This time they lined up and kicked the field goal and we eventually settled for a 13-13 tie. Their damn band cost us a victory.

We went back to the Sun Bowl.

Sure did. With a record of 5-4-1. Can you believe it? We had accepted an invitation to the Sun Bowl.

Nebraska beat the slop out of us, 45-6.

They gave us one of the worst whippings we ever received. I remember two things about that game. The clock went haywire in the first quarter and the official had to keep the time. The wind was blowing about 50 miles an hour and they had the wind in the first period. Every time they crossed the 50-yard line they kicked a field goal. It was the longest quarter I'll ever remember and they had us, 18-0, as the quarter ended.

By the way, Jean still hadn't discovered that vodka made flying easier. So this time, I took Jay on this Sun Bowl trip. He was 10. And I hated for him to see us get beat that badly.

14 THE WHEELS ARE STILL OFF

1970 was the "Chinese Year of the Dog" and I featured that in our Friendly Reminder Calendar. It turned out not to be Georgia's "Year of the Dog." We ended 5-5, which certainly wasn't a good season at all.

We started off by getting beat by Tulane. And later, 7-6, by Mississippi State in Jackson. That was the only time I really broke down and cried after a game. It was to me the kind of game that you feel like you should have won. I didn't do a good job with what I was supposed to do.

Archie Manning of Ole Miss had beaten us the year before and he did it again in 1970 in Athens. I was tired of looking at Manning and I knew our players were tired of chasing him.

In the Florida game, we fumbled the ball going in for what would have been the clinching score. Florida recovered the fumble and went on to make two late fourth quarter touchdowns to beat us, 24-17. That one hurt.

It was during 1970 that one of the most memorable games for me took place. It was against Auburn.

Auburn had a great year. I'm not certain if they had lost. This game often decided the Southeastern Conference Championship. There were representatives at the game from the Orange, Sugar and Cotton. Any of those bowls were Auburn's for the picking as soon as they did away with the Dogs. Georgia versus Auburn, 1970, falls into the most gallant efforts because the Tigers were supposed to win handily. We were 4-4 going into that game. We weren't going anywhere. They were headed anywhere they wanted to go.

On the very first play of the game, their back ran into our line and one of the damnest collisions took place. Ronnie Rogers and "Rubber Legs"

Woods separated the runner from his helmet. This set the tempo for the rest of the game. It gave every indication our guys were ready to play and it held true throughout the contest.

We upset "Shug" Jordan's team, 31-17, on the road. Was it considered an upset?

Yes.

Isn't it amazing what a positive state of mind will do for a football team?

We got beat by Georgia Tech for the second year in a row, which is an awful way to end any season. We were 5-5-1 and leading the Southeastern Conference in mediocrity.

15 ALMOST - EXCEPT FOR AUBURN

In terms of Georgia teams with great ability and potential, the '71 team placed high in that category. I'm talking about the teams I knew during those 17 years in Athens.

We opened with Oregon State. We felt like those Oregon boys would come south and melt in our hot weather. And they did. That first game was highlighted by the kick return heroics of Buzy "Super Frog" Rosenberg.

We won the game, 56-7.

Rosenberg scored on punt returns of 79 and 66 yards. He had three other returns of 37 yards, 4 yards and 16 yards for 202 total on the day. An average of 40.5 yards per return, which is an NCAA record.

This was a 10-1 season. And the game we lost I'll never forget. It was against Auburn, who came to town with revenge on their minds because of what the Dogs had done to them the year before.

I have always felt that game was one of the poorest planning jobs I ever offered as a defensive coordinator. We had opportunities to win the game, but we allowed them to do things they never should have had a chance at. Pat Sullivan, their quarterback and an eventual Heisman Trophy winner, threw a lot to their star receiver, Terry Beasley.

They beat us, 35-20.

The story goes, the Auburn team, headquartered at the Athens Holiday Inn, was harassed all night by our devoted fraternities. The Greeks took shifts standing outside the motel yelling and hollering, the attempt of which was to keep the Auburn players from getting a good night's rest. The Greeks figured Auburn wouldn't be able to perform well the next day.

I don't think they could have performed any better had they gotten 14 hours sleep. Although those guys might not have gotten the sleep they needed, they probably sat up and feasted on more revenge. They were good and took a game from us that might well have kept us from gaining the number one spot in the country.

The next game was on Thanksgiving night against Georgia Tech at Grant Field before a nationally televised audience.

Much to our discomfort, to put it mildly, the Yellow Jackets jumped out to a 14-0 lead. At halftime, we had taken a good shot at them and trailed by three, 17-14. Later Georgia went ahead, 21-17. Tech came back and made it 24-21.

With a minute-twenty-nine left in the game, Andy Johnson took the team 65 yards to paydirt. During this drive we had to make two fourth down plays to stay alive. That's how close it was.

I did not know this story until much later — but the phone from the pressbox to the sidelines went out shortly after the drive began. James Ray, our other quarterback who had the headset and was signaling the plays to Andy, simply continued to do so ... without getting the plays from upstairs. In other words, our quarterback handled the phone on the sideline and called some of the plays for that winning drive. Thank you, James Ray.

Jimmy Poulos dove over for the final yard with 14 seconds left. We won, 28-24.

Vince took the troops to the Gator Bowl where he beat his brother Bill's North Carolina Tar Heels, 7-3. We ended with an 11-1 season. We badly needed this good year because of the previous two.

One more thing, I was really proud of our defensive squad that year. We led the Southeastern Conference in rushing defense, averaging 97.8 yards per game, which is pretty darn good. And we led the nation in shutouts with four.

Andy Johnson was a sophomore that year and I consider him one of the best athletes I have ever had the pleasure of being around. Poulos was a sophomore that year too. I had been assigned to recruit him.

Poulos was from Atlanta. It came down to us and Alabama. His dad, Pete, sold cars in Atlanta and really knew all about selling. Finally, when Jimmy did decide to go to Georgia, I remember his dad telling me that I was a great salesman but I was the worst "closer" he had ever seen. I respected him for his observation. He sold Cadillacs. His son Jimmy was a Cadillac of a player too. "Top of the line."

Before we look at 1972, I want to go back to that '69 Sun Bowl when Nebraska gave us a good lesson on how to play football. The only good thing to take place that trip was a phone call form Coach Mike Castronis in Athens telling us Andy Johnson had committed to come to Georgia. That made things a little brighter for all of us.

16 | *TO SQUAT OR NOT TO SQUAT*

In 1972, our captain, fullback Robert Huneycutt, led us to a 7-4 season. We opened with a win over Baylor. Lost to Tulane. Beat North Carolina State and Lou Holtz by six; the Bear came to town and left Crimson everywhere, 25-7.

The next week we slipped by Ole Miss, 14-13. Beat Vandy pretty good. Won at home over Kentucky by six, 13-7. Tennessee came to Athens and shut us out, 14-0. We beat Florida. Auburn beat us. We beat the Industrial Arts School in Atlanta, 27-7. And that was it.

A pretty good season. But without a bowl bid.

This was the first of a three-year period of mediocrity for the Dogs. It wasn't because we didn't have good players. We certainly did. I'll have to take the responsibility because I started screwing around with our defense and got away from the "Split-Sixty" defense and tried to do something that I didn't know well.

This is about the time the real feud got started between two of the greatest guys I've even been associated with: Sam Mrvos and John Kasay.

Both were from Pennsylvania and both were long-time assistants at Georgia. Both played for Georgia and had sons who played for Georgia, and both helped me tremendously during my 17 years there.

The feud developed because the strength program had become such an important factor. Kasay believed in squats as a basic exercise for leg strength, and Mrvos was violently opposed. Kasay worked with the offensive players in our strength endeavors, and Mrvos with the defensive players. Mrvos also was my right hand man as he assisted me with the defensive line for many years.

Both being from Pennsylvania and sometimes talking in a strange language, they had strong arguments regarding the good and the bad of squats. Kasay felt this was the most important leg exercise a lineman could possibly do. Mrvos thought it developed bad habits because in order to execute the squat properly, one had to turn his feet out. He believed the only good obtained by executing a squat would be a slew-footed way of walking, which would be ideal for kicking dog turds from the sidewalk.

Eventually Sam resigned and devoted fulltime to his Physical Education position at the University of Georgia. Kasay took over the strength program for the entire squad and today is recognized as one of the best in the business. Needless to say, everybody in the program squats these days.

Kasay was also the long-time athletic dorm coach-in-residence. One of these days, he'll write a book and will fill the whole thing with nothing but funny stories that occurred when he made bedcheck.

I wanted to mention these two guys for their assistance to me during my years at Georgia, and I consider them two of my best friends.

17 | *ME, A BIGOT?*

n 1973, we made two bad mistakes. I discarded my beloved "Sixty" defense in favor of the "Universal Five-Four." And for the first time since I had been at Georgia, we were beaten by Vanderbilt.

That first mistake led to the second one.

This was a roller coaster season much of the way. However, we finished strong with victories over Auburn and Georgia Tech to end the regular season. We traveled all the way to Atlanta and got a 17-16 win over Maryland in the Peach Bowl.

This season provided me the opportunity to coach my first black defensive lineman, Chuck Kinnebrew, from West Rome High School. He was an outstanding prospect although at the time he was not a first-team player. He later became one of the best defensive linemen we had.

I thought everything was going pretty good until I received word that Chuck thought I was a bigot.

I wasn't sure what that meant. But I was sure that it was not a compliment. Still I figured things would work themselves out.

Now, let's go to the Tennessee game, where Chuck and I were standing together on the sidelines.

We had this black sophomore linebacker from Augusta, Georgia. His name was Sylvester Boler, who had the potential to become as good a linebacker as Georgia ever had. Boler was chasing Tennessee's quarterback, Condredge Holloway, right into our sideline. Holloway was also black.

And a collision was imminent.

At this point, Chuck Kinnebrew began to jump up and down on the sidelines and he is screaming, "Come on Boler, kill that black "m— — f— —.""

I knew right at that moment Kinnebrew and I were on the same team. We became great friends for the next two years.

We closed the '73 season 7-4-1 including the bowl victory.

It was in 1973, the first of my two sons joined the team. Rusty took a scholarship to Florida State and played his freshman year there, but the next year transferred to Georgia. After a redshirt season, he played linebacker from 1973 - '75. He was a three-year regular at Georgia.

Jay, his younger brother, was a wide receiver, playing behind Lindsay Scott. He was a starter when Lindsay had problems. Jay messed his knee up pretty bad and missed the 1980 season when we were national champs. That was a tough break for him. He played well for us in '78 and '79.

Although both those guys were really good high school players, they didn't quite measure up to the ability standards we had set for scholarship players at Georgia. But both "walked on" and proved as many have that height, weight and speed are not the only qualities of a good college player. Actually, both had pretty good speed and, at one time, Jay was the fastest white boy in Athens. Both earned scholarships after one year, without any help from me. The three of us enjoyed great football experiences at Georgia. I am proud to have been on the same team with them because they were Junkyard Dog-type players, and that's the highest compliment I could pay them.

Rusty and Jay were the kind of players who gave great efforts on Tuesday or Saturday. It didn't matter if it was a practice scrimmage or game day. And that is all I ever asked of any player. To be perfectly honest, I expected more of Rusty and Jay than our other players. I let that be known rather often.

As a dad, I was proud. But as a coach, I stayed on them pretty good. In fact, I kicked Rusty in the butt on national television when we were playing in the Cotton Bowl. I didn't think he had made a good enough effort in getting to a fumble.

Rusty and Jay both graduated from Georgia. Rusty has a business degree and Jay has Bachelor's and Master's in Physical Education. Both are football coaches. Rusty coaches linebackers at SMU while Jay coaches quarterbacks and fullbacks of Georgia Southern.

Without hesitation I'll tell you they are outstanding coaches. I hope they inherited some of my good fortune and will be as happy in coaching as I've been.

18 | *POLKA DOT PANTS AND JACK DANIELS*

T he '74 season was a long one thanks to my decision to go with the "50" defense and our performances in the very last two games. Somehow, we beat Florida, 17-16. I'll never know how. Our record was 6-3 and that ain't too bad except we had Auburn and Tech left. We lost at Auburn, 17-13. After the Auburn game, we gathered at Vince's house and he told us the Tangerine Bowl (now the Citrus Bowl), was extending an invitation for us to play Miami of Ohio in Orlando. I spoke up and said I thought we should wait until after the Tech game to accept.

I really didn't believe any of us would want to go to a bowl with a 6-5 record, especially if Tech should beat us. Vince allowed that he wasn't about to let Georgia Tech determine our bowl plans. So I was out-voted, one-to-one. Georgia was to play Miami of Ohio in the Tangerine Bowl.

The worst happened when Tech came to Athens and proceeded to beat us just about as soundly as a Georgia team has ever been beaten.

Pepper Rogers was Tech's coach. And although his personality was different from other coaches, his teams were always well-prepared and they executed the wishbone offense as well as anybody we ever played — including some great Alabama wishbone teams.

Rusty told me in later years that the Tech contest was his most embarrassing moment as a player. And his good old-fashioned hate for Georgia Tech stemmed from this very defeat.

It was gray, cold and raining during that Tech game. I mean North Pole weather. There were two big barrels sitting on each end of our bench with roaring fires putting out some much needed warmth. It was obvious that our offense would rather have been huddled around those barrels than on the field. The defense had those same feelings. Our guys just couldn't wait to get around that fire. While on the other side, the Georgia Tech people seemed to be warm, comfortable and enjoying themselves.

After the game, it was reported that as the field crews began cleaning up the stadium and picking up under Georgia Tech's bench, they located several empty Jack Daniel bottles. This evidence is not conclusive of anything. However, 34 is a hell of a lot more than 14.

Vince later made the statement he'd never have any more of those damn fires on the sidelines.

In Orlando for the Tangerine Bowl festivities, we had two brand new buses, I mean the latest in bus transportation, sleek and beautiful. The bus driver got lost trying to get us to a barbecue out in the country planned by the bowl committee for both teams. We were almost an hour late which didn't speak well for our organization.

As we pulled up in these two beautiful buses, I saw the Miami of Ohio team had been transported to the party in two old yellow school buses. I can remember turning to my wife and saying, "Oh hell, we've had it."

And we had.

Miami beat us 21-10. I think all of us were ready to get back home, right then.

This story came back to me years later-involving the only funny thing to occur during that entire trip.

The game was played a week before Christmas. So Jean had done quite a bit of holiday shopping in Orlando. Among the items she had purchased, a navy blue and white polka dot polyester lady's pantsuit with bell bottoms for my mother.

Rusty and a teammate, Jim Baker, had taken off in our car one evening when they found this place where the dress code didn't allow blue jeans. And that's all Baker had brought. So Rusty and Baker walked back to the car and began going through Jean's Christmas packages. Rusty came across his grandmother's pantsuit, which would stretch from here to eternity. Baker donned those blue and white polka dot pants over his jeans. The guy at the door took Rusty's cover charge. But when he looked at Baker's attire he said, "Buddy, anybody who wants to get in a place as bad as you do, doesn't have to pay. Go on in."

Until this day, I don't believe Rusty's grandmother knows that pretty outfit we gave her for Christmas had made the rounds in Orlando on a University of Georgia football player (in places Rusty's grandmother would shudder just to think about!)

19 | THE JUNKYARD DOGS

1975 was a turn-around season because we had come off consecutive years of 7-4, 7-3-1 and 6-5, and the fans were beginning to mumble.

Two things came about that fall. The "Spilt-60" defense was back and the Junkyard Dogs came on the scene. Both situations made a difference. We weren't very good on defense the year before and the prospects for the '75 season didn't look much better.

So there I was in the summer of 1975, trying to come up with something our defensive unit could rally around. Something we could call our own. Something we might take pride in that would make us play even harder than we could play.

Jimmy Mathews from Albany, Georgia, was visiting my house. I believe it was July, 1975. We were sitting at the bar in my kitchen having a couple of cool ones. We were talking about the condition of the Dogs and the prospects for the '75 season. On paper, things didn't look good.

I said to Jimmy, "I'm looking for something we can do to make our guys take pride in their work. Something we can hang our hats on and rally around." So we talked about different things. Then Jimmy suggested, right out of the blue, "How 'bout the Junkyard Dogs?"

My reply was I didn't consider that original enough.

Then we got to thinking about the song, "Bad, Bad Leroy Brown." If we ever did anything good maybe we could get the band to play that Junkyard Dogs tune. When we finished our conversation, I was still looking for something else. I just didn't think it was original enough.

Fall approached and I still had yet to improve on Jimmy's idea.

So, I decided to give Junkyard Dogs a try. After checking around, as far as we could tell, no living creature is more dedicated to his task than the Junkyard Dog in defending its territory.

On defense, we wanted to keep people out of the end zone. That was our territory. And if we could be just half as dedicated as a Junkyard Dog, then good things would happen.

I approached Roger Dantz, our bandmaster, and told him what our idea was. I asked him if our defense ever did anything good, would he "crank out" that song. He said he'd love to do that. The band had been looking for something different anyway.

I talked to the players about the challenge of our new statement. Believe me, it did make a difference.

Two things I want to add: a thanks to Jimmy for the idea. Jimmy lived and died with the 'Dogs. And the other involves how and when I told Vince. Believe me folks, it's a humorous account but there's just no way my editor would allow me to share it with y'all.

Ask Vince sometime where he was and what he was doing when I asked him if he had any objections to my calling our defense the "Junkyard Dogs."

In our first game against Pittsburgh, although we lost, 19-9, our defense played with a renewed enthusiasm that made me feel good. At the gathering of sports writers after the game, I told them we were calling our defensive unit the "Junkyard Dogs," and that explained why they had heard the song, "Leroy Brown" several times that afternoon.

Things just kind of grew from there.

We beat Mississippi State, South Carolina, and Clemson, but lost to Ole Miss in Oxford before rebounding to beat Vandy and Kentucky. The Richmond game was supposed to be our tune-up for the Gators. Florida ran the wishbone and ran it well. We had not played against the wishbone that year and Vince thought we could get by Richmond without a great deal of trouble. He wanted to practice for Florida during the week prior to the Richmond contest.

I was opposed to that because I didn't think we were that good. Our other defensive coaches agreed with Vince so I was out-voted. We went out and practiced Monday, Tuesday and Wednesday against Florida's wishbone. On Thursday, we spent what time we had left working against Richmond's "I" formation including their running and passing plays.

Anybody who knows anything about football knows that ain't much time to prepare a team for what might be forthcoming.

Be that as it may, we scored late in the fourth quarter to beat Richmond, 28-24. But the best part of the story is we defeated Florida the next week, 10-7. In terms of physical mismatches, the 1975 Florida game again stands out to me as an example of a team overcoming great physical odds. To me it might have been our greatest test of determination with as bad a case of the wants as I can ever remember.

Time after time the Junkyard Dogs turned Florida away and held on to have new life. It was Florida coming at us fourth-and-one, third-and-two. Our guys just dug in and did what they had to do. They stopped those drives just an inch or two short and that made all the difference in the world.

Our winning touchdown came in the fourth quarter when Richard Appleby threw the "end around pass" to Gene Washington. We won a game we couldn't have won had our guys not played like Junkyard Dogs.

One of my fondest memories of that game was the sight of two of our coaches, Sam Mitchell and Jim Pyburn, rolling around on the muddy Gator Bowl floor doing a dance called "the Gator."

That year our match-up against "Georgee Tech" was nationally televised. It was a night game. Might have been Thanksgiving.

It was cold. It had rained, or Georgia Tech had wet the field down pretty good. Parts of it were frozen.

Pepper was still the coach. Old Pepper, he was loose as a goose. I liked watching his TV show. He'd say anything and was always laughing.

On Tech's first possession, they threw a pass. Bobby Thompson, our defensive back, picked it off on about the 30-yard line and ran it back to the six. We scored right off the bat. From that point on things got better. On the series before the end of the half with the score, 21-0, our way, Georgia Tech fumbled the ball and it ended up on the back of a Tech lineman. It was just sitting there, seemed to rest there momentarily before Lawrence Craft, one of our defensive ends, just grabbed it right off the back of that unsuspecting lineman and took it in for a score.

The best part of the night was that the network had arranged to visit the Georgia Tech dressing room at halftime. Nothing folks, could have been better.

National television in the Tech dressing room and they were behind, 28-0. Serves them right for the '74 fiasco.

So the two teams went to the locker room to talk about things. Meanwhile, all the restrooms in the stadium were jammed. Finally, with just a few minutes left before the second half kickoff, these two guys were standing in the men's room at the trough. You know, the kind that starts high on one end and slants down to the drain?

Get the picture. Nobody left in the men's room except two guys taking a leak. One's a Tech man. The other's a Georgia fan.

The Georgia Tech man had on his gray flannel suit, blue button down shirt, gold and white tie, topcoat and his fur-lined gloves were tucked under one arm. Next to him was the Georgia fan in an old red jacket with a scarf around his neck. A half-pint of Early Times in his back pocket.

There they were side by side relieving themselves. Somehow, this guy from Georgia Tech standing to the left of what's going on dropped one of those fur-lined gloves and it fell into the trough. It proceeded to float downhill in front of the Georgia guy, who took aim and followed it with a good stream all the way down to the very end of the trough. The Georgia guy, as he finished, turned to the Tech fan and said, "You know buddy, this just ain't y'all's night, is it?"

I know a lot of folks may have heard the story. But it bears repeating when it comes to any encounter the Dogs had with Georgia Tech.

The final score was 42-26. Georgia!

We got to play everybody who made the trip. Vince didn't like the idea of Tech scoring that much on us late in the game. Neither did I. The '75 team could be classified as the greatest overachieving team ever, going 9-2.

In spite of that overachieving manner, in the Cotton Bowl that year, we were ahead of Arkansas, 10-0, with just three minutes left in the first half. We fumbled. Arkansas kicked a field goal. It was now 10-3. Remember, all this happens within three minutes before halftime. Jim Pyburn, our defensive coach, left the pressbox early to beat the crowd on the elevator. He wanted to be in the dressing room when the Dogs arrived. He saw the score, 10-0, our way.

Back to the game. In our next series, maybe with two minutes left, we lined up to try to run a shoestring play. That's where the team huddles up on one side except the quarterback. Ray Goff's over the ball and all of a sudden, he picked up the ball and tossed it to our back behind the team. We had done this earlier against Vanderbilt. But Arkansas was waiting.

Why we ever chose to run that play at that point on the field, none of us will ever know.

Arkansas damn-near intercepted the flip from Goff to our back. They got the ball and went on in to score.

Now here's Pyburn coming down the elevator all excited about our lead. How well we'd played. He was putting all the diagrams on the blackboard, cheering us on. All of sudden we asked him if he knew what the score was. And he said, "Hell yes, it's 10-0."

I said, "The hell it is, it's 10-10." Boy, did he hit the roof.

The life of a coach can go from real good to real bad in just one ride on the elevator. If you don't believe me, give Jim a call.

The score ended, Dogs 10. Razorbacks 31.

But still, a great year for the "Junkyard Dogs."

20 | *THOSE CRAZY TRACK PEOPLE*

I believe the '76 squad was one of the best offensive teams while I was at Georgia. We ran the veer and it was a high-risk offense. Vince never really did like it much for that reason. He'd rather run the "I" formation lead play and make four yards in a safe manner. So would I. But when the veer worked, it really worked.

Whatever we did that season, we did right. We won the Southeastern Conference Championship with 10 wins and two defeats: Ole Miss beat us, 21-17, and later in the Sugar Bowl, Tony Dorsett brought along the University of Pittsburgh and they beat us, 27-3.

During those nice pre-game Sugar Bowl festivities, I looked up and there was Coach Bear Bryant, who had stationed himself at the bar in the hospitality room and was there when anybody came in. I can remember his telling me, "You know Pittsburgh might beat me, but that Tony Dorsett wouldn't."

I asked him how he'd keep Dorsett from beating him since Dorsett was the eventual Heisman Trophy winner and Pittsburgh's biggest threat. I never could pin Coach Bryant down to find out exactly how he'd keep Dorsett from beating us.

As it turned out, I obviously didn't know the answer either, because Dorsett had a pretty good day and Pittsburgh won the game and became National Champions.

One of my best experiences of all time was our getting after Alabama, 21-0, in Athens before one of the largest crowds in Bulldog history.

We had two quarterbacks, Ray Goff and Matt Robinson. Goff was the runner, Robinson was the passer. The irony of the situation was in high school, Goff was the great passer. He was recruited on that basis by every-body. The book on him was, "Great arm, could throw it a mile, but couldn't run." He was the lumbering type runner. Matt Robinson, on the other hand, ran the "Power I" offense at North Springs High School in Atlanta, and rarely threw the ball.

But when they got to Athens, Goff became the running quarterback. Robinson threw it for us.

In the 'Bama game we had a great day. We had some terrific plays that kept things going. We led, 7-0, until a minute before the half. I can't remember why Matt was in the game. He came up to the line of scrimmage. The ball was like on the 3-yard line.

Would you believe he lined up with his hands under the guard's butt, instead of the center's?

He got "unconfused" and scored on a keeper to put us ahead, 14-0.

Again, the life of a coach: like old Jim Pyburn on the elevator, or Vince watching Matt bark signals all crouched down behind one of the guards.

Makes one wonder what we're doing in this business. I know. It beats the hell out of work,

On the Friday afternoon before that Saturday battle with Alabama, we were in Sanford for a light workout. It's a loose-type of practice. My chance to throw passes to the defense and show off my arm.

But already at four o'clock that afternoon, at least a dozen of those nuts had begun to gather to find themselves a place to sit on the railroad track overlooking the stadium. One guy even had a deer stand mounted on a telephone stand.

Free seats were up high looking down through the south end zone. Choice spots on the track were tougher to come by than a seat on the 50 yard line.

Our business manager, Kermit Perry, came by the railroad track at seven o'clock the next morning headed for the locker room. By then, hundreds of the "track people" had gathered. Seven in the morning. They spent the night there.

Kermit said he hollered and asked somebody he recognized how long he'd been sitting there. The guy hollered back and said, "About two fifths of vodka."

By the way, the "track people" were one of the greatest assets and one of the greatest features of Georgia football tradition during my 17 years at the University.

They showed total commitment to the Georgia program every Saturday. They were a point of inspiration for me. And I salute them as the finest illustration of "loyalty" I've ever seen. They were my kind of people.

Our team bus would pull up to the stadium to the cheers of the worlds' nuttiest fans packed on the bank and on the tracks. It seemed like thousands. You couldn't find a more rabid, enthusiastic Georgia supporter anywhere.

There were those who felt the "track people" were an undesirable element. But those track folks hated Alabama, loved the Dogs and stamped out the kudzu. And that ain't all bad.

As our players got off the bus, those people yelled and yelled and cheered to the extent if anybody who had on that Georgia jersey and walked down those steps to the dressing room couldn't get excited about playing football, then something was wrong with them.

There's no telling how many games Georgia won over the years because of "the edge" provided by the railroad track gang.

That's the truth.

Along with that is another story that touched me.

I got off the team bus one day not long after I had arrived at Georgia. There was this big, one-armed black man standing right by the bus door. I was always the last one off the bus. As I passed him, he asked if I had a ticket.

I reached in my pocket and gave him a sideline pass and moved on with the team. Never said a word to him.

That happened in 1964.

From that moment on, every Saturday when that bus door opened, that guy was standing there. And I never would say anything. I'd just give him a ticket. He came to be my good luck omen. My genie. Everything was going to be okay, as long as that exchange took place. Just me and that one-armed, black man. All those years. Never any contact with one another except on game day. I'd give him a ticket, we'd shake hands and I'd get the feeling we would do all we could to win the game for him and those loyal track fans.

Every home game, folks, I was thrilled to the deafening cheers of our 80,000 fans. During the game, the close plays, the thrill of the competition of two teams getting after one another.

But for me, it started when I'd climb off that team bus and my one-armed, black man would be there.

A football game can really create good quotes. One that I'll always remember came out of our game with Florida that year.

They led Georgia at halftime, 27-13. Doug Dickey was their coach. They ran over us pretty good during the first half with a wishbone attack. On their first series of the second half, they had a fourth down and one yard to go. The ball was on their 35-yard line. For some reason they chose to go for it.

They ran an option pitch. Our safety, Johnny Henderson out of Macon, came up and tackled their guy with the ball at the line of scrimmage.

That play went down in Florida's history as "Fourth and Dumb," according to the Jacksonville papers.

"Fourth and Dumb" just flipped the switch and it became our game. We went on to beat them, 41-27. The lights went out for Florida, you might say, and came on for us.

We scored 28 points in the second half. The Gators scored none.

"Fourth and Dumb!" They said it. I didn't

The Junkyard Dogs did it again. By that time, you have to know the entire team had taken on the Junkyard name. Something I had chosen for just our defensive unit.

When that took place, what with the entire team being the Junkyard Dogs, I decided I wanted my squad to have its own identity. So I looked around our unit that year. We had one semi-big lineman. His name was Ronnie Swoopes. He was six-three and weighed 240. He wasn't all that big. But it was big for us. My other players, when they stood around Ronnie in a huddle, were amazingly small. Linemen and defensive backs, all of them were small.

So I was going to call the group, "Ronnie and the Runts." I had these t-shirts made up that said, "Runts have to try harder."

"The Runts" never really caught on because Junkyard Dogs had done so well. But that was my intent.

It was during 1976 somebody started a campaign against brutality in football. How players used their helmets as impact weapons. How people were getting hurt and mangled. This came out pretty strong about the time we beat Alabama, 21-0, that season.

As a matter of fact, Sports Illustrated ran a picture of an Alabama back being tackled by nine Georgia Bulldogs. You could hardly see the Alabama player. Maybe a part of his helmet and a leg. He was completely engulfed by red players. After the article came out, somebody from SI called me and asked what I thought about brutality in football, as they had used that picture to depict brutality.

Nine guys tackling one little old ball carrier.

I told the SI reporter that after looking at the picture they had published, my question was, "Where in the hell were the other two Georgia players?"

21 | *THAT ONE LOSING SEASON*

1977 was the only losing season in Coach Dooley's 25 years at Georgia. We opened at our place by beating Oregon. But then Clemson beat us, 7-6, which by the way, was their first victory over Georgia in Athens in 63 years.

However, the next week Coach Dooley got his 100th victory when we beat South Carolina, 15-13. In just 12 more years, he would have 200.

We had a chance against Alabama in Tuscaloosa.

Our guys really played hard. In the fourth quarter, an obvious pass reception for us was ruled caught out of bounds. The films later showed our guy well in bounds. But they went on to beat us, 18-10.

I haven't said much about officiating. And I probably won't! But it's amazing how an official's decision can have such a drastic effect on a coach's life.

We beat Vandy in Nashville. And played Kentucky the next week in Athens when Prince Charles of England was the honored guest. Kentucky proceeded to beat us, 33-0. The worst numbers posted since we've been at Georgia. I'm not superstitious or anything like that. But I hope Princess Di keeps things interesting enough for Charlie so that he will not want to attend any future Georgia football games. We closed out our worst year with three straight losses to Florida, Auburn and Georgia Tech. We finished the season 5-6.

We had gone from the penthouse to the outhouse in one year.

22 | WHICH WAY DO THEY GO?

Going into 1978, the experts analyzed our opportunities for the upcoming season by making us underdogs in eight of our 11 games. We suggested "Let's go from underdogs to wonderdogs." We were probably the only ones stupid enough to think we could ever pull off such a thing. But then nobody thought Willie McClendon out of Brunswick would give us a season like he did.

It was his senior year. All he did was establish a Georgia rushing record and took us along for one hell of a ride. Nine wins, one defeat and one tie.

We lost to Bill Walsh's Stanford team in the Bluebonnet Bowl, 25-22, and earlier to South Carolina who had a guy by the name of George Rogers, a freshman who could really run the football and later won the Heisman. But in our other "outings " it was a "W" for the Dogs over Clemson, Ole Miss, LSU, Vandy, Kentucky, VMI and Florida.

Our bubble almost burst when we went to Kentucky. We were behind, 14-16, with 4:03 left on the clock when Jeff Pyburn, our quarterback, directed a long drive that got us to their 12-yard line with three seconds left in the game. We ran our field goal team onto the field, and as we looked out there, low and behold, we lined up to kick with only 10 men. Now, you can kick a field goal with 10 men, but the rule says you must have seven on the line of scrimmage to make it a legal play and we had six. We had no time outs remaining and we couldn't get a lineman out on the field in time to execute the play. What to do? Kentucky did it for us. They called time out to give our kicker, Rex Robinson, some extra seconds to think about his task. During the time out, we found Tim Morrison, sophomore tackle, who was our missing person. We got 11 players out there. Rex made the field goal and we won,

17-16.

Naturally, Coach Dooley inquired of Morrison as to his whereabouts when we needed him. Tim's reply: "Coach, I was on the bench praying."

Tim's prayers for the team were answered, but he would have had to do a heap of praying for his own personal safety if Kentucky hadn't called that time out.

Tim was an outstanding offensive lineman for three years, and contributed greatly to our success. However, if things hadn't worked out the way they did. I'm afraid he would always be remembered as the missing lineman on the field goal team.

This is like life. A man can do so many good things during a lifetime and "screw up" just once. Chances are he will be remembered not for the good things, but for the mistake he made.

We beat Tech, 29-28, scoring with two minutes left in the game. A back-and-forth game. It seemed whoever had the ball last would win. We did.

But listen to this. When we scored with just 90 seconds on the clock, it was Georgia 27, Tech 28. The week before we tied Auburn, 22-22, by choosing to kick an extra point. I don't think anybody wanted to kick an extra point and tie Georgia Tech this week.

Our offensive coaches decided to run a pass play for the two point try..

We ran the pass. It was incomplete. But hold on. Georgia Tech was called for pass interference in the end zone. We had another chance. I knew then the good Lord wore a red and black robe. But we still had to push the ball over to win.

We were at the one-and-a-half-yard line. We called time out to think about what we wanted to do. Vince wanted to run the lead play, the same play Jimmy Poulos beat Tech with in '71! That's a hard rushing play. Just for a yard and a half. Bill Pace, our offensive coordinator in the pressbox, wanted to run an option play.

They argued. Vince on the sideline. Pace in the pressbox. One wanted to do something. One wanted to do another. So they finally, almost at the expense of taking too much time during the time out, decided they were going to fake Vince's play and make an option out of it, the lead option.

I'll never forget Vince saying, "Oh hell, go ahead and run it."

So we lined up in our "I slot" formation. We were going to run "43 lead option." We were faking Vince's favorite play. The quarterback was going to take the ball, ride the tailback, pull it out, and either keep it or pitch it to the trailing back coming around.

Well, as we looked out there, we saw Buck Belue, a freshman quarterback; Jimmy Womack, a sophomore fullback; and Matt Simon from Statesboro, a freshman tailback. Right off the bat when the ball was snapped, Womack, the lead blocker went the wrong way. There's Simon, who ain't a Rhodes Scholar (and we could see the wheels turning in his head), saying to himself, "Old Jimmy's played here longer than I have. He must know where he's going, so I'm going to follow him."

This was a moment when everybody's life depended on what was is happening. It was critical. And here we saw our fullback and tailback going the wrong way. Well, poor old Buck wheels out of there. He's supposed to fake the ball to the tailback and there ain't no tailback. The Georgia Tech defensive end was bearing down on Buck.

But Amp Arnold, the wingback, along with Buck, did what he was supposed to do. Buck simply tossed the ball to Amp and he walked into the end zone. Our fullback and tailback, having gone the wrong way, sucked Tech's linebackers all to the wrong side, allowing Buck to flip it to Amp, who went in for the two points.

Well there's a situation: Georgia against Georgia Tech and it couldn't be more critical. You either win or lose the game on one play. And the play is a complete abortion. But it worked.

Try and figure that out. I suppose it's moments like those, when everything goes wrong and also those moments when everything unfolds just as you have practiced it, that have made coaching a maddening, marvelous experience all these years.

I'm sure somewhere along the way, some sportswriter gave our coaching staff credit for making a great call and praised our players for great play executions. If we had executed perfectly, it might not have worked. That's coaching.

I'd rather be lucky than good.

23 | *ACC SPELLS TROUBLE*

This was one of the most unusual years I've ever experienced. As everybody knew, Georgia was supposed to beat all those Atlantic Coast Conference teams and struggle with its Southeastern Conference opponents.

In 1979, we promptly lost to Wake Forest, Clemson and South Carolina. But then, we came back to beat Ole Miss, LSU Vandy and Kentucky. Virginia showed up in Athens, our eighth game in, and they beat us badly. Then we traveled to Jacksonville, and whipped Florida.

Now we are 5-4. All our wins are over Southeastern Conference opponents and all our losses, against Atlantic Coast Conference teams. South Carolina was an independent, but they are first cousins to that Conference.

We were going to Auburn with an opportunity of winning the Southeastern Conference Championship with four losses on our record. By winning the conference championship, Georgia would be the host team in the Sugar Bowl. We could possibly beat Auburn, lose to Georgia Tech and represent the Southeastern Conference, with a 6-5 record.

But this didn't happen. Auburn beat us, 33-13, and we beat Tech, 16-3.

Another most unusual thing about this particular Georgia team was that we led the nation with 49 takeovers (fumble recoveries and interceptions). One would think with that many takeovers, we'd have beaten everybody.

We would return a number of good players from this team. Surely not enough to give us any reason to think we might go from 6-5, to 12-0 the next season but ...

24 | *THE DAWGS - ALL THE WAY*

I would like to open my review of the 1980 season and the many events which took place with this letter I sent to our squad in the summer of 1980.

July 7, 1980

Gentlemen (and Linemen):

The football season of '80 will be my 17th as a Georgia Bulldog. During this time there have been many thrilling Saturdays of competition, each with its individual memories, because each game has its own personality.

There are two Saturday traditions and experiences which have remained basically the same throughout the years for me and I would like to share them with you.

The first one concerns THE RAILROAD TRACK CROWD. These are my kind of people because they love the Dogs almost as much as I do. Oh, I know they do some crazy things — like turn over our opponent's buses sometimes, and now and then they throw one another down the bank and into the street below. But they stamp out kudzu and they pull for us to win and that ain't bad.

If you can get off the bus to the cheers of THE RAILROAD TRACK CROWD and walk down those steps to the dressing room and be inspired to play football as best as you possibly can, something important is missing beneath the Georgia jersey you wear. It is impossible not to be inspired. They choke me up! The season of 1980 will be the last for THE RAILROAD TRACK CROWD. A great Georgia tradition will have passed with the new addition to our stadium. The view from the tracks will be no more.

Your team will be the last Georgia team to be greeted and cheered by THE RAILROAD TRACK CROWD. Wouldn't it be fitting if their last team was also the best Georgia team ever? Think about it!

Another Saturday tradition which has meant so much to me over the years can be stated very simply: "THERE AIN'T NOTHING LIKE BEING A BULLDOG ON SATURDAY NIGHT ... AFTER WINNING A FOOT-BALL GAME." I mean like whipping Tennessee's ass to start with, then 10 more and then another one.

This is the Game Plan. We have no alternate plan.

Sincerely,
Coach Russell Assistant Head Football Coach

There are many reasons I could offer for Georgia's National Championship in 1980. We had Herschel Walker. We had a lot of good players. The kicking game was super. The offense and defense made timely plays. We did so many good things. Yet, deep down, I really and truly believe our guys became a TEAM because five good seniors including Frank Ros, Hugh Nall, Nat Hudson, Scott Woerner and Chris Welton, caused "The Hog Incident" to take place in the spring that year.

Following spring practice every year, it was a tradition for our players to celebrate the end of such drudgery with a combination picnic and freshman initiation. This always took place out in the country at Mr. Seagraves' lake. Prior to this year, some of the locals always provided the food and "beverage" for the occasion.

As far as I know, there had never been a "serious" incident associated with this party, but Coach Dooley wanted to head off any possible trouble before something serious did happen. The word came down from the top that there would be no further "Seagraves" parties.

This is such a great tradition, thought these five seniors, it would be a shame to discontinue it. They could control the tempo of the thing, keep the action down. Nobody would get hurt, nobody would get drunk and nobody but the team would ever know about it.

The local people who had furnished the food in the past had gotten the word from Coach Dooley about no party, and so there was a problem of what to eat and how to get it. That question was solved when one of our guys remembered there were some good looking hogs in a pen out at the college experimental farm. They would get one of these choice animals and have a barbecue. The choicest product of the brewers' art was always easy to come by.

The menu was set, but how would they get a big hog out of that pen without making a lot of noise and bringing out the people who worked there? Hugh had a hunter's bow and it was decided that the quietest and most humane way to get their prize was with bow and arrow.

They went out to the farm in the wee hours of the morning and picked out the best looking specimen in the lot.

Hugh later told me he missed the whole damn hog with his first two shots and this was from his position atop the fence shooting straight down at a still target. The third arrow got him in the back of the head and "done him in." They had one helluva time getting that 400 pounds of dead weight over the fence and on to the pick-up truck. Nat was one of the strongest players on the team and he couldn't budge the beast. It took all five of them straining to get the job done.

With that, "Seagraves" went on one more time and all went well, no problems, until several freshman (who had been duly initiated by chugging hot beer until they threw up), drove by the hog's carcass and head, which was hanging from a tree limb.

They cut it down, threw it in the back of their pick-up truck and drove to the campus. They saw a group of girls gathered in the parking lot and for some crazy reason, threw the hog carcass into the crowd. Somebody called the campus police and the freshmen were "nailed."

A few days earlier, a hog had been reported missing at the college farm. Between the campus police and the people at the farm, it was decided the head and hide in the parking lot came from the missing pig.

All the papers carried the story. Sports Illustrated picked it up. We laugh about it now, but we can't stand publicity like that and you can imagine how it was reported. Coach Dooley had to take action.

Several squad meetings were held and Vince asked me to head the "investigation" of the incident. All players were aware of what was taking place. It was even brought out at one of the meetings that the hog they ate was being given steroids and those who had partaken "might be" subject to impotence and sterility. Boy, did that get their attention!

The five organizers of "Seagraves 1980" were called in by Coach Dooley and the conditions of their punishment were spelled out. They would spend the summer in Athens being paid minimum wages for doing anything around the athletic complex they were told to do. This included painting the huge concrete block wall that surrounded the practice area. This job alone must have taken them a month to complete. They would pay for the hog and for their "keep" during fall quarter.

Everyone thought that was a pretty tough sentence and it was. The five accepted their plight. They felt they had no choice, so they did it. You gotta do what you gotta do.

Last year at the 10th reunion of the 1980 team, Frank Ros reminded me that from the first day the case was judged, players (all of them, not just a few) came to him and offered to chip in and pay for the hog. This was the beginning of a new spirit, a feeling of unity, a togetherness which had not been present before.

The players felt the five seniors were taking the punishment for the whole team. Instead of a possible demoralizing effect, the incident had a bonding effect. It brought the team together.

Isn't it amazing how something like this can be the foundation for a National Championship? I'll guarantee you, "The Hog Incident" was that important to us. It brought us together as a TEAM.

During spring practice of 1980, Coach Dooley made it a point every day during squad meetings to emphasize the importance of TEAM play as opposed to individual play. If the TEAM was successful, each individual player would be successful. If the TEAM won, everyone was a winner. There is enough for everybody when the TEAM does well. The theme was TEAM and he did an outstanding job of getting their attention focused on that point.

It impressed me, and during the summer I designed the first "TEAM-me" t-shirts. (The word "TEAM" was very large, with the word "me" in very small letters underneath.) Every player became a walking picture of the theme.

Bill Pace was our offensive coordinator from 1974 through 1979. He was a fine person and an outstanding coach. After the '79 season, he took a similar position at the University of Tennessee.

Before Bill left, he and the offensive coaches asked if we wanted Robert Miles, a senior-to-be and a two-year performer at tight end, as a defensive player. I said, "Shoot yeah, we'll take him." I remembered Billy Payne in 1968. After we had switched Miles from offense to defense, Coach Pace said, "Robert Miles is a pussy. He can't play defense." I'm sure this was a tongue-in-cheek statement, but somehow it stuck with me. We moved Robert to defensive end. He had a great spring practice and he was a starter as we got ready to open the 1980 season against Tennessee (remember, Bill Pace is now Tennessee's offensive coordinator).

On Monday before the game, I was out front leading calisthenics. I had done that over the years and I'll always appreciate Vince letting me do that. It gave me a chance to express myself.

For some reason, and certainly it wasn't planned, I pulled a piece of yellow paper out of my pocket and announced that I had received a telegram from Coach Bill Pace, offensive coordinator, University of Tennessee, and it said, "Robert Miles is a pussy." The squad roared. I knew Robert could take that kind of kidding. He was a good man. He was a good student. He had walked on. He had earned his scholarship. Now he had begun his senior year and he was starting at defensive end against Tennessee on Saturday.

Since we beat Tennessee, we couldn't stop a good thing. The next Monday, I got a telegram from Tom Wilson, head coach at Texas A&M. It read, "Robert Miles is a pussy." The team laughed. Robert laughed and he was playing good and the team was winning.

We had something going now that we couldn't stop. Every Monday, even if I forgot, the players started to holler, "How about the telegram?" Every Monday, the head coach of that week's opponent would send the same message. Twelve opponents. Twelve head coaches. Same message, "Robert Miles is a pussy."

Let's get something straight, right now. Robert Miles ain't no pussy. He found his home on defense in 1980 and he played like a champion. I'd like to think those telegrams made him conscious of being a better player. The point of the story is I had fun and the team had fun. It was another "together" thing.

Ten years later as we gathered for that championship team's reunion, I got up before the group, reached into my pocket and pulled out a piece of yellow paper and announced, "I have just received a telegram from George Bush, President of the United States, it reads, Robert Miles is a pussy."

Robert laughed just as much as the others. Just as he did throughout the 1980 season. Thank you, Robert Miles.

1980. This was the year all the good things seemed to happen. The pieces of the puzzle fell into place, like the 16-15 win over Tennessee. We were lucky to win that game, but nobody anticipated the impact of Herschel's debut ... likewise, the big play in the Florida game — Buck Belue to Lindsay Scott. Good things certainly happened.

Many folks have asked me what I was doing while Lindsay was running past our bench and toward the end zone in his dramatic play. I was looking for yellow flags.

Likewise ... the Clemson game. They made 26 first downs to our 10. Good gracious, how did we ever win that one? The difference was by Scott Woerner's punt returns. Likewise, the South Carolina game and Heisman Trophy winner George Rogers, fumbled the ball on the 10-yard line going in to help us preserve a 13-10 win. Likewise, the Auburn game and Greg Bell who blocked a Tiger punt on a designed punt return, to turn the game in our favor.

And, of course, Herschel Walker, a freshman from Johnson County High School in Wrightsville, Georgia. He became a "difference maker" for the team. If you don't believe me, check the numbers.

But before we came to know that, the question was, could he do in the Southeastern Conference what he did back at Johnson County High?

At our first practice, all the coaches were at their stations testing the freshmen. When it was Herschel's turn to be timed in the 40-yard dash, all the coaches left their stations to go to the finish line to put watches on him. My watch read 4.35, as did a couple of others. Somebody got him at 4.3. Somebody else had him at 4.4. Mike Cavan, who recruited Herschel, clocked him at 4.2. We knew Mike was prejudiced, so we threw his time out.

Still, that 4.35 was the fastest time in the 40-yard dash I had ever recorded on my watch.

We had Herschel in football camp the summer before his senior year in high school, so we knew something about him. But still the question remained, could he make that transition from Wrightsville in Class A high school football to Knoxville and the Southeastern Conference? Everybody found out in the second half of the Tennessee game.

Herschel was genuinely nice. One of the most polite youngsters I've ever been around. He told me on many occasions that he'd just as soon play linebacker as running back. As I have said before, every great team must have its "difference makers." This young man was certainly that. And on this team there were others too.

About half way through the season, the philosophy, "the only game that exists is next Saturday's," began to pick up with do it "just one more time."

This was in reference, of course, to that next game. Anybody can do anything "just one more time."

Each game became a "just one more time" by not looking ahead, just doing it that week. After we had done it "just one more time," 11 times in all, I had t-shirts made up with "Just...one more time," and gave them to our players as we boarded our plane for the flight to New Orleans. In a few days, we would tee it up against Notre Dame in the Sugar Bowl.

I brought that saying with me to Georgia Southern, where it got considerable play each year as we went into the Division I-AA playoffs. Our crowds picked up on the chant "Just...one more time." It sounded good coming from the stands.

The Sunday following the Tech game, Vince and I were putting the finishing touches on a good lunch at the athletic dormitory dining hall. The Georgia coaches often took their families to lunch there on Sunday. It was a good place to visit with players and coaches in a different atmosphere.

When the room cleared out a little, Vince asked me to sit with him over in a corner and he said, "Erk, I am going to Auburn tomorrow to talk about their head coaching job. You'd better make plans to take the team to New Orleans." I said, " Are you serious?" He responded, "Damn serious. They've made me an offer I don't think I can refuse." We chatted further but that was the real substance of our conversation. The tone of our discussion led me to believe he was serious and I had been around Vince long enough to know.

It didn't take long for the word to get out that Vince was in Auburn, Alabama, and that negotiations were going on. The newspapers and television had that as the number one sports story. You can imagine what big news that was, especially at this particular time of the year.

All the assistant coaches got together immediately to discuss what might possibly happen if Vince should take the Auburn job. Our concern was not for the upcoming game with Notre Dame, we could handle that. But what about next year, and the next? What about our future at Georgia?

Vince would probably take some of these coaches with him to Auburn. Some he would not. That's the way it works. What if an "outsider" got the job at Georgia? Traditionally, the new guy brings most of his own people with him.

This is how assistant coaches are left scrambling for jobs when the head coach moves on. Not a very good situation to be in, but it happens all the time.

We decided for our own protection one of us should apply to take Vince's place, on more than an interim basis, if he should leave. We also decided it should be me.

I contacted the university president, Fred Davison, and members of the Athletic Committee. I told these people I wanted to be the head coach at Georgia if Vince left.

In every conversation, the response was very positive and in two days, I had every reason to believe that if Vince did leave Georgia, I would be the head football coach. Let me just call it like it was. If Vince went to Auburn, I would be named head coach at Georgia. It was that simple.

As a staff, we continued preparation for the Sugar Bowl. We had tons of work to do since we had a 10-game film swap with Notre Dame.

What happened is history. Vince decided to stay at Georgia. He would assume the title of Athletic Director. That was a large factor in his decision.

People who were close to the situation decided that my disappointment in not getting that job led to my leaving Georgia. I can honestly say that series of events had nothing to do with my departure. I was disappointed, but I've been around long enough to know there is nothing certain until the fat lady sings.

Let's look at the whole situation from a realistic and positive standpoint. Vince remained at Georgia and did very well. The Georgia people were happy. Pat Dye went to Auburn and started winning big and the Auburn people were happy. I went to Georgia Southern and good things happened. The Georgia Southern people were happy.

The best part of the whole situation is I'm happy and I'm so glad things happened just like they did.

Have there been other job offers? Yes!

I interviewed at The Citadel in 1967. I was impressed until the General (president) called me in and explained what he expected of his team. He knew a captain stationed at Fort "Something" who would be an excellent offensive coordinator, and a young major who would be a real good coach. I got the feeling this was going to be the General's team, not mine. I got back to Athens, called the Athletic Director at The Citadel and said, "Thanks, but no thanks." Red Parker took the job.

I had a good man pushing me for the at North Carolina State job. As a matter of fact, he was chairman of their search committee for a new head coach, and he appeared to be excited about the upcoming interview we had arranged. I was too. This all happened during the 1971 season. I was to fly into Raleigh following our game with Kentucky, interview with the committee, then return to Athens on Sunday afternoon.

I went in to tell Vince of my plan. He reasoned that if those people were genuinely interested in me halfway through the season, then they would still be interested when it was over. He made another point that if word got out that I was thinking about another job, it might not be good for the morale of the troops. We were undefeated, 6-0, and I sure didn't want to screw that up.

I returned the plane ticket, called the man and told him I'd see him after the season. He never called back.

A skinny, little guy by the name of Lou Holtz got the job.

Coach Bobby Dodd called one evening and asked if I would be interested in the head coaching position at Iowa State. Their committee had called him for a recommendation and he wanted to pass on my name.

Arrangements were made and I took the trip. It was a great interview and the hospitality was super, but have you ever been to Ames, Iowa, in January? It was gray and cold and bleak and there ain't no Spanish moss hanging on the trees up there. I couldn't wait to get back to Athens and thaw out.

A fellow by the name of Johnny Majors took that job.

There were Vanderbilt and Kentucky, and other brief encounters with job possibilities, but the time and place never seemed to be right for me. Besides, I wasn't one who was "driven" to become a head coach. I had the best coaching job in America right there at Georgia.

The Sugar Bowl game, that contest where the Dogs did it just "One More Time," has been recorded in the book, "Glory! Glory!," and other published accounts. Not much need in my writing a lot about the game except to say it was a time of great emotion.

We had good practices both in Athens and when we went on to New Orleans. That unity was still there from the "Seagraves" incident, and even stronger now as a result of eleven straight victories. The players were never a closer group than in the locker room just minutes before the Sugar Bowl game got underway. They were tight in the sense of talking to one another and getting ready for "the last game in the world."

What do I remember about the 1980 Sugar Bowl? Notre Dame was big. Yet, we won, 17-10. Our defense played like crazy and so did our offense. Terry Hoage, a thin freshman from Texas, made the trip. His only job was to block kicks. He blocked a Notre Dame field goal and his play turned the game around by giving us momentum.

One situation about "good things" continuing to happen as they had all season long took place right after Hoage's play when Rex Robinson tied it up, 3-3, with a 46-yard field goal in the first quarter. He kicked off to Notre Dame. The ball sailed down field and their two deep backs do that thing of,

"I've got it — you take it," and the ball bounced between them and here came those Kelly boys from Savannah, Bob and Steve. If Bob hadn't gotten it, Steve would have on the 1-yard line. This has to go down in history as the longest "onside kick" ever executed in football.

Herschel plowed over and it put us up, 10-3. The Irish scored once more, we held on and scored seven more and the dream was real: Dogs 17, Notre Dame 10.

I don't know how many of those 77,895 attending that game were Georgia fans, but there were enough to completely cover the Superdome playing field when the final whistle let loose. Our coaches and players had to fight for their very lives to get to the dressing room where we celebrated with those "special" cigars I had brought along for this occasion.

How do I feel about that 1980 season and team? I guess it is best summed up in the letter I wrote to the team as I was leaving for Georgia Southern — when the University of Georgia was Number One and National Champions.

June 8, 1981
Gentlemen (and Linemen):

I thought about calling you together to say "adios," but I knew I'd bust out crying and wouldn't be able to say what I wanted to say.

I want y'all to know that the toughest part of making a decision to leave Georgia was the thought of leaving you. After all, you, the players, are Georgia football and you are not only good players, but you are good people, as well.

At this time you are riding the crest of collegiate football. You have as fine a coaching staff as has ever been assembled at Georgia and as players, as much potential as I can ever remember. The future seems as bright as you want it to be. I know you want to be good and I know you will be.

Here are a few things I have believed in and have tried to emphasize during my time at Georgia. I hope you will remember them.

1. G.A.T.A.
2. Every practice is a rehearsal for the game. As you practice, so shall you play.
3. The best way to win a game is not to lose. The best way not to lose is to not make mistakes.
4. I'll believe this wherever I am. "There ain't nothing like being a Bulldog on Saturday night ... after winning a football game."

I'm moving down the road about 160 miles to Statesboro, Georgia I don't have an office or a football field yet, but I have a house and my door is always open to you. Holler at me!

Y'ALL BEAT EVERYBODY!

Sincerely
Coach Russell

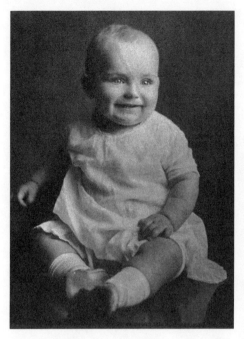

Erk, at six months, with strong arms and legs, looked ready for his future in Ensley High sports.

MAY-DAY MONARCHS CROWNED

HONOR ROLL

All A's

First semester: Ann Blaylock, Joan Cozart, Billy Lou Estes, Billy Foster, Joyce Lenderman, Marjorie Snow, Judy Sprague, Betty Weed, Mary Alice Worrell.

Second semester: Charles Cox, Don Davies, Bruce Greenhill, Richard Morgan, Frances Taylor, John Thies, Nancy Trainor.

Third semester: Louise Baker, Betty Jo Brown, Jacqueline Lenderman, Joy Love, Bob Owens, Sarah Pass, Mary Ellen Stammer.

Fourth semester: Peggy June Creel, Reginald Ginn, Susie Ann Nix, Olene Stone, Barbara Thomasson.

Fifth semester: Doris Atkins, Margaret Finlay, Dorothy Mae Hawkins, Carolyn Tate, Betty Waters.

Sixth semester: Helen Adams, Pauline Anselmo, Lenora Best.

Seventh semester: Billy Chalker, Marilyn Kelly.

Eighth semester: Janie Lou Akins, Jo Ann Culp, Bettye Davis, Jane Love.

A's And B's

First semester: Edna Earle Anthony, Virginia Armstrong, Hamlin Caldwell, Marion Caldwell, Johnny Mac Driskoll, Dorothy Duncan, John Cameron, Joyce Gann, Fred Globetti, Mary Alice Heap, Miriam Jackson, Doris Kladden, Johnnie May Krats, Billy Kremer, Dolores Middleton, Virginia Miller, Ann Mims, Jones Moore, Cheryl Mosteller, John Orr, Martha Jane Price, Harold Proctor, Richard Ray, Betty Jean Sellers, Betty Straiton, Sudie Wilson, Joyce York.

Interesting Picture Is Shown

Tuesday, April 18, most of the History and Geography classes saw a technicolor picture on South America. It was based on Walt Disney's trip to South American.

In the picture he visited Rio de Janeiro, capital of Brazil; Buenos Aires, capital of Argentina; Chile, Bolivia, Columbia, Peru, and Paraguay. The strange kinds of flowers were very interesting. They saw the way in which the rich and poor people live in South America, the way they eat and dress, and the way they entertain themselves. Their dances were quite different from ours, and so are their clothes.

All the students who saw the picture liked it very much, and hope to see more like that one.

Peace Program Presented

Recently at the residence of Mrs. Joe McMillen, in Ensley Highlands, the Study Club met for a peace program. The basis of the program was "Peace Through Poetry."

Margaret Findlay began the program with "Poetry Through the Ages," and Isabel Holmes gave "Elegy To a Dead Soldier."

The responsive reading, titled, "The Profits of All Lands Speak Friendship," was given by Jewel Alexander and Christine Sannermann.

Jacqueline Jones followed with "He Stirred the Eagle's Nest." Christine Sannermann presented "The Unknown Soldier Walks Again." Isabel Holmes concluded

Pictured above are the Queen and King of Ensley High: Dot Burford and Erskine Russell.

N. H. S. Holds | **Pvt. Auston Dies As**

Durant-Richard Team Wins Jitterbug Finals

BY CECIL DAWKINS

Along with spring comes the birds and the bees and the flowers, but in the minds of the E. H. S. students, first comes May Day.

This year, May 1st hit the old high with a bang, bringing such delightful events to the stage as Martha Jo Riddle in a ballet specialty, and Nellie Ruth Hardin in the Evolution of the Dance. Other dancers were Sarah Durant and Robert Richard, contest winners, who really shredded the old rug with their popular "Chicken Walk." Jean Sellers and Guy "Honey" Lillian gave the "Camel Walk" a whirl, while Melba Mills and Hilly McWhorter doubled on the doublestep. A hilarious novelty number was done by Red Martin and Fred Norton in comic costumes.

Blond beauty, Jean Heath, with Richard Hunter, showed the old school how the waltz should be done.

Two one-act plays were presented by the speech department. The characters of "Three's a Crowd" were Wilmore Beckers, Lenora Best, Esther Sarasohn, Dan Douglas and Jack Williams. "Glamor in the Pocono" starred Billy Alth, Ann Hinckman, Isabelle Holmes, Laurie Tranham, Jack Kimbrough and Hubert Harper. Billy Chalker directed the plays.

Uniforms of a young man: high school May King; military duty; at Auburn; and later as Grady High's head coach.

Russell, end, Aub.

Goal line

Hipps, back, G

Erk grew hair for the family; offered the Tiger look; and relaxed with the family — Jean, Rusty and middle son Don.

Squab Jones, long-time all-purpose manager for 50 years, loved the Dawgs as did Head Coach Vince Dooley.

The many faces of Erk: hugged by Jim Pyburn; "hanging tough" with Vince; relaxing with Herschel; and telling it like it was.

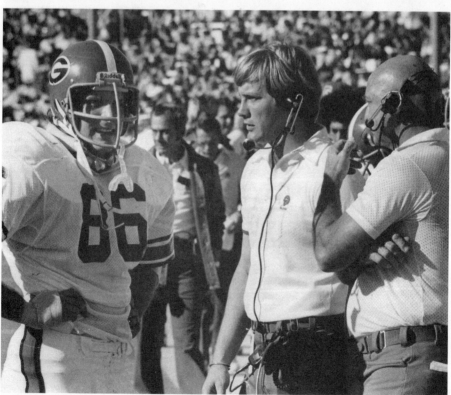

It's GATA on the sidelines; with son Rusty ('86); the Junkyard Dogs; with sons Rusty and Jay ('81); with "The Look."

'Dogs Eighth in SEC?

COURAGE
HUSTLE
ATTITUDE
MORALE
PRIDE
INTELLIGENCE
ONENESS
NEVER QUIT
SACRIFICE

A Champion is one who holds first place, having defeated all opponents.

FRIENDLY

SUNDAY	MONDAY	TUESDAY

MAMBO GOOK   TEAM   GATA

Go To Church — Select a church two miles away. Run there in thirteen minutes. After church run home in twelve minutes.	**4** "Straight Arrow" — Nall says: "Join Hudson, Woerner, Ros, Welton, & me in going Hog Wild about beating everybody in 1980. We're in the best condition ever. How about you? Only 12 more days 'til Homecoming!	**5** Your Horoscope — The alignment of the stars indicate you will make several short trips soon. May I suggest about twenty, 40 yard sprints today! Eighth in S.E.C.?
Go To Church — Do not hate Tenn. While in Church 23 hours will be adequate today) A hard workout this afternoon will be good for the soul, brother.	**11** A Fact of Life — Work a little -- Win a Little. Work a Lot -- Win a Lot! No Deposit --- No Return. Run! Run! Run!	**12** First Sunrise Service — Will be held one week from today for those who fail the test. Will You be there?

19 August 80

▶ PREDICTED FINISH
Southeastern Conference
1. Alabama
2. Auburn
3. Kentucky
4. Tennessee
5. LSU
6. Mississippi
7. Mississippi State
8. Georgia
9. Florida
10. Vanderbilt

REMINDER CALENDAR

WEDNESDAY	THURSDAY	FRIDAY	SATURDAY
1980 GamePlan BEAT TENNESSEE AND GEORGIA TECH AND EVERYBODY IN BETWEEN. THEN WIN ONE MORE!		**1** 3,000 years ago Moses said: "Take up your tent and get on your ass. We're going to the Promised Land." Today I say to you, "Take up your running shoes and get off your ass. We're going to to the Sugar Bowl!"	**2** Today's Poem There is a young coach named Kase Who wears a big smile on his face My test is so great I hardly can wait For you and the big Two mile race 17 Days 'til the test
6 <u>Humor</u> <u>for</u> <u>Today</u> Morrison: Do you know what has 16 balls and sings? Harper: No Morrison: A male quartet Harper: That's only eight balls, stupid. Morrison: One of them is a Tenor. Have you run tenor twelve miles this week?	**7** <u>Don't</u> <u>Be</u> <u>a</u> <u>Glutton</u> A glutton is one who eats fried chicken all day and wakes up in the middle of the night with a breast in one hand and a thigh the other. How Is Your Weight?	**8** <u>If</u> <u>It</u> <u>Is</u> <u>To</u> <u>Be</u> <u>It</u> <u>Is</u> <u>Up</u> <u>To</u> <u>Me</u> The Best Day -- Today The Best Time -- Now The Best Person To Do The Job -- ME	**9** The Epitome of Living There ain't nothing like being a Bulldog on Saturday night after winning a football game. Only 4 more Saturdays 'til Tennessee
13 <u>Get</u> <u>A</u> <u>Big</u> <u>Neck</u> Do Neck Iso with Earnest. If Earnest is not available, do neck bridges with Gusto. A players best friend Is A Big Neck!	**14** <u>Rope</u> <u>a</u> <u>Dope</u> Womack: Did you hear the story about the rope? Stewart: No, Jimmy Womack: Skip it! Then Run Like Crazy!	**15** <u>Welcome Home!</u> Your kind, friendly, thoughtful, courteous coaches are anxiously awaiting your arrival. Please Drive Carefully! Three days 'til the test!	**16** PICTURES AND PHYSICALS. THE CAMERAS ARE READY DR. HUBERT IS READY IS YOUR BODY READY?

Erk, the communicator through the Friendly Reminder Calendar; or in person, formal or informal.

Erk, the Eagle, holding high the "skin" with A.D. Bucky Wagner; handing it off to Southern President Dale Lick; and starting over with new players and coaches.

Erk communicates with his young Eagles.

Say what? Ham the Man! The Hugo Bowl; a "Runt" talk; Allen Paulson presenting his "million"; and Erk starting early.

A victory stogie; sideline drama; two Big Boys

1989 — the moment before the last game of Erk's career. Three hours later: Eagles defeat S.F. Austin; 37 straight wins at "Our House"; a 15 game winning season and a third national title within five years.

Tim Stowers, Eagles offensive coordinator, assumes head coaching duties and Erk begins to relax.

25 | *BECOMING AN EAGLE*

T he first time I heard Georgia Southern College was thinking about starting up or returning to football, is when I became interested in what was going on.

So many have asked me when I became interested in that situation. That's when!

In fact, Frank Inman, a former coaching colleague of mine at Georgia who had moved down to Brunswick to become director of athletics for Glynn County, called me one day and asked me if I had heard about what was going on in Statesboro and would I be interested in that coaching position.

I told him yes to both questions ... with a lot of reservations.

Seems Dr. Dale Lick, Georgia Southern's president, had gotten in touch with Frank for some recommendations. That's when he mentioned my name and asked Dr. Lick if it would be alright for him to give me a call.

Lick said, "Fine." And Frank did and later Dr. Lick got into the picture. (Wasn't he already in the picture — from the beginning?)

I had been doing the same thing for the University of Georgia for 17 years as defensive coordinator. I felt I had been looking out the same window all that time. A good window, but I really thought I was in need of new and different challenges and experiences.

I could see starting a new football program from scratch as an opportunity to do different things. Let me assure you, every day at Southern for the next four years brought forth new experiences.

I knew I was going to have to raise money. Although the idea of doing that didn't thrill me all that much, I knew that was going to be a big portion of the job. But to think, to be able to start from zero and to do something, to be totally "on your own" was an opportunity very few coaches have.

Ninety-nine percent of the time you move into a new coaching job, you're taking over somebody's successes or failures. Here was a chance to start literally with nothing, and to see what could be done.

I knew very little about Georgia Southern except what I had read in the newspapers from time to time and through folks who had gone to school there.

There was nothing I had heard from anybody that would be a factor in my choosing Georgia Southern.

I had contacts with Dr. Bucky Wagner, Director of Athletics at Georgia Southern, and the guy helping me do this book, Ric Mandes, who at that time was assisting Dr. Lick in putting together a feasibility study and a steering committee that would provide Lick some important information.

From the beginning, I kept this whole thing quiet at the University. I did ask some general questions about Georgia Southern, but as far as saying anything about taking a new job, I didn't talk to anyone. There wasn't enough information available at this time to even have a serious discussion.

Actually, there wasn't anyone in particular, especially the coaches, to talk to. They would have thought I was crazy, that I was seriously considering taking the job at Southern.

My first trip to Statesboro? It took place the weekend I had gone to Jackson, Mississippi, to lecture at a high school coaching clinic. That was a Friday. I had a luncheon appointment with Dr. Lick on Saturday. Which meant I had to be in Statesboro by noon the next day.

So I drove to the Atlanta airport, flew to Jackson, did the clinic, returned to Atlanta the next morning and headed for Statesboro. My timing was tight to say the least. So when I pulled out of the airport parking lot, I was hustling.

I kept the needle somewhere between 75 and 80 and I almost made it. In fact I was passing through Metter, a small town less than 20 miles from Statesboro on the interstate, when I saw a State Patrol car coming the other way. I was flying like crazy — I knew he had me.

Five seconds after I passed him, I saw his blue light pop on. So I pulled off the interstate. As he crossed over the median, I got out of my car and was waiting for him.

He recognized me and said, "Coach where in the world are you going in such a hurry?" I told him I had an appointment with Dr. Lick. He snapped shut whatever little book he had in his hand and said, "You get back in that car. Be careful, but don't keep the president waiting. We want you to come down here and coach our team."

My lunch with Dr. Lick took place in the spring of 1981. I believe it was April. It was the first time I had gotten to meet the man who everybody thought was a little eccentric but very energetic. I had talked to him on the phone, but this was my first time being with him.

So there we were, just the two of us, sitting by a full window in the local Holiday Inn dining room overlooking the swimming pool. Dr. Lick had some difficulty getting the conversation started because he was taking in the heavenly bodies surrounding the pool.

I did, too.

My first question to him was, "At what level would you like your football program to be?" Without flinching, he smiled and said, "Division I!" I wasn't sure what Division I meant to him. But I knew what it meant to me: Georgia, Notre Dame, Southern California — all those kind of folks.

I knew right away Dr. Lick was serious about football.

But on the other hand, I thought he might be a little crazy too.

My next question was, "Dr. Lick, how long do you plan to be here?" I damn sure didn't want to take a job with aspirations of Division I and then have this guy go somewhere else, suddenly!

He told me he was on a 10-year plan. That sounded pretty good to me. That was about my plan too, as far as future coaching was concerned.

The point is, I didn't want to move to Statesboro and then Lick leave and another president come in who might not care about athletics.

I stayed with Dr. Lick for a couple of hours and then Mandes took me to play tennis, some doubles. On the way to the courts, Mandes explained to me this would be "the" tennis competition I could enjoy in Statesboro.

After the match, I thought if that was challenging competition, then I had a feeling I would be the best tennis player in Statesboro. By the way, Freddie Blitch, a local farmer and one of our foursome, got a call that his cows were loose and he had to leave. That ended the match.

Heading back to town, I stopped by Johnson's Beverages and asked for a quart of beer. The young man who waited on me later mentioned my order to Sammy Johnson, who owns the place. Sammy told his clerk to tell Coach Russell that if he'd move to Statesboro, he could have a quart of beer, every day, "on the house."

Hell, that's the greatest fringe benefit I've had in all my years of being in this business!

Back in Athens, I sat down and told Jean where I had been and what was going on.

Remember, during that time from everybody else's point of view (except mine, Lick's, Wagner's and a few others), this was a far-fetched thing for anybody to do or to think about doing. I mean, that was everybody's natural reaction.

If I had gone back and told anybody, "Boy, I'm really considering taking that Southern job," well, you can imagine what they would have thought. Besides that, I wasn't ready to make such a statement.

Not by any stretch of the imagination.

Jean reminded me as we talked, she would do whatever I wanted to do. But I found out she later told her friends she thought her husband had lost his cotton-pickin' mind.

Vince and I never really sat down and talked about my going to Southern, not seriously. He was aware I had made a few trips down there. Vince was in Tampa attending a Southeastern Conference meeting, when I made up my mind. I called and told him of my decision. He said he couldn't believe I was going to make a move like that. I explained that it was something I had given a lot of thought to. Vince wished me luck and thanked me for the work I had done and the things we had accomplished together. Later, those folks had a nice "going away" party for me. And I really appreciated that.

Where did I actually make up my mind? In Waldo, Florida. I was returning from a speaking engagement at a Florida high school coaches clinic in Gainesville. By the way, on my way down to that meeting, I was riding along and bit into a new plug of Taylor's Pride chewing tobacco, and one of my front teeth fell out.

As I stood in front of folks and talked about my favorite subject football, I provided some extra humor this time as I whistled and talked my way through that clinic.

On the way home, I stopped in Waldo, and called Mama from a pay phone. I asked how she was doing and passed the time of day for a while. As soon as I finished, I called and asked Dale Lick if he could pay me one dollar more than the University of Georgia. He said, "Erk, we can work that out."

That's when I made my decision to come to Southern. In Waldo, Florida, which by the way, was where my Mama was born. Seemed sort of fitting to me that all that took place there.

Both the boys, Rusty and Jay, were grown and had finished college, so I really didn't have to worry about where they'd live. I was excited about doing something new and different. Somewhere along the way I convinced myself, or I was convinced this is what I wanted to do — maybe not what I ought to do, but it was really what I thought I'd like to do.

I didn't have to worry about my kids. It wasn't like they were in high school and we'd have to move them. Jean was my only consideration.

At one point, the four of us sat down and I outlined what I thought the Georgia Southern situation might be, although I really had no idea. Truly, what I had was just some sort of visualization of the situation.

I asked Jean what she thought. She said, "I'll do whatever you think you need to do." Her answer wasn't, "I don't want to do it," or, "I think you ought to do it." It was, "If you think that's what you want to do, then that's what we ought to do."

Rusty said, "Go for it."

Jay said, "Follow your gut feeling."

Those were the comments my family made when I put it to them. All were good comments. I liked them.

Football at Georgia Southern College was Dale Lick's idea. It was his baby. It was his brainstorm. I felt he, the president, would have the support of the administration. He was the administration, wasn't he?

As for Bucky Wagner, I liked him. Of course I had no idea of his administrative abilities. Since then, however, his abilities have proven to be pretty good ... in fact, he is very capable. Especially for a guy from Ohio.

At the time I was visiting Georgia Southern and having a good look around, Bucky came off as a likeable guy and seemed to have a strong background in athletics. Of course he, like Dr. Lick, would be cooperative with this big step they were about to take.

Keeping in mind I would be active as a fundraiser, I called to ask if Georgia Southern had somebody who could go out and get money or who was already doing those things.

I found out they did.

Dale Lick!

I'm here to tell you right now, Lick had very little fear of asking for something when it came to Georgia Southern. In those tight moments when it's a "fourth-and-one" and there are just a few seconds left and this one is for all the marbles ... Lick would get the ball. This was good because I wasn't an "asker." Later, I became one ... through necessity.

He was calm under pressure. So calm that he almost got fired by the Board of Regents for aggressively promoting Georgia Southern. By the way, you can imagine my consternation when I picked up the *Atlanta Journal* and read, "Lick 5, Regents 4." They almost fired the reason I came to Southern.

Nothing was too good for his institution — books in the library, students working with the right kind of equipment, whatever. He'd go after it.

That's the way he approached football. He thought is was important. It was so important it was going to be his vehicle to university status.

Ironically, the first team Georgia Southern ever squared off against was the Florida State Junior Varsity. You know who the president of Florida State is now? Dale Lick.

26 | *STARTING FROM SCRATCH*

I t was on the morning of May 26, 1981, at a press conference, that Bucky introduced me as the head coach for Georgia Southern football.

There were about 500 folks in Hanner Fieldhouse on the Southern campus waiting to hear what I had to say about a place that had no equipment, no stadium, no scholarship money, no staff and really, not even a football. Earlier that morning Bucky had run to K-mart and bought a football to hand to me during the introductions.

Just the night before, I had spoken at the Johnson County High School sports banquet in Wrightsville. They were honoring one of their own who had gone out and performed pretty well. His name was Herschel Walker.

After the dinner, Herschel walked with me to the car, shook my hand and said, "Good luck, coach."

Herschel was headed back to Athens where there was adequate equipment, money, staff, just everything. And here I was headed for Georgia Southern which didn't even own a football. I think Herschel might have thought I was crazy like a lot of other people back at Georgia.

I drove on to Statesboro where I met Mandes. He took me by a local gathering and that group included a number of Georgia supporters and they still couldn't believe I was doing this thing.

Later, he dropped me off at Dr. Lick's house where I spent the night. I felt like a blue chip high school football prospect who was being stashed away so the competing coaches couldn't find him.

The next morning I got up, ate breakfast and went out to the campus to make the announcement. Dr. Lick welcomed the folks, telling them how things were really going to work out now that Erk was here. I was thinking to myself, "That's easy for you to say, Dr. Lick. You ain't gonna be down at the practice field come August trying to find 20 or 30 guys to play ball." But Lick had by that time proven himself tough and ready to go. So I knew I would be able to count on him hanging in there with me.

Then Bucky got up and did his thing.

Finally, it was my turn. Bucky handed me the K-mart football and I held it up high for everyone to see. I wanted to make certain everyone knew why I was there. And of course, the press needed some pictures.

My remarks were brief and to the point. I thanked everyone for making me feel at home. I mentioned how important Dr. Lick had been in my deciding to take the job. And then I just told them, "Folks, I'm 54. Turn that around and it's 45. Age is nothing but two numbers to me." I certainly am glad I became 10 years younger with that statement, because being 45 really came in handy while we were taking all those 12-14 hour bus trips later as the Eagles traveled to play away and as I spoke to groups anywhere who would listen to the Georgia Southern story.

I went on to share with them that morning two very important things I had come to know in coaching football — that every team needed the loyal support of the fans, and a place to play. A nice stadium, where on Saturday afternoons the Eagles would put it together. And where football "tradition" would resound down the aisles onto the field.

I then made a really bold statement, but I meant it. I said to the group that if they would help me with those two things, within 10 years we could line up and compete with anybody.

The place went crazy, which was fitting because I thought to myself, "Russell, you're crazy for having made such a statement." But it was too late then, and suddenly everybody was caught up in a dream.

It was my idea to hold the press conference on Saturday morning. I felt that having made my decision, we needed to go ahead and make the announcement.

The newspapers and the rest of the media were full of speculation by that time and I thought we had speculated enough. We ought to get it completely out in the open. Get it over with.

It had been a tremendous decision for me to make. There were a lot of University of Georgia fans really pulling for me to stay with the Bulldogs. There were telephone calls every day with people giving me advice, telling me I had no business going to Georgia Southern, which had no program ... when after all, in their opinion, Georgia was the best place to be. I suppose I was impressed more by one such comment when Charlie Whittemore, one of the young assistant coaches at Georgia, and I were playing racquetball.

This local fan saw us playing. He opened the door and stopped the game. He proceeded to tell me that I had no business taking on the Georgia Southern job, because that was a job for a young man. Honestly, this statement aggravated me to the extent that I beat Whittemore for one of the few times, ever.

I suppose I made about four trips to Statesboro. I met with college officials, the athletic staff and many folks from the community, especially the so-called "Dirty Dozen." Those guys had done so much in getting the idea of football at Southern off the ground, even before I came into the picture.

One person I called and talked to was Bruce Yawn, the cashier at Snooky's Restaurant which, by now, has become my second home. Bruce had played offensive guard for Georgia in the late '60s and knew the game and knew the local temperature. So, now and then, I'd call Bruce and we'd talk about how things really were going. He would give me his honest opinion.

Really, Bruce owns Snooky's. I ought to straighten out that fact. But he did run the cash register because that was his best vantage point to check out the coeds who were bold enough to venture into the joint.

Once, Jean and I tried to slip into town just to look around. But that didn't work out too well. I had wanted her to see beautiful downtown Statesboro and some of the neighborhoods. But we were spotted. So we just bought a copy of the local paper and headed on back to Athens.

From the time Dr. Lick, Bucky and I stood in front of the crowd the morning of May 26, to when I reported in at Southern on July 1, I closed up shop at the University and said goodbye to many dear friends and associates, which leads me to say that leaving wasn't all that easy.

Oh, I was really excited about having the opportunity of starting a program from scratch and was full of anticipation about what was out there for me. But still, you have to remember, Jean and I lived in Clarke County for 17 good years and while we were there, we experienced many nice things. We had deep roots in Athens. It was a great place to live.

One guy I knew I would really miss was Dr. Fred Davison, the president of the University.

Fred and I were good friends. It went beyond his being the "top dog" and me being just one of the dogs.

Often times after our home games, Fred and his wife and the Georgia coaches and their wives would go over to Vince and Barbara's to rehash the game and shoot bumper pool. Fred was a pretty good player and a terrific president. The University of Georgia did well under Fred's leadership. I admired him greatly. We laughed together when we won and we cried together when we lost.

When he heard I was thinking about leaving Georgia, he called me into his office and we had a good down-to-earth conversation. I told him the reasons I was considering taking the job at Southern and how much I knew I had going for me at Georgia. Fred is a good listener. When I finished, he told me that if I ever wanted to get out of football, there would be a place for me at the University.

Fred Davison is a special kind of guy. It's unfortunate the University let him get away.

One of the items that really took hold of me from the first time I met Dr. Lick and then later when I met the rest of the Southern people, was just how serious they were about starting a football program.

They were dedicated to anything it would take to make things happen.

I found that out when I mentioned to Dr. Lick how I had been trying to get myself placed in the Teachers' Retirement System of Georgia, and at the University of Georgia that situation had proven very difficult. I wondered if Dr. Lick might have a new point of view on this subject.

I was 54 and retirement at the time loomed as a large factor in my future. So I talked to Dr. Lick and his personnel officer about my situation. Later, I received a call. Dr. Lick said he had worked it out for me and I was now with the Teachers' Retirement System of Georgia. "Anything else?" he asked. That guy could get serious about a project.

Interestingly enough, the University of Georgia, where for a long time I had tried to get some help with my retirement, let it be known that that could now be arranged.

It was too late. I had already made the commitment to Georgia Southern.

During the latter part of May and all of June, I worked hard back at Georgia, wrapping up things as far as my responsibilities were concerned. I had a football camp to conduct and many other activities to carry out. All the while though, I have to admit, I was thinking about Statesboro and Georgia Southern football.

That's when I thought of our equipment manager at the University ... one of the best I've ever known, which means he was one of the stingiest. His name was Howard Beavers and I respected him tremendously because he was one of the finest in the business. He was the kind of guy if he issued you a pair of socks, he expected two socks back. If you gave him one sock, you got one clean sock the next day for scrimmaging.

Beavers had a simple rule, "A sock for a sock; a jock for a jock."

Anyway, before I left Georgia, I went over and talked with him about my situation down at Southern. Beavers dug around and found at least 250 old cotton jerseys in various colors, a bunch of pants, a truck load of shoulder pads and other football items which could be reconditioned.

I even called Georgia Tech, can you believe that? And how about this, they sent me a set of old yellow jerseys for a dollar each. Georgia Tech! I was the enemy for 17 straight years, and now they were helping me.

I never thought I'd coach a team with yellow shirts.

Honestly folks, we wouldn't have started football at Georgia Southern without Beavers' contributions.

We got stuff from Vanderbilt and Ole Miss. We also bought a seven-man sled from Dunwoody High School in Atlanta for $100, which is less than one tenth of the normal cost. Si Waters sent one of his furniture trucks to Atlanta and picked it up for us. Everything we did as we started our program was through necessity. It was "bargain basement" time at Southern but with a good purpose.

Dennis Nelson owned a steel construction company in nearby Pembroke. He built a coaches' tower for us, one of the nicest ones I've ever seen. Coach "Bear" Bryant had his famous tower in Tuscaloosa. And I would have one in Statesboro! Whereas, Coach Bryant conducted his practices from his tower, I climbed the ladder to mine the first day it arrived and never returned. It was too far from the action to fit my coaching needs. We used it to video tape practice sessions. Dennis also built "chutes" for our offensive line plus our other blocking and tackling sleds and anything else we could draw up. He wouldn't let us pay him for those items. And it was a good thing too. We didn't have any money.

If it hadn't been for good friends like Beavers and Dennis, we just couldn't have gotten started. That's the truth.

27

GIVE IT ALL YOU GOT

From the very beginning, I knew Statesboro was a place I would like to live. But in all honesty, I'm a pretty simple guy when it comes to locating. I've always enjoyed the places I've lived during my career. I suppose the closest I have come to not enjoying "quarters," were those first few months in Nashville when I lived in a dormitory and my family was still in Auburn.

That really was no fun.

I feel I can live and adjust to almost any situation, and so can Jean. We've always been fortunate to live in good places and be surrounded by good people.

I felt I could fit in with the people of Statesboro. We talked the same language from the very beginning. I found this out early on when I would go to Snooky's and sit around the table with the folks who frequented that place and realized these were great people.

They weren't "football experts" like you find some places. I liked that. I discovered there were other things to talk about. I got involved in discussing fishing, farming, fighting and all the other "f" words they used as much as I did football.

During those visits to Statesboro, I met Cohen Anderson, a local attorney who was extremely excited about the new football program. It was almost as if he was getting ready to play again. Cohen had been born and raised right there in Bulloch County. He was up in age and he knew everybody. He had been a football player for the Georgia Teachers Blue Tide back in the late 1930s before World War II broke up everything. When I reported to Georgia Southern on July 1, 1981, for my first work day, there was Cohen waiting for me. He made it a day I'll never forget.

We got in his pickup truck and started down Highway 80, one of the main branches tying Statesboro to the rest of the world. Cohen was fired up about raising money. Our first stop was a boat place out in the country. Later we went by a lumber yard, then a farm supply store. He introduced me to everybody he saw.

We stopped by a feed and seed mill filled with a bunch of Georgia Tech people. You can imagine how glad they were to see me as the new coach of Georgia Southern. And how willing they were to contribute money to my cause. I figured they still had me pretty well set in their minds as a coach at Georgia, the enemy. I was received warmly enough at all those stops but it was obvious football wasn't the most important thing in their lives.

This was my first experience on my first day with an enthusiastic Southern alumnus doing the best he could do to raise some money for football.

Cohen and his wife, Newell, came to be my good friends and supported the program all the way down the line. We lost Cohen in 1989 after a long illness. But you know, almost until the day he passed away, if the Eagles were home, somehow he'd climb those stadium steps and sit and cheer as long as his strength allowed him to.

Another interesting individual to whom I was introduced that first day was Lincoln Womack.

I met him in Cohen's office. Lincoln Womack wore overalls and a blue work shirt and boots and carried a roll of hundred dollar bills in one pocket and a pistol in the other. Mr. Womack came from about as far back in the woods as anybody could. There he was sitting in Cohen's office. And on top of that, Cohen was going to ask Lincoln to give me some money for football. I'm not certain Mr. Womack knew what a football looked like, but I liked him and I think he liked me. We just didn't share the same major interest. He was into pine trees.

I'm sure he wondered who in the hell Erk Russell was and what Cohen was talking about. So Cohen went ahead and mentioned we needed money for this cause. And with that, Lincoln pulled out a hundred dollar bill and handed it to me. When I saw that roll, I got greedy.

From there on, whether in my office, on the street ... whenever, he'd hand me a hundred dollar bill. Unfortunately, I didn't bump into him enough. As a pine tree farmer, Lincoln once told me he didn't have a million dollars but he did have a million pine trees. I got to thinking that a million pine trees and a million dollars have a lot in common, possibly a stadium.

He was in his 70s when I first met him. He was friendly. He was straightforward. He'd see me, hand me the hundred dollar bill, say a few words and keep on going. Lincoln looked good in those overalls. Comfortable.

Lincoln wore his outfit because it was what he wanted to have on and he figured a guy like himself ought to wear them. I agreed.

I had talked to Bucky Wagner along the way as I was making my decision to come to Georgia Southern about how we were going to buy equipment, offer scholarships and where we were going to play. And where we were going to get the money to pay a coaching staff.

I did two things during the interim of my move from Georgia to Georgia Southern. The first was to start rounding up a coaching staff and finding some equipment.

But I knew the rest of what I needed would have to come from some strong funding. That's why that first day with Cohen meant so much to me. He had given that trip much thought. He couldn't wait for me to get to town so he could grab me and take off talking about our needs and how these folks should invest in this dream that was now about to become a reality.

By the time I had arrived in Statesboro, some efforts had been made by the college administration to begin a Boosters' organization. Not much had happened. So I found myself expanding those roads traveled like the one with Cohen that first day. I would go anywhere, anytime, as long as it didn't interfere with my duties as a coach. I would talk to folks about our needs. I would ask for $2 for a pair of socks or a jock or a chin strap; 4$ for a t-shirt; $10 for a jersey; $75 for a set of shoulder pads or a helmet. (A million dollars from anyone who wanted a stadium named for him!)

Anything they would give, we would take back to Statesboro and put into our football program. I traveled night after night after night throughout South Georgia with the message, "Folks, we need your help." I felt like I spoke to every civic group in Southeast Georgia, some of them twice.

There were great people out there. All this football stuff was just new to them. Sometimes we convinced them with our story. At other times, to be perfectly honest, we came home empty-handed. But at least we had called the play and tried to reach our goal.

I went to Eastman, and spoke in a cafeteria and had about 70 people there. I don't know how much we brought home, but we had something in the way of funds. And remember, we were selling football in this area as a new experience for these folks. We were telling them something they had not heard for a long time — you won't have to go to Athens or Atlanta to see good college football. You can come to Statesboro.

I spoke in churches, back rooms, Sunday school rooms, tents, bank board rooms, you name it and we were there, carrying the word, talking about our needs. Encouraging everybody to get interested and give. We needed the money.

In Lyons one night, we ate barbecue off paper plates and drank good homemade iced tea from styrofoam cups. I got up and began to talk. As I talked I really felt good about the way these folks were listening. They were nodding their approval as I told the story of our needs. How football would help expand the services for the Georgia Southern students. How it would be a great place to be for everyone on those autumn Saturday afternoons.

I swear right in the middle of my talking I thought I heard an, "Amen." What a night! Lewis Grizzard was there.

Lewis is a dyed-in-the-wool Georgia Bulldog and will go anywhere for good barbecue. They told me he had tears in his eyes that night I spoke in Lyons. Maybe he was crying because he wanted me to shut up so we could go drink a beer. He couldn't believe old Erk had turned tailcoat and wasn't up there talking about the red and black anymore.

But this is typical of how I spent those first summer nights and all the next year into 1982, traveling and talking and asking people to support football at Southern.

You know in life, if there isn't some humor, then trying isn't worth much.

Bucky, Mandes and I went to Pembroke for a breakfast meeting. We were invited by a good friend of ours, Danny Warnell. He said, "Come on down and talk to my people. They are really enthusiastic about what you're doing."

When we arrived around 7:30 that morning we were shown to a back room of the Cowart Cafe. There sat about 20 men who looked about as interested in hearing what I had to say as if Lyndon Johnson had just been resurrected.

It was the kind of place where the waitress knows everybody and what they want — eggs, no eggs, whole wheat toast, coffee with cream, coffee with no cream.

The guy in charge said to me, "Erk, why don't you get things started and tell us about football at Southern." So I moved to the front of the room and thanked them for getting up so early and meeting us and expressing an interest in what we were doing just up the road in Statesboro.

I was about five to 10 minutes into what I had to say when the waitress came in with the first of many breakfast trays. She commenced in a pretty good sounding voice, "Pass that down to Joe ... and Harry, here's yours ... and John, you had plain coffee." This went on for a long time, while I was supposed to be telling the story.

Now these guys were eating their breakfast and the waitress kept bringing in more and more for them to eat.

And old Erk just wasn't too sure he was getting the job done, particularly when I looked to the back of the room and Wagner was doing his damned best to keep from busting a gut at the situation I now found myself in. Folks, I'm here to tell you, I've been in some tough situations and had to keep on with whatever I was doing. But let me go on. Things got worse.

Being in the cafe's back room at that time of day, I didn't realize this was when the grocery man did his thing. That is, filling up the stock closet located just behind where I was standing. I had thought it might be a restroom. I was wrong.

So the grocery man, while the waitress continued passing out plates of eggs and bacon, started pushing his dolly full of boxes behind me into the stock closet. He made five trips, each time never saying a word.

There I was, trying to talk about football, looking at a group of hungry men putting away their breakfast, a lady in white making certain everyone got a refill of coffee, and the grocery man, making certain nothing detained his purpose in life. Meanwhile, Wagner had now buried his head in his hands and was shaking with laughter.

And with that, I just started laughing. Hell, what else was there to do?

Finally, the guy who had invited me down started laughing and was joined by the rest of those good people. I told them just to give Southern football everything they had. I illustrated my point with this story.

Seems this young couple who had not been married too long took a weekend trip to a professional seminar. The husband was just starting out in his career and was taking every advantage he could in preparing himself for the future.

The meeting started the next morning with coffee at 7. So the couple set their alarm for 6 and went to bed and proceeded to do the things young married couples do. There wasn't too much sleep that night. Consequently neither of them heard the alarm.

They jumped out of bed with about 20 minutes to go. The guy told his wife to go ahead and take her shower first and he would follow.

This was a pretty nice place where they were staying and it offered amenities such as shoeshine service. If guests wanted to have shoes shined, they just left the shoes right outside the door before retiring. The next morning the shoes would be polished to a nice sheen and would be relocated where they were the night before.

As the husband got into the shower and his wife was drying off, he asked her if she would reach outside the door and get his wing tips.

So he was showering and she had the room door slightly opened, trying her best to get the shoes, which were just out of her reach. Seems she kept reaching farther and farther 'til she was out in the hall when a draft hit the door and it slammed shut, leaving her unclad in the hallway with nothing but those nicely polished wing tip shoes.

As luck would have it, the elevator bell rang and off stepped this really drunk guy who began weaving down the hall toward this lady in distress. Get the picture. She's naked with a pair of shoes and a drunk is moving toward her.

Slowly she began sliding down the wall with those shoes placed strategically. And there she remained while the drunk kept bumping around moving toward her.

He got right in front of our gal, took a long look at the situation — her being naked and those wing tips right in front of her delicate parts — and winked at the shoes and said, "Attaway to go buddy, give 'er all you got." Just then the grocery man made his final trip across the front of the room. Everybody busted up. I laughed so hard I just sat down on the floor. For the first time, he spoke, "What kind of meeting is this, anyhow?" I had to reply, "I'll be damned if I know."

That punchline was my message to those in attendance to give us all they could offer.

We had fun that morning in Pembroke. 'Til this day I'm not certain whether it was the waitress getting her job done or the grocery man getting his work finished or my joke. Regardless of the reason, they had a good time and I'll never forget those last five minutes of that meeting for as long as I live.

What started out as a total disaster, ended with our getting some $3,000 in pledges to our program.

After that meeting Bucky, Mandes and I drove on to St. Simons Island for an alumni social that night. Standing in front of the group, I couldn't bring myself to use, "Give 'er all you got" again, but it was a productive meeting. The president of that local chapter handed me a check for a $1,000. It seemed like a million.

I went back to Statesboro late that night, woke Jean up and showed her the check. She gave me that look of, "I still think you're crazy."

Sometimes we wondered if the word was getting out. And if so, how far.

What with all these stories about my traveling here and there and answering letters, I was really and truly touched when I got a letter from a couple living in Alaska with a $10 check and another one from an alumn in Japan with $10.

What great gifts, at a time when we needed $10 in the worst way.

I figured if what we were doing had gotten out that far, then we must be doing something right and that we should keep on keeping on.

Wherever we could get a few gathered to talk about football — we'd be there.

28 | *MIRROR, MIRROR ON THE WALL*

When I settled in at Southern, as I said, I did extensive traveling and talking. I hired a couple of young coaches (I'll get to them later on), and of course, I did a lot of thinking about that first group of young men who would be showing up come September with football on their minds.

As far as facilities were concerned, they let us have one of the physical education dressing rooms, which had adjacent showers. We pulled out the small lockers and replaced them with bigger ones. Right off the bat we had some good quarters as far as that part of the program was concerned.

I called Mr. I.V. Chandler in Dalton, Georgia, who had provided carpet for the Georgia program and whom I considered a good friend. Mr. Chandler was an avid Bulldog follower. But being the gentleman he is, he overlooked the fact that I had switched areas of the state and provided carpet for our dressing room floor at a greatly reduced price. I'm sure he must have taken a long look at that blue stuff being loaded up, since he was so devoted to bright red.

In terms of what we had available to begin a program, our dressing room was an outstanding feature.

Sammy Johnson, my good friend who offered me that special fringe benefit of a free quart of beer every afternoon when I knocked off, gave us enough weights from his old weight room to get us started with our new one. That was a terrific gift.

A weight room is as good a selling point when it comes to recruiting as just about anything, including the kind of coaching that is available, the stadium or the uniforms. Many folks just don't know that. Conditioning is the key to any athletic endeavor, especially football. Athletes spend a considerable amount of time in the weight facility.

If they aren't on that field or in that library studying, we like to know our guys have the stuff in them to get in that weight room and pump iron.

Practice fields were an absolute necessity. But what wasn't a necessity that first summer in '81 as I looked around? Fortunately we had an area that pretty well fit the bill. In fact from day one, where we now practice, we have always practiced. The location for those fields at one time was part of a small five-hole golf course which was no longer in use. It wasn't really a bad location, but there wasn't much grass.

Actually, there was so little grass and so little rain during those first two years, we'd scrimmage a play then have to wait 15 seconds for the cloud of dust to clear before we knew the result of the play. Unintentionally, our offense really was "four yards and a cloud of dust."

I remember the day Bucky and I went out to that spot and tried to imagine two football fields. I took a hard look around, and I told him I thought this place would work. We could put one football field going one way and another one going a different direction. A place for the offense to do its thing, and a place for the defense to get after it. We could put goal posts there, there and there.

We cut the grass — more weeds at that time than grass. And we put down lines. It wasn't exactly the most ideal of situations, but at least it was something. Later, that location turned into what today are two of the best practice facilities anywhere in the country.

The way those old fields took on such a beautiful identity was, I mentioned at Snooky's one morning that our old facility wasn't really what it should be. Wayne Johnson and Joe Smallwood took it from there. They just did it by rounding up others who wanted to see us do good and went to work on the project. In a year we had great practice fields. Community effort. That's what made my job so easy.

Right at first, the fields were not bad at all. They had potholes, of course, but with the cooperation of Southern's Plant Operations, we got them filled. We couldn't do too much about the black dirt. Football practice is an activity of profuse sweating if one is really trying.

At Georgia Southern those first couple of seasons, our guys looked like coalminers headed out of the shafts when they moved toward the showers after a good workout. Sometimes, some of the guys would jump in "Beautiful Eagle Creek" for a preliminary wash job. Which reminds me. The very first day we put on the pads and went to work, one of our managers came to me in the middle of practice and said, "Coach, we don't have any soap in the showers." How about that? We had scrounged around and outfitted more than a 100 young men for football and I had forgotten the soap.

I saw Jimmy DeLoach standing on the sideline watching practice so I went over, handed him $20 and asked if he would go across the street to Piggly Wiggly and buy all the Ivory soap he could get for the money.

We got the soap, but the store manager wouldn't let Jimmy pay for it when he explained what it was for.

This is an example of how it was when we got started. Everybody in the community was doing all they could to help the cause. We just couldn't have gotten it done, otherwise.

I referred to Beautiful Eagle Creek earlier and will continue to do so as the rest of the Georgia Southern story is told.

Beautiful Eagle Creek is actually a drainage ditch, I suppose. However, after a good rain and the water rises it can take on the appearance of one of those pretty South Georgia black water streams.

On other occasions, when it doesn't rain much, the water recedes and one can see various items such as beer cans, old softballs from the adjoining area, golf balls, bottles and all kinds of stuff lying on the bottom.

I have always maintained that Beautiful Eagle Creek must surely be the original habitat of gnats and mosquitoes because so many of those two species still remain in the area.

Our practice fields lie gently along the banks of Beautiful Eagle Creek and every day our players must cross that small bridge coming to and going from practice. During two-a-days they cross Beautiful Eagle Creek four times daily.

As we began our program in 1981, we didn't have a "hedges," or a "Death Valley," or a "Rock." As I looked around, the only thing we had we could call ours was that drainage ditch and I named it Beautiful Eagle Creek. Every practice session when we'd finish calisthenics, I would have my squad face the stream, ditch, whatever, and have them salute Beautiful Eagle Creek.

The players took to it. They looked upon it as theirs and it became a part of our everyday life as we practiced along the banks. We were the only football team in America that had its own creek.

It has become a part of the history of Georgia Southern football. Beautiful Eagle Creek has made football history at Georgia Southern.

Who's to say there really is no magic in that murky water? Who's to say those powers possessed by that stream will not beat Furman and Arkansas State and others in seasons to come? Not me. I'll never doubt the waters of Beautiful Eagle Creek contains some mystic element which makes it "special" and in turn will make Georgia Southern football "special."

Let me tell you about our offices — where we went to work each day to have meetings, discussions and watch films.

Our office was in a trailer. That's right, a mobile home Robert Mallard let us borrow. Like I said, we'd take anything and make it work ... as long as the price wasn't too high. And when things were "free," we found that most affordable.

Our football office had two bedrooms, a kitchen, a living room and two bathrooms.

If you came to see us, you would enter and walk into the living room with a naugahyde brown sofa, allowing you a place to sit down. When you sat, it sank so low you had to be an acrobat to get up. To the right was a bedroom and an adjoining bathroom. It was nice for my assistant coaches to have an office and a place to go to the bathroom. There was a bar that separated the living room from the kitchen. We had a sink, stove and refrigerator. What other coach in America had an office complete with a stove, refrigerator and that kind of stuff?

Through the kitchen was another bedroom just a little larger than the other one. That became my office.

The most outstanding feature of the whole place was the bathroom that joined my office. It had all the necessities of any bathroom. But the greatest feature of all was that sunken bathtub surrounded by mirrors. Get the picture? There I was sitting in a nice office and if somebody needed to excuse themselves I'd say, "Go right ahead." And he or she walked into that bathroom and suddenly was surrounded in luxury. It was great seeing the looks on peoples' faces when they returned to my office and proceeded to talk to me.

Our young graduate assistants used that mirrored bathtub to great advantages while we were living in that office. Your imagination can be your guide.

The trailer took good care of us. It was a little crowded at times. Other times, it was packed. But, it was a "fun" place. It was ours and now as I look back, we got a lot done in that make-do environment. It was right there that we first watched Tracy Ham on film, the images projected on a window shade we used for a screen.

I remember it was the local Kiwanis Club that contacted me and asked me what I really needed. I told them a Kodak projector. And I'll be darned if they didn't go out and buy one for us. This was a terrific gift. Those things ran about $800 back then. Again, the folks in the community were pulling for us to do good and thanks to them, we did.

The only thing that really bothered me about our office was they left the wheels on it. I could visualize coming to the office after losing badly — and they would have rolled us right out of town.

When you consider the facilities we had in the beginning, it led to our taking on the philosophy, "If you don't have the best of everything, make the best of everything you have."

I brought in three young men who had played for me at the University and who wanted to get into coaching while finishing their undergraduate degrees.

Hugh Nall, who had "shot the hog," had played on the '80 National Championship team and needed just a couple quarters to finish his college work. Hugh saw Georgia Southern as a good opportunity to start a career in coaching and complete his degree. He was our offensive line coach. Ricky McBride, a Savannah native, had finished his eligibility at Georgia but had a way to go in completing his course requirements. He was our linebacker coach. Pat McShea, who also played on that great Georgia championship team, served as one of our defensive line coaches. These three guys played for the Dogs and they loved the Dogs. But they completed their undergraduate work at Georgia Southern. They loved the Eagles just as much as they did the Dogs. We called them "Bull-Eagles."

When it came out I had been named head coach, I started getting hundreds of letters from prospective coaches interested in being a part of our staff.

The fact we didn't have hardly any money to offer the candidates really limited the field to those who were just hungry enough to come coach with us for almost nothing. Because that's what it was ... almost nothing in terms of what coaches are paid.

The two guys I invited for a final interview were Ben Griffith, an assistant at Elbert County High School, and Mike Healey, who had been head football coach at Bishop-Kenny High School in Jacksonville, Florida, but had resigned that position and was waiting to take the state bar exam. Mike told me if it came down to coaching at Georgia Southern or becoming an attorney, it wasn't even close. He wanted to coach at Southern. Both were good high school coaches with excellent reputations. Ben and Mike were the two full-time coaches I hired. I was lucky, again. They did a great job for Southern.

I needed them in Statesboro by the first of September. Hugh and the others had things to finish up at the University.

For Ben, it was a little more difficult. He had a wife and two children and had a tough time deciding whether he could walk away from a fairly good position and come coach with me. And I really couldn't blame him. But it was his decision — a chance to go from the high school level to a college program. In our case, a prospective college program.

I can remember Ben's high school was already practicing when I called him one more time and asked him if he wanted that job. He finally agreed and came to Statesboro.

Mike stayed with me until I retired. He was an important part of our three National Championships and has since returned to high school coaching. Ben left our program in 1983 to become offensive coordinator for the University of New Mexico, and later moved on to the University of Arizona as their offensive coordinator. He is now at Kansas State.

I think Ben made a good decision back in August of '81. Not that Elbert County High School is a bad place to coach. But since that time, he's had an opportunity to work on the major college level. Speaking of those two guys, when we all huddled up that September, I asked what they wanted to coach, offense or defense?

They said it really didn't make too much difference. So Mike took the defense and Ben, the offense. That's how we started.

I have already mentioned that to have a successful team, there needs to be "difference-makers" present. Let me share with you how I came to know one such "difference-maker."

One August morning in 1981, I got a call from Dr. Lick. He told me about a faculty member, a Ph.D. in the English department, who had a strong background in coaching football and who might be interested in helping with our program. You can imagine what ran through my mind. Doctor of philosophy? English department? I'd never seen any of these among the coaching ranks.

But what do you say to your president in a situation like this except, "Send him by my office and we'll talk."

The next day, Patrick O'Dyer Spurgeon walked into the trailer and introduced himself. That was the beginning of one of the best things that ever happened to Georgia Southern football.

It didn't take long for me to realize that Spurgeon was dead serious about helping our program. Neither did it take long for me to realize he, indeed, had a strong background in football. He had been a college player in a very successful program and a high school coach as well.

Right off he let me know that he would not be the "token English professor" on our staff. If he was going to work for us, he was really going to work. And work he did ... without pay. No paycheck for Spurgeon. He did it for the cause: Football at Southern.

From the beginning, he coached our kickers and our snappers. The entire kicking operation was his. Check the record. These guys have all done well.

While he was doing this, he coached our offensive "scout team" — that group which imitates the opponent's offensive picture for our defense. Already, this is basically more responsibility than the average assistant coach. The thing he did better than anybody I have ever been around is "scout." Each week's upcoming opponent should be presented in an expert manner because this is very valuable to the success of any football team. Every Monday, it was the way in which Spurgeon presented his report to the squad that made the difference. There's no way I can describe one of his presentations. All I can say is there's never been one better. He's the guy who got our squad started every week in focusing on the upcoming game.

He'd use a little Shakespeare, a little "blood and guts." Sometimes it was "Shakespeare's blood and guts" that got his point across.

Pat Spurgeon would leave town on Friday, drive hundreds and hundreds of miles, sometimes a thousand miles. He'd drive all night, collect his thoughts, present them to the coaching staff on Sunday night and then deliver his masterpiece to the squad on Monday.

During this period he may have slept a few hours or he may not have. Remember, he was still teaching English five days a week.

Over the years, he served as "Father Confessor" to many of our players. The players felt right at home as they confided in Spurgeon. He helped us recruit, and was instrumental in selling many of our top athletes and their parents on the advantages of coming to Georgia Southern.

With all this, when I got down in the back and when my old knee was about to blow, he's the one who would pick me up and help me go just one more time. He's still there, thank goodness, doing his thing, "Being a difference-maker."

Not bad for an English professor — recommended by the president.

I'll always remember Mike, Ben, Pat and our original Eagle coaching staff with great respect and gratitude. They were with me when the going was really tough. I put those moments of glory I shared with that staff right up there with the ones who were with me for those three National Championship seasons.

29 | MEETING MY KIND OF FOLKS

That first year I received a lot of letters from people coming out of high school or guys who had been in the Army or married people who had always wanted to play college football. Hundreds of people wrote. I always wrote back, telling them they had to be enrolled at Georgia Southern and what the academic requirements were. With that letter I'd add, "Bring your own shoes and anything else left over from high school."

In addition to answering those letters, of course I started looking for football players ... pretty good players who might not be going anywhere. I remember around July 15, I got in my car to go to a private school all-star game to see some people play. I thought private schools might be a good source of players for Georgia Southern, because by and large, private schools were not recruited too heavily by the football playing institutions. I didn't know that a few years later, I would find out just how good some of those guys could play.

I was leaving Statesboro driving down Highway 67 to get on the interstate for Charleston, South Carolina, to watch this game when I stopped at a general store along the way. It was 5 o'clock on a hot summer afternoon. There must have been seven or eight farmers who had just knocked off. They were standing around in that general store talking about whatever farmers talk about that time of day. As I walked in, a couple of those guys recognized me and said they were glad I had come to Georgia Southern. That made me feel good about the fact they knew who I was and they knew we were going to have a football program later that year.

As I walked back out to my car one guy followed me and seemed to know something about my background at Georgia. I was having a hard time saying goodbye to him. Finally, I got in my car and pulled the door shut. He was still talking to me through the window. I told him I had to go and I'd see him later. That's when he said, "Coach you know it's all off, don't you?" And I said, "What's all off?" He grinned and said, "All the hair on your head!" He laughed and slapped his leg. I never will forget that. Going into a place as a complete stranger and having some guy follow me out to the car and kid me about my bald head. These were my kind of people.

Anyway, I drove on over to Charleston to see the game. From that contest we got two or three good players — Tommy Raye and a guy who played fullback back home in Bulloch County, Mike Seamens. Plus a kid named Dennis Cheeks. It was a pretty successful trip.

I had never been to Charleston from the direction I had taken. So on the way home, I got up on I-95 and before I headed out I stopped at a place and went in the men's room. I was standing there doing what needed to be done when this guy walks up and asks, "Coach, what are you doing way over here?" I told him I had been to a football game over in Charleston.

And right there in the men's room he introduced himself. I'll never forget his name, Anton Borowsky, which right off didn't sound like a typical South Georgia name to me. Anton said he was in the produce business back in Statesboro. "I'm headed home and I know a shortcut if you want to follow me," he said. I thought that would be a terrific idea.

So I started following Anton Borowsky. We stayed on about five miles of paved road and then he turned off onto a dirt lane. I'm talking about those two-rut jobs. The trees from one side had grown over the road and they met trees from the other side, forming a tunnel. Here was old Anton whipping that truck along pretty good hitting those tree branches. I tried to keep up even though the tree branches were giving me a licking.

After about 10 miles of those two-rut roads, the tree branches banging around and Anton's canvas covering flapping everywhere, I asked myself, "Now who in the hell is Anton Borowsky and does he really live in Statesboro, or is he leading me somewhere out here in the swamp to knock me over the head?" I got downright edgy.

But sure enough, Anton did live in Statesboro and he did share his shortcut home with me.

Coaches will do just about anything. I've always said you've got to have two things to stay in this business: you have to be just a little bit crazy and you must have a lot of trust in people. Those two things were put to the test during that ride home from Charleston.

At Georgia I was used to driving to the Atlanta airport and going anywhere in the United States where there was a good defensive football player. Did I mention that at Georgia our conservative recruiting budget was around $500,000? At Georgia Southern in 1981, mine was $2,000.

One such trip I used to take at Georgia would completely exhaust my entire Georgia Southern budget. This is a description of one of my first full days of recruiting for Georgia Southern.

I left the fieldhouse at 7:30 in the morning. My first stop was Claxton. Then to Baxley and over to Alma. On to Waycross, then Nahunta and Blackshear. My last stop was in Jesup. Then I was on my way back to Statesboro. In order to get to Statesboro from Jesup, one has to go through Ludowici.

Ludowici is a nice place. When there was no interstate going down the east coast, Highway 301 was the main source of tourist travel ... which took everyone right through Ludowici.

Word had it that Ludowici had one red light with the fastest trigger in town, better known as a tourist trap. Don't let a Yankee move through the yellow light 'cause it would turn red just at the right moment followed by another light going off — the blue of the dome sitting on top of a police vehicle.

Warnings were rampant about Ludowici.

But then that was many years ago. As I moved into this now-quiet hamlet, I pulled up to that one stop light. It was red. There was a car in front of me. I could see through my front window a gray-haired lady was driving. And she had this huge sticker on her back bumper that read, "Honk if you love Jesus." Well I do love Jesus and it had been a great day. So I let her have a long blast ... two full seconds.

I watched this stately looking lady get out of her car and start back toward me. She was well-dressed with mature, gray hair (well, blue actually). I thought she was going to commend me for what I had done, so I rolled down my window.

Instead she stopped about six feet from my car door, put her hands on her hips and said, "You old bald-headed bastard, can't you see the light's red?"

The humor in recruiting at Georgia Southern! I like telling stories about my first days down in Southeast Georgia looking for football players. It illustrates the vast difference in recruiting for Georgia Southern and the University of Georgia.

Often, parents would stop by and ask how their son was doing in football and academics. On one such occasion a good friend of mine, Gilbert Hastings, and his wife visited me. We had recruited their son, Gib, out of Atlanta. I had known the dad for quite some time. He was a graduate of Mississippi State, where he played ball. He was also a Southeastern Conference football official. He had called some of our Georgia games and even helped with some scrimmages.

Anyway, Gilbert and his wife had a nice chat with me in my trailer talking about Gib and about other things. As we were leaving the office, I invited them to come by the house for lunch before they headed back to Atlanta.

They accepted. So I told them to follow me.

Let me give you the setting. There is a family in Statesboro who built the largest home I believe I've ever seen. It is an exact replica of George Washington's Mount Vernon — big, two stories. I swear, it looks like it would take up a full city block. It sits gleaming, a white mansion of sorts in the middle of the finest lawn I've ever seen, surrounded by tall Georgia pines.

The driveway could be the landing strip at Hartsfield International, except it's lined with those pretty flowers I can't pronounce.

The carport is larger than my football team's dressing rooms. All in all, it is impressive and cannot be missed, no matter what time of day or night. It is a fine piece of real estate.

And I had to go right by it headed to my house.

Well, there's old Gilbert and his wife following, with their heads full of stuff that I'd told them about how good Statesboro had been to me.

As I approached this mansion, I noticed there were no cars to be seen. This was a great opportunity to exercise my humor and to impress the visitors. No one was home. So without any hesitation, I just wheeled into the long drive and parked my car right there next to Mount Vernon. I motioned to the Hastings to get out and come on in.

Gilbert just sort of stepped out of his car with the look on an official's face I've seen plenty of times, and he said, "Erk, you're shittin' me, aren't you?" I laughed and said I was. We drove on to my moderate, affordable, comfortable dwelling and had a good lunch. And laughed.

But it's those kinds of times that have always kept me from getting too serious about myself.

30

DALE KICKS OFF!

Before I get too much further into the story, I want to take a time out right here to report without a doubt it was Dale Wesley Lick, Georgia Southern's president from 1978-86, who got football going again. And it took a guy with a pretty heavy "set" on him to, "go for it."

Following is some of the historical background Mandes shared with me upon my arrival to Statesboro, which chronicles the rebirth of Southern football.

Through the years, those who led the college before Dale arrived in the late '70s were all sports-minded. I have heard each of them led the college in a good way and supported all the athletic activities on campus during their time. And I'm sure there were many campus visits by alumni and local citizens who asked about football.

I am in no position to compare Lick with any of those who preceded him, but I do know Dale and the way he went about doing things or getting them done. Prior to my coming to Southern I understand he was the type of individual that, no matter how large or small the question or request from folks in South Georgia, he'd look into it. Within a matter of a few days, whoever had asked the question or made the request got a reply from Lick or one of the officers from the college.

A lot of criticism was thrown Dale's way because he tried to look into almost anything anybody expressed an interest in. I know the way he treated my interest. He was on the phone every day, filling in some answers, providing me the information I needed and offering suggestions and advice. That's a good leader to me. Like I said, I am not comparing Dale to any of the other presidents. I didn't know them with the exception of Dr. Harry Carter, who worked as acting president after Dale left until the arrival of Dr. Nick Henry, the current GSU president.

But a leader has to be a special kind of person. And Dale was. That's why finally in the late '70s and early '80s, he looked into this 40-year-old question of football. He told his close colleagues that when a few other things were accomplished, he'd find out if football would work at Southern.

Remember, I was at the University of Georgia when all this was happening. But across my 10 years at Georgia Southern I have heard the story many times about how Lick finally said to Mandes, "Get me a feasibility study committee and call Dr. Bill Bolen in marketing and ask him to put together a survey. We're going to find out once and for all if football is possible and if the folks of Southeast Georgia will come watch."

The feasibility committee went to work. So did Bolen, and to the disbelief of many (but to the joy of more), Dale stood up in 1980 and said, "Football is back." I found that out by reading it in either the Atlanta paper or my local paper, I'm not sure. Right then and there, I became a part of the group that kept up with this tall northern farm boy.

When I came to town in early 1981, really even before I left Athens, I picked up on a catchy phrase, "The Dirty Dozen."

Again, through a lot of conversation after moving to Statesboro, I found out this was the group of community folks who joined in on Lick's wild idea about football. They went to work writing letters, having meetings and, in general, making a strong statement to the college that Statesboro and Bulloch County were behind the idea of football ... again. It seemed appropriate their meetings were held in the small back room office at Snooky's.

"The Dirty Dozen" should have been called "The Daring Dozen."

Each of them left Snooky's after every meeting and went out and worked on the idea of football at Southern. Each faced the question from so many, "Are you crazy?" Or, "Where are you going to get a coach, players, a stadium and for hell's sake — the money?" "The Dirty Dozen," individually or together, said, "In time, it will happen. In time there will be a coach, a stadium, players and fans."

As I understand it, "The Dirty Dozen" was that core which got out and talked and raised money and let it be known far and wide that come hell or high water ... football was coming to town.

Appropriately enough, there is a plaque saluting the work of "The Dirty Dozen" on our stadium wall. It says, "Thanks for making it happen, for believing and for never giving up on the dream."

Who are they and what did each one of them do individually? When asked, they all say, "It's not important. What is important is the fact that we got folks to believe." And the crowd of believers grew and they went out and got some more. In 1990, when the Eagles won their fourth national title, CBS-TV was there, and so were 25,000 fans jammed in Paulson Stadium.

And that's about all any one of "The Dirty Dozen" will say 10 years later. What they did is theirs. What they accomplished is their individual memory. They didn't want plaques or praise.

The story of football, I know for sure, cannot be told without "The Dirty Dozen" being remembered and recorded as a force that would not lie down, would not shut up, would walk through eating places where grinning faces would signal, "Here come the fools."

But they were not fools.

They were that group brought together through their love for the idea, the dream of football at Southern.

To me, though I didn't see them in action early on, they were Southern. They were committed to the mission.

They were not going to give up on the idea of bringing football back. Especially in light of the fact that finally, there was a Georgia Southern president who seemed interested in taking a look.

I wish I could have been one of them. But I was back in Athens reading about this crazy group of folks who believed they could bring the game to town again and of all things ... were looking for a head football coach.

And so who were they?

I considered this group to be friends in general, each with that basic characteristic of being involved in community activities: Roy Akins, director of marketing for a local bank; Al Burke, trust officer for a bank; Hugh Colson, an industrialist; Jimmy Deloach, a state Labor Department officer; Sammy Johnson, a beer and wine store proprietor; Robert Lamb, a haberdasher; Morris Lupton, owner of a convenience store chain; Donald Nesmith, building contractor; Bobby Olliff, a revenue agent; Frank Pearson, a forester; Ronnie Pope, another haberdasher; Bobby Underwood, an insurance agent; Si Waters, a furniture store owner; and of course, Bruce Yawn, owner and cashier at Snooky's. Thirteen in all, but still a baker's dozen for history's sake.

I believe in fundamentals.

That's a coaches mentality. Blocking, tackling, throwing, running, any of it. The game cannot be played without fundamentals being understood and carried out to the fullest. Fundamentals are those little things that, when developed, allow the big things to happen.

Naturally, I would use the game of football to make the point. Always try to be around the ball, is what we taught. Keep your eyes open and hit everything you meet straight on. Keep your legs driving whether you're a runner or a lineman. Understand the assignment so it comes as naturally as breathing.

The little things allow big things to happen: a recovered fumble, a break away run, an interception, stopping them on fourth-and-one.

In the case of Dale Lick and "The Dirty Dozen," they worked hard on fundamentals, i.e., getting the message out that a study was underway which would clearly determine something one way or another about football at

Southern. Talking it up among folks everywhere. Setting a budget for equipment, uniforms, a place to play, a coach and staff, facilities — beginning a
campaign to bring in money!

As I understood it, the message went beyond Bulloch County. Folks
began joining forces with "The Dirty Dozen." People began to notice Dale
had not lost his cotton pickin' mind. Questions and comments of interest
started moving down highways 301 and 67 and 80, across Statesboro into
Snooky's and out to the campus and into Dale's office. And that's the way the
story was told to me.

After I got to Statesboro and joined forces, Sen. Glenn Bryant of the
Georgia General Assembly, an astute businessman and a devoted south Geor-
gian from nearby Hinesville, called.

A Savannah building contractor, M.C. Anderson, whose two daughters
were attending Georgia Southern, made contact with us. Morris Lupton, one
of "The Dirty Dozen," stepped forward. And Bo Ginn, our congressman,
visited Allen Paulson in Savannah at Paulson's multimillion dollar Gulfstream
headquarters.

What Dale had done ... what "The Dirty Dozen" and the many others
had done ... all brought the attention of Sen. Bryant, Mr. Anderson, Rep.
Ginn, and ultimately, Mr. Paulson, to Georgia Southern.

When Dale, Bucky and I visited M.C., before we could really get into
our pitch, he just came right out and said he was planning to give us
$250,000 whether in cash, check or by starting to dig the hole for the
stadium ... whatever we wanted.

We decided on our drive back to Statesboro we would take the offer in
the form of stadium site preparation. Our reasoning was once M.C. got
started, he wouldn't stop until he completed the site. And that's exactly what
he did, moving his gift in value from $250,000 to nearly $1 million.

Folks, M.C. Anderson was the first to step up and give us the big push.
He was the one who got it all started as far as big gifts are concerned. No
doubt in my mind.

Sen. Bryant donated the property on which the stadium now stands.
M.C. Anderson moved his heavy equipment in and dug the bowl for the
stadium. Morris Lupton invested $480,000 for the dressing rooms and the
Booster complex in the south end zone of what became Paulson Stadium.
And one night in 1983 after Bo Ginn's visit, Mr. Allen Paulson handed me
and Dr. Lick that check for $1 million to complete the project.

I'll never forget Mr. Paulson looking at me and saying, "Erk that check
won't bounce, it's on my personal account."

Small things ... large projects are results of fundamentals.

It all works together. A 40-year-old question asked of a whole bunch of
presidents across those four decades. An answer from Dale. "Digging in" by
"The Dirty Dozen." The ground swell of followers. And the stepping forward
of Anderson, Bryant, Lupton and Paulson.

I wish I could take credit for what those individuals did. But I can't. I pass it on to the spirit of the community and these leaders who chose to believe, and most of all, the goal they set for themselves.

It has been said that my accepting the coaching job did some good. Maybe. I don't know. That's a call for someone else to make. All I know is that much work had been done by the time I arrived and had put a couple of seasons under our Eagle wings. During that time Bucky and others had started the Southern Boosters organization and had been getting some funding, while Dale was steady taking his lumps from some of the faculty and community disbelievers.

Every day I'd get up and go to my office on wheels and meet with my coaches and go out to practice. Later I'd meet whoever was riding with me that night and we would take off for some far distant community to talk about football at Southern.

I coached. And I let "The Dirty Dozen" and Dale tell me when to speak.

But it was the furniture store owner, the insurance man, the independent — whoever of those 13 special guys and Dale and Bucky who got the stadium built. And a lot of other projects completed.

It took devotion and the never-ending belief that anything is possible.

Thanks are in order for the individuals who gave $10, and to those commitments from Sen. Bryant, Anderson, Lupton and Paulson.

Large or small, gifts given in the spirit of seeing the Eagles fly were of equal importance to me. And it all began, believe me, with the little things being taken care of.

31 | *A THREE-GAME SEASON*

By the way, in my 50 years associated with competitive sports, the only opportunity for me to sit in a stadium and watch a game took place in 1981 when I came to Georgia Southern. Fall quarter had not yet started. But I had been working, taking trips, writing letters, making phone calls and getting my Eagle coaches appointed. We were busy. But that fall would be different than any I had ever faced since I started coaching.

I mean, come the first of every September, I had been on the sidelines somewhere with somebody.

So on that first weekend in September of 1981 in Statesboro, I knew Georgia was opening the season against Tennessee in Athens.

I fully intended to go to that game. But as the time approached, I just couldn't make myself go back to Athens having been there the past 17 years. I just felt kinda funny doing that — sitting in the stands.

Old Danny Warnell, who was responsible for that back room breakfast over in Pembroke, offered me his place on Hilton Head, South Carolina, for the weekend. So Jean and I went over. It was a beautiful day, the first Saturday in a hundred years that I hadn't been involved in a football game. There I was sitting out on the beach on Hilton Head, and Georgia was playing Tennessee in Athens.

I couldn't believe there were people anywhere in America who weren't intensely engrossed — compelled to follow football on a Saturday afternoon during football season. Yet, there they were, walking back and forth on the beach with no apparent thought that football was being played in the United States. There were people swimming, flying kites, fishing, laying around asleep. For the first time in my life, I realized that people do something on a

Saturday afternoon during football season other than go to the stadium.

What an experience!

It also gave me a chance, as Jean and I listened to the game on the radio, to hear "The Voice of the Dogs," Larry Munson.

See, I knew what Georgia was doing on defense. I knew what they were doing on offense. But for the life of me, I couldn't get that impression by listening to Larry.

And Larry said, "... the Dogs are in a four-man line, a three-man line..." and I knew they weren't doing that. Because I knew what they did. I did understand when he said, "There goes Herschel."

Anyway, that was quite an experience. The first Saturday I can ever remember not coaching during football season, or being in the stadium somewhere.

I had always thought, "Isn't everybody's Saturday afternoon wrapped up in a football game like mine had always been?" I was really surprised that right in front of me were just a whole bunch of folks laughing and carrying on and not giving a hoot about football at all.

I was impressed there was something else in life going on during football season other than football.

Two weeks later on September, 16, 1981, we put out a call which read, "All y'all who are interested in coming out for football at Georgia Southern, come on out."

We were greeted by 126 of the most enthusiastic non-athletes I have ever seen in my life.

Our first session called for timing this group on the 40-yard sprint. We did this on the tennis courts because we didn't have enough football shoes to issue. The fastest 40-yard time recorded was 4:67 seconds turned in by David Shields of Waycross. He was white and I knew we were in trouble.

I was used to looking at players weighing somewhere between 240 and 260 and standing in the range of at least 6'2" or 6'4". I didn't see any of those there. My mind went back to that one Georgia season when I developed the phrase, "Runts try harder."

We had a real assembly of people who wanted to play. One guy, who later became one of our managers, had a left leg that was two inches shorter then his right one.

The line I gave Jean down in Orlando when we looked out and saw the Miami of Ohio team had arrived at the Tangerine Bowl barbecue in two yellow school buses, came back to me as I looked into that sea of anxious faces. "We've had it."

But unlike the Orlando situation, we were the guys in the yellow buses. These kids were probably not outstanding football players. But, I knew if they didn't want to play they wouldn't be there. Like the hotel drunk and the young lady behind the shoes, I had the feeling these guys would give it all they had.

We scrimmaged in that black dirt. Roger Inman, our equipment man, was always having trouble with the washing machines. We had two machines and one of them was always out of order. Everybody's work load increased when we started football at Southern.

Tom Smith, our trainer, had expertly cared for the baseball and basketball teams. With football, his work load increased ten fold. No complaints. He took care of 126 then.

My coaches could tell if a guy could play. Slowly, we put that first team together. My squad in '81 was something I had never quite seen in all my years of coaching.

There we were with 126 guys and our new coaching staff grinding in that black sand on our make-do practice fields. We were trying to find out just how many football players we had in this group. Damned if we didn't find that we had some pretty good ones and all of them really wanted to play. We were working toward that upcoming date that we had in a few weeks with the Florida State Junior Varsity.

Billy Hobbs and Mike Cummings from Dublin called me one day and suggested we bring the team over for an intra-squad game, a situation where we could get after each other under actual game conditions. I thought it was a good idea.

Billy, who's in the sporting goods business, and Mike, who has a men's clothing store, knew just about everybody in Dublin and really got a pretty good crowd that night — upwards of 3,000. It was cold and we played in the Shamrock Bowl. I'll never forget that name. I suppose it's stuck with me because somehow I associated a shamrock with luck. Believe me, we were going to need lots of luck.

Lewis Grizzard, my good friend, heard about the event and drove down and held a portable megaphone and made a funny little talk to the crowd before the game. We had a scratchy record of the National Anthem. I believe Dr. Lick said a few words and then we all stood while the Anthem was being played.

Dublin is about 75 miles from Statesboro, so we had a nice crowd from home with us that night.

It was a good experience. A piece of the dream so many folks had held on to, even before I became interested in this situation, came alive that night. They cheered like crazy. I looked back into the stadium now and then and there the fans were, standing and yelling like it was the Sugar Bowl.

The game gave us a good look at some things under game-like conditions, and helped us recognize those who might be players.

I understand that Bo Whaley, a local newspaper columnist in Dublin and a graduate of Georgia Southern, took a group of our fans down on the other side of town to a place called Estes after the contest. Estes is a beer joint where you really need to know somebody on pretty good terms before you go in and order at the bar. Bo knew. And there he walked in with a bunch of folks dressed in blue and white, and all happy about the football program.

Bo had offered our fans a few suggestions about the personnel at Estes. He said, "The individuals sitting at the bar — give them time to start the conversation. You will be served the coldest ale anywhere. And the little old fellow sitting at the jukebox who never says a word, well, he will be the one to really decide what music will be played."

It was understood clearly by our group through Bo, if this codger didn't like a song someone punched in, he would hit a button and the gracious old hymn "In The Garden" would suddenly start playing. Honest!

Before the night was over, the innocence of our group had taken over Estes totally. At one time Alan Tyson, who serves pretty good barbecue in Statesboro, was standing on the Estes bar leading everyone in a loud rendition of "In The Garden." Old, young, new and different people just sort of came together that night. People talked and things got happy. As Bo tells it, "A good time was had by all."

Someone told me about an Eagle fan who stayed over that night because he had a funeral to attend at a nearby church the next day. The story goes the guy got up very hungover and showered and shaved and tried to drink a Coke to settle his stomach and barely got to the church.

Being a good friend of the family who was in a deep grievous state, he was asked to walk with them to the very front of the church. So there he was, his head killing him, his stomach creating a total revolution to the rest of his body — everything sort of out of focus. Finally the service began with a big fat soprano who yelled open the service by screeching all four verses of "In The Garden."

Our fan just put his head in his hands like he was overcome with grief. In truth, he was somewhere between throwing up and doubling up with laughter. No disrespect for the bereaved intended.

Dublin was the first outing for the Eagles and the first sort of tailgating our fans enjoyed down at Estes.

We were able to come up with a three-game schedule that fall. We played the Florida State Junior Varsity, the Fort Benning Doughboys and Magnum Force, a team of policemen out of Jacksonville!

So we came home and got busy getting ready for that J.V. game down in Tallahassee.

I remember Cohen, Jake Hines and Si Waters attending the Florida State J.V. contest. As I looked behind our bench to see who was there, there were those three. They made up the Georgia Southern cheering section that day. Jake back in the 1930s was an outstanding runner for the first football team, the Georgia Southern Blue Tide. In fact, before his death in the late 1980s, he was inducted into the Georgia Athletic Hall of Fame right up there with Frank Sinkwich and Charlie Trippi. It was a fitting and proper tribute to a great player and a fine man.

And Si Waters. We used his horse truck as our equipment van in 1981. And in 1982 as well.

This was Georgia Southern's first game of the new era. We played hard.

We had them on the ropes. Fourth and 11 with 2 minutes left. They were on their own 30. They completed the pass and went on to score. I should have called a blitz. We lost!

I never liked to walk off the field after losing. No coach likes that feeling. But I have had moments in defeat when I knew we had put forth the best effort we could, and things just didn't work out for us. This was one of those moments.

Our helmets weren't all the same color. We played in our practice pants. They were supposed to be white but the black dirt had taken its toll. We weren't pretty, but boy, did we compete.

I told our players after that game, I never wanted them to be proud of themselves in defeat, but I felt they had made every effort possible to win the game and I would be proud for them.

Coming back in those buses, with that team and with Si's horse truck behind us, I knew I was a long way from what I had been used to. All the equipment I ever needed. Lots of good players. Facilities that would stand up to anyone's, anywhere. And a running back by the name of Walker.

I knew something else too. I was involved in the most exciting experience of my life. I was basically in charge of a large dream made up of a lot of small dreams found in the minds and hearts of "The Dirty Dozen." And in the minds and hearts of the coaches working with me. But most of all, in the minds and hearts of those young college guys riding, now asleep after having given such great effort.

We went on to beat the Fort Benning Doughboys and we beat the Jacksonville Magnum Force, which, by the way, was our very first home game. We played them in the local high school stadium, Womack Field, at night. We had a pretty good crowd to come out. In fact, we played in Womack during '81, '82 and '83. We moved to lovely Paulson Stadium in 1984, which was the same year we became a member of Division I-AA and were recognized as an NCAA football program.

From '81 through '83 we played as a "club" football team. We had no NCAA affiliation. It was like we got up a football team at Georgia Southern and called folks and asked, "Y'all want to play a game?"

We began an 11-game schedule the fall of '82, but as far as official records of winning and losing, that began in 1984. But you can bet your life, when we went after each other in practice and against the Little Seminoles and the Doughboys and Magnum Force and on into '82 and '83, we were serious as hell about what we were doing.

Keep in mind, that was the first three months, six months or whatever, of football at Georgia Southern. We had taken some guys who wanted to play and made a team. We took what we had in the way of facilities and held scrimmages and taught formations and selected certain people to play certain positions.

One of the guys who played his position pretty good for us that first year was Pat Douglas, a defensive back. Pat had been a walk-on player at Georgia and thought Southern would be his opportunity to play football. It was and he played well.

The Fort Benning Doughboys had an outstanding quarterback with some professional experience. I believe Pat intercepted him four times in that game. The next year we gave Pat the first Georgia Southern football scholarship we issued in this era. He was a good one. Pat provided us with a real example of what could happen if hard work and dedication were applied in everyday practice.

Jesse Jenkins was another guy on that '81 team. He had been an outstanding football player at Warner Robins High School in middle Georgia. But Jesse hurt his knee his senior year and was too small to receive any really serious offers from major colleges. He came to Statesboro and from the very beginning became an outstanding football player for the Eagles. He wore a huge knee brace. I use these two young men as examples of how lucky we were in that first year when it came to people showing up who could really play. From the first day of practice until each graduated, they led by example. Good players with the "wants."

Pat Douglas became a graduate assistant for us when he finished his eligibility. Then he became a full-time assistant and was our secondary coach through 1986. From walk-on, to football scholarship, to football coach.

When we had a prospect on campus, the first thing he looked for was the weight room and the dressing room and the stadium. We really didn't have much to sell in those areas. They wanted to be a part of a strong program. To a talented player, the physical things like weights, where they hang their helmet and where they play every Saturday are just plain factors which cause them to go to one school or the other.

Sure, they'd take a good look at the coaches and listen to what the coaches said about what's in the future for them. But when we had a kid who had just come from taking a good look at some of those established football programs around our area, I'm afraid our impression wasn't too good. We'd take him down to the practice fields and his shoes would get messes up in that black dirt. Then we'd mention playing in a high school stadium. Not exactly the ideal recruiting circumstances.

But we had a great academic institution for which to recruit, although that fact was not well-publicized in the early '80s. Yet, we sold that! And we sold opportunity, "Opportunity to play football now. You don't have to wait for our juniors and seniors to move on, we ain't got no seniors. You can play now." We sold, "Be a part of the beginning of something that's going to be special."

We believed we were going to make it happen. And if we could get some good players coming to Southern, it really didn't make any difference what kind of helmet that kid had on — reconditioned or brand new. If he wanted to put a stop to somebody, he would. If he wanted to find the end zone, he would. That was my feeling then and that was my feeling the day that great team of '89 closed out my career with a 15-0 season and a third national title.

Some things never change.

It was when we got the stadium in 1984 that we really had a physical facility working for us. Later in 1988, through community effort, we got a super weight room. Like everything in the world, time is the factor, the stage on which we do our thing ... each day trying to make things a little better. And believe me, 1982 and '83 were full of that stuff. Don't forget luck. We had lots of that, and the harder we worked, the luckier we got.

We appreciated what all went into those first three seasons when we were playing at the club level — trying to raise money for quality players — mixing it up in the black dirt during our scrimmages.

Let me wrap up this first season and all the things that went with it by going back to that Florida State J.V. game. The difference between our people and their people was a mile. The difference between our equipment and their equipment was a mile wider. The fact that our guys went out and did as well as they did gave us what we all needed at that very moment: a display of heart and courage.

And though we did lose that first game, we surely did scare the you-know-what out of those Seminoles.

Finally, I was pleased that my office sitting on those tires had not been moved. Had that happened, of course, it would have meant I was out of a job. And that bathroom with all those fine mirrors would have been out of my life. At least we were safe until the next year.

32 | *CBS IS HERE?*

This was a special day for me, the first game of the '82 season. I had been in the business over 30 years when we moved toward the "Eagle Special" in front of Hanner Fieldhouse that morning.

The "Eagle Special" was the bus used by the athletic department at Southern. It was a 1954 model Greyhound Scenic Cruiser, which had been purchased by the school in 1981. At that time the vehicle had logged some 10 million miles. By the time it completely wore out in 1988, the "daddy" of the bus, Roger Inman, estimated that we had put another 250,000 miles on that baby.

Roger was officially our equipment manager. He had graduated from Southern in 1979 and had stayed on to work for the college at several jobs while he got his master's degree. Roger knew more about what was going on at Southern than anybody. He knew where everything could be located and who to call if something was needed. He just knew how to get things done. He circumvented enough red tape for us to operate somewhat efficiently.

He was also the driver and chief mechanic of the "Eagle Special." He knew every inch of the machine. He could tell by the sound of things where to start looking in order to get it fixed. Roger was the damnedest "fixer" of anything I've ever seen. We couldn't have made it without his help.

Anyhow, the "Eagle Special" was our method of transportation — at least half of it — in those early years. And although we had some minor problems, we always got there with the help of Roger, his trusty tool kit and his knowledge of how to keep the bus going.

That September day in 1982 brought the same feeling I had on other buses, on the planes ... an excitement hard to describe. This was to be

Southern's first game against a true college team in 41 years, in the Gator Bowl, of all places, where I had been so many times before.

We were now a team facing an 11-game schedule. I was excited. This was the only game in the world as far as I was concerned. Down the road in Jacksonville, we would meet the University of Central Florida.

One of the longest bus rides I took while coaching at other places was probably 250 miles. However, before I retired after nine years of directing the Eagle program, I knew what traveling on a bus was really like. We logged more miles on the roads of the southeastern United States than any team ever has.

The trip to Jacksonville took about three hours. We stopped in Brunswick to eat our pre-game meal.

The Gator Bowl was in the process of being expanded and at the time there were only about 40,000 seats available for the patrons of the game. Needless to say, we didn't need them all.

Central Florida had been playing three years of club competition. We only had that three-game schedule the year before.

We won the game, 16-9.

With less than two minutes left, we were ahead, 16-9, and we could have run out the clock with the quarterback taking the snap and just kneeling down. I told Ben, our offensive coordinator who was calling the plays, to tell the quarterback to just, "Sit on it."

Of course we hadn't been together long enough to have faced that situation before. The communication between Ben and myself was not all it should have been. To my horror, I watched as our quarterback handed the ball to the fullback, who promptly fumbled, giving Central Florida a minute and a half at mid-field. They drove down to the 10-yard line where, with 30 seconds left, they threw four incomplete passes into the end zone. We won our first college game for Georgia Southern in over 40 years.

Needless to say, the next week while preparing for our opponent, we worked on communication between me and Ben, and Ben and the team.

In that Central Florida game our first touchdown came on a 13-yard pass from Rob Allen to Scott Conners in the second quarter. Since then, I've seen a bunch of passes thrown and caught. But somehow, that one from Allen to Conner remains special.

There we were, with our crowd that followed us on our first road trip. I'm telling you folks, we were lost in that big thing. But we won. And our people were happy and so were we.

We played our second game of the season against Baptist University in Savannah. We were trying to schedule some contests during those first years in places other than Statesboro in order to raise the interest of folks throughout Southeast Georgia.

That game was one for the record books.

At the end of the first half the score was, 42-0. I remember walking over to the Baptist coach before the start of the second half and asking him if he didn't want to shorten the third and the fourth quarters. He hugged my neck and said, "You're the kindest man I've ever seen in my life." We cut the quarters down to 10 minutes instead of 15, and let the clock run. The game ended, 42-0.

By the way, Melvin Bell became Georgia Southern's first 100-yard rusher with 107 yards. We only threw one pass!

So we came home with two victories. And the Valdosta State Blazers were coming to Statesboro. We would play at home for the first time. What a moment!

It was a beautiful Saturday afternoon at Womack Field, the scene of our local high school games. Records show that Womack, with a capacity of 3,500, somehow allowed 7,000 fans as we went at it.

Valdosta had started its program in 1982 and had gone right into Division II, the Gulf South Conference. We were thinking the best thing for us to do, for many reasons, was to wait and see. Geographically, the Gulf South was not convenient. Our plan took longer to develop. I'm glad we waited and studied it.

I had it in the back of my mind we needed to belong to the Southern Conference. It took longer than I thought to realize this ambition.

The Blazers had recruited some junior college players and had several already on scholarship. I remember their outstanding passer, a fine drop-back thrower. And he liked to throw it to an equally talented wide receiver — someone we really never covered in the two years we played them.

That was the difference in our personnel. They had decided to jump into a conference and start giving scholarships right off the bat, and they took several junior college guys and other transfers to play for them.

So this was it. This was the moment we had all been waiting for. A real team. A real season. A real schedule. Womack Field. We were at home. We even had somebody out there selling popcorn, hotdogs and cold drinks. I believe we had blue and white buttons and stuff like that to sell as well.

There was some sort of pre-game ceremony recognizing a few of the folks who had worked hard in getting football started.

I remember running out on the field for the kickoff and some of our students had printed on big red sheets, "Hi Mom, send money," like they do when one of the TV networks covers a game. Little did I know that three years later we'd be playing for the National Championship and be on television.

Our kickoff man, Damon Wickham, set the ball down. It was 1 o'clock. Everybody was up and yelling. That moment of anticipation was there and we heard the whistle.

Damon's first kick went out of bounds. So we moved it back to the 35-yard line. We kicked from there. His second effort went out of bounds. This time, groans quickly took the place of cheers. By now we were back five more yards. The next kick went out of bounds. By then everybody was sort of looking around, wondering if we'd worked on this part of the game.

I was ready to shoot Damon. So I made him move all the way to the far hash mark because he was pushing the ball out to his right. It took three kicks for me to realize it. He managed to get the ball to their 40-yard line and they returned it into our territory. That's the way we started things that day.

It ended just about the way it began. We scored our last touchdown and they were two points ahead. We had to go for two to tie. Things were tense on the sidelines. I got somewhat exasperated with our coaches beating around with this and that play and wondering what to do. So I told them to line up in the "Power I" and run the toss sweep to Gerald Harris.

That wasn't a popular decision with our coaches because as we looked out there, it seemed every one of Valdosta State's players was positioned in the very area we planned to run. We had no built-in system for checking off, so we ran the play anyway, right into the teeth of their defense. Somehow, Gerald threaded his way through and scored those two points.

We ended up, 27-27, and all the fans really got into it. We had not won, but we had not lost either and we came through with an exciting finish on a badly-called play by me.

I remember some of our fans got more involved in the game than others. Rick Sellers, who used to be a deputy for the Bulloch County Sheriff's Department, was up from Baxley to watch his first Eagle game. I was told later that just before the half, Sellers got so excited he ran down to our sidelines to be with the team. Back then, there just wasn't much need for security.

As we headed for the lockeroom at halftime, Sellers was running along with us. Nobody knew who in the hell he was. Sellers was a big, husky type so no questions were asked. He loitered around for awhile, and I remember asking if he had any eligibility left.

When it was time to break for the second half, Sellers was first out of the gate, leading the team back to the field. His friends and wife were sitting up in the stands, asking each other what happened to Rick, when here he comes. Folk's that the kind of enthusiasm we were starting to experience.

Now we were 2-0-1. And our first home game had been played.

Because so much of what happened to us during those early years came about with Tracy Ham as quarterback, I will share a brief history of his development that fall. On September 1 we had four quarterbacks. According to my depth chart, Tracy was fourth on the list. I won't go into who the other three were, suffice it to say, that's the way I thought it should be.

September 7, 14 and 21, Ham was third on the chart. We went all the way to October 20 and Ham was still third. But by November 8, Ham was number one.

How stupid could I be to wait that long to move Ham up? He came on to establish himself as the number one quarterback. I'll have to give myself credit for making one smart move. Some of our coaches suggested we switch him to defense. I said, "Hell no!"

But as good as he was, Tracy didn't do it all by himself. I know he would be the first to admit that. He was surrounded by a bunch of young guys who wanted to play. We had some good ones sprinkled in there too, who later developed into a fine supporting cast.

So now we found ourselves into the first real season with this group with a record of 2-0-1. I continued to remind them how concerned I was with doing good on the field, as I always remembered my office had those wheels. I didn't ever want to have the slop beaten out of us and come home to find my office vanished, hidden somewhere, while they appointed a new head coach.

That's just what I said as we headed toward our fourth game against Gardner-Webb in their stadium.

Gardner-Webb, in Boiling Springs, North Carolina — a bus trip of some eight hours — was in the NAIA SIAC Eight Conference and was a powerhouse in that league. This was to be a true test as to how far along we had come.

We were over-matched in this game. It was obvious from the beginning that it would be a long evening.

At halftime they led us, 35-0, and as we walked to the dressing room, Mike Healey said, "Coach what are we going to do?" I replied, "Don't ask me, Mike — I've never been this far behind at the half."

They beat us, 44-6, behind the throwing of their fine quarterback, Chip Stuart, who threw 57 passes for 391 yards. Our only score came when our defensive end, an ex-Marine by the name of Jimmy Kerfoot, intercepted one of those thousand missiles Stuart released that night and ran it in for a touchdown in the fourth quarter.

Their coach kept Stuart and his first team in the game until the end of the contest, throwing the ball like crazy, trying to add to his already impressive numbers.

I remember calling my team together about a minute before the end of the game. I told them when the whistle blew we were going to run straight to the dressing room, get dressed, get on those buses and go back to Statesboro. I did not appreciate the other coach keeping his first team in the contest. I didn't even say goodbye or congratulate him.

To not congratulate a coach in victory was another first for me, but during this new experience, there would be a number of firsts.

We came back home the next week and played the Fort Benning Doughboys in our house ... Womack Field. We won, 56-6, and it looked like I was doing the same thing I was complaining about earlier ... running up the score. No. We played everybody that day and that is always good for a squad's morale. That is especially true with a new program.

The highlight of that day was when a CBS crew came in and did a special on the Southern story.

John Tesh, the CBS guy, took me somewhere out on campus. We sat on a bench and talked about what was going on.

When he finished with me, he took his microphone and camera to our Southern Boosters' office, which was also located in a mobile home, but without wheels. That kept Kenny Winstead, our first director of that operation, about as nervous as I was about getting the job done each week. He was fortunate to have a good assistant like Wanda Parrish.

On Saturday mornings those few diehards who were the spirit and core of our fans met and had a few drinks and got fired up before the game.

I remember Tesh and his crew came in and filmed Morris Lupton, one of those special individuals who had stepped forward and put a lot of money where his spirit was. Tesh fired away with his taping and caught Morris standing in the middle of our cheerleaders with a glass of some clear liquid in his hands, leading a mighty yell.

Later they taped some of the game action and saw our fans filling up that tiny Womack Field. They sent the story to New York and, a few weeks later, Brent Musberger introduced it during one of the CBS games that day.

That was the first real exposure our program had received. Folks, we didn't have money to buy that kind of advertising. For the first time people all over the country heard about Georgia Southern, Statesboro and what we were doing with our new football program.

After Fort Benning we hosted Newberry, another pretty good team which had been playing for years. It was the Eagles' first victory over an established football program. It continued Southern's unbeaten streak at home. The score against Newberry was, 36-14, with one of our guys, Ben Holt, running the ball 19 times for 121 yards. It was a good victory for us.

Catawba, another NAIA school, came to town for the first homecoming involving a football game at Georgia Southern in 41 years. Our little stadium was jammed, but none of that meant very much to a tough Catawba team which beat us that day, 10-7.

They led, 10-0, with less than five minutes in the game. It was then we released the first long pass of the Eagles' young history. A 41-yard toss from Rob Allen to Robert Baker for six. We got the ball back but were unable to do anything. In all honesty, I felt our team was better than theirs and we should have won. But that's what makes football interesting. You never know. In this instance, I knew. We played awful. It's really bad when you play badly at homecoming.

We had over 8,000 folks at home to watch us that day. That was a lot to get into that stadium with a seating capacity of 3,500. I felt we had a real chance to promote ourselves in front of such a large group of people.

That next weekend we played Wofford under the lights in Statesboro. Wofford was a true powerhouse and they enjoyed a great tradition in small college football.

They ran the wishbone and we turned the ball over seven times. You can't expect to beat a team when you hand the ball over seven times. One is too many.

We lost, 28-7.

This took place on November 8. The reason I remember it so well is that's when Tracy Ham became our first-team quarterback for keeps.

I can't really remember distinctly what Tracy did that day. One thing he did do was hand the ball to Ricky Harris, who ran 147 yards, which was pretty good.

Our next outing took place at Mars Hill and we won, 17-3. Mars Hill is a lovely small school in North Carolina. The campus was picturesque in November, the way a college campus is supposed to look. In that contest the Harris boys, Gerald and Ricky, combined their running skills for a total of 215 yards. After a slow first half, Ham came forward and showed that he was going to be a fine option quarterback.

A lot of things brought adventure into our lives back in those days.

Like for instance, the buses we used to go to Mars Hill. We rode the "Eagle Special" and another bus. And to put it bluntly, we sort of walked onto those buses for those away games, never quite certain as to what would take place between here and there.

Our slogan that year for marketing our program and for ticket sales was, "Get that first-class feeling."

But on that long trip to Mars Hill, we were just over the South Carolina line when the radiator began running hot. Steam everywhere. There we were out in the middle of the country, but right in front of a pretty farmhouse occupied by a nice lady with a long garden hose.

While she and Roger Inman pulled on that hose and filled up our "Eagle Special," the team started singing, "Get that first-class feeling."

Out there in the South Carolina countryside, with a bus that had long since seen its days, there we were relying on this long garden hose and a kindly country lady to get our team on the road again. We got to our destination in good shape, won the game and got home. Who cared if it was 4 a.m.? We were Georgia Southern and we had won. There are two important things one can get so far behind in and catch up on so fast. One of them is sleep.

We began closing out that first season by going to Valdosta State and playing them one more time. It was tough to play the same team twice in one season, but both of our institutions had just started our programs. We both needed that game.

We bused down remembering how we had to stretch in that first game with them back in Statesboro to tie, 27-27. We wanted to do better on this occasion. We were 5-3-1 now.

It was in that game Ham had his first really great night, rushing for 120 yards. Melvin Bell took it 130 yards. The score was, 45-29, our way.

Melvin had played for Ben Griffith at Elbert County and then went on to Presbyterian College. Melvin wasn't feeling too much at home at Presbyterian, and as a result of his relationship with Ben, transferred to Georgia Southern at the beginning of the 1982 season. As I have said earlier, a lot of players from other schools showed an interest in the Southern program and several had transferred. It was never my intention to deliberately go after a kid at another place.

But if one called me and wanted to talk, I'd talk. I would have been stupid not to. Most of those who inquired about changing schools were advised to stay where they were.

Not only did Melvin come down from Presbyterian, but another player showed some interest. He lived in Statesboro. With that, the word got out I was hitting on that college pretty heavily, which was as far from the truth as anything could get.

We had two men living in Statesboro who had some affiliation with Presbyterian. They took it upon themselves to visit Dr. Lick, requesting that he advise me to leave Presbyterian alone and quit hijacking their players.

The man that he is, Dr. Lick asked me one simple question, "Are you doing anything like that?" I told him no. He said he believed me and was behind my efforts all the way. He wanted me to run the football program and he was going to get back to running Georgia Southern.

Lick was like that. Touching base with me was his way of handling folks who dropped by with some bitching. He had the patience of Job. Honest to God, I don't see how anyone would want to be president of a college or university. Every day it seems to me somebody showed up complaining or wanting a change.

I took Melvin and put his desire to play in an Eagle uniform and hoped those two guys who visited Dale would just come out each Saturday and watch Melvin run. I didn't have time to waste on whether they liked it or not.

The whole thing reminded me of the coach running up the score on me. Totally unnecessary.

The 11th game — the finale of 1982.

We went to play those junior varsity guys from Florida State in Warner Robins, which is located in the middle part of our state. Again, the location indicated our interest in getting fan support everywhere. Besides, they had a nice stadium and we had a good crowd in attendance.

We won the game, 31-20.

In that contest, Tracy continued to do what he had started doing the past three weeks, becoming the quality player he was. In that contest Ham was doing his thing against some real quality players. Those big Seminoles were on scholarships and would move into varsity positions the next season. At least some of them would.

But Ham's quickness was already beginning to show up. It was a tough type football game and he took some hard knocks. He threw nine for 17 for 114 yards. Melvin Bell ran 20 times for 201 yards. Tracy started to take charge of our team. It is always nice to have good players, but it was becoming noticeable that we had some good players who really liked to play. I felt good after that contest.

We completed that first season 7-3-1. Not bad. It was a winning effort. Seven is more than three, and that is the way I've always looked at a season — how many wins and how many losses. I did that at Grady High right on through the Georgia years and brought it with me when I moved to Statesboro.

The toughest team we faced that year was Wofford. I believe they went undefeated and if they didn't win the NAIA championship, they came close.

How did I record our kids' effort and skill? I thought for the most part we had a group comparable to the NAIA schools, which was a long way from what we would see when we started into that circle of NCAA Division I-AA. There was an indication we were getting better, especially when Ham started running the team.

The emergence of Ham, the Harris runners, Bell and Pike, Jesse Jenkins and Monty Sharpe gave us the good players. We had good people. But we felt we needed more depth and there were gaps we had to fill to build a strong program.

Our chart showed that Georgia Southern scored 290 points to our opponents 190. We beat people 26.7 to 17.3 points per game. We had five touchdowns scored on us by the run and 18 in the air, which meant it was tougher for a new group to defend the pass than the run. And of course, with that Valdosta State quarterback and the Gardner-Webb air attack, those two games put the passing touchdowns way up there.

1982 was a tremendous year for Georgia Southern. In looking back we got a lot better with time and particularly when we introduced Ham. We were able to utilize his abilities and the abilities of the skilled people. The skilled people were the key to our success. This would continue to be our strength for the next few years.

Beginning with those hot August days down in that black dirt next to Beautiful Eagle Creek with gnats all over the place, we had fun. It was fun because we were winning and we needed to win in the worst way. I had left the University of Georgia and the best coaching job in America. We had to make it work!

33 | *AND THE HARRISES RAN ON*

Many things happened from the time we closed out the 1982 season against the Florida State Junior Varsity.

Those "players" I mentioned earlier came on the scene and really got things going. Sen. Glenn Bryant, M.C. Anderson, Allen Paulson and Ann and Morris Lupton in their individual ways built "our house," which we began using in the fall of 1984.

It was this "squad" who took that message from 1981 of, "Give us a place to play," and built the prettiest little stadium in America.

But in 1983, another 11 games faced us. It was a tough schedule for a one-year-old. We dropped the FSU J.V. and the Doughboys and replaced them with college teams. We would travel for hours on that "Eagle Special" with the "First-class feeling." I wasn't sure we could beat anybody, but I now had an idea we could be competitive if we continued to get better. That's what we had to do, get better ... if we were to win one game.

We opened against Central Florida. I looked across the field and there was Lou Saban moving up and down the sidelines, pumped up like he was still in the NFL. I don't know this for certain, but I'd bet you a dollar there wasn't another game in America that day which featured two head coaches with as much coaching experience and who were as old as Saban and me. (I was 56 and he was older.)

Our team led, 15-9, at halftime, but the numbers changed in the second half and the final score was, 29-33. We lost. That "old codger" beat me.

Tracy ran it in twice in the fourth quarter, from the 15 and the 13-yard lines. Gerald Harris carried it for 102 yards. Melvin Bell gained 130. You figure it out. With that kind of offensive production, we should have beat anybody. I'm afraid I didn't help our defensive troops in their efforts to stop the pass and draw.

The next weekend we went to Savannah to play that team I was supposedly raiding in an unprofessional manner — Presbyterian.

We won, 35-21. Ham carried the ball 15 times for 90 yards. He threw it 10 times and completed four of them for 139 yards. That's 30 yards a catch. We began to see him find the open man.

We played in Savannah, continuing our efforts to be available for still many of the patrons to see what we were trying to accomplish. Savannah was a pretty tough crowd to get to. It took us awhile to convince that large town it had the chance to drive up the road just 50 miles on I-16 and enjoy football at Georgia Southern. I'm happy to say, they got the word and now do so much for the program, in addition to coming to the games.

Savannah and its good people helped us in gaining the bid to host the National Championship games in Statesboro in 1989, '90 and '91. They really rolled out the blue and white carpet for the two teams appearing in those championship games. Savannah Mayor John Rousakis worked closely with our Statesboro and Bulloch County officials and the folks at the college to pull that off.

Savannah's support was slow in coming, but in a few years, the city became a source of great support.

Who would have ever thought back then in the fall of '83, I'm talking about less than six years, that CBS and ESPN would bring in those big vans and cameras and we would be seen all across America? I wouldn't have.

The third game of the '83 season was against a really good Troy State team. In fact, they might have gone all the way and won the Division II championship that year. They beat us, 28-27, when we went for two after scoring late in the game. I'd rather tie than lose just about anytime, but our team had played just as hard and they deserved a chance to win. Down in that dark, hard left corner of that high school field, Tracy couldn't quite cover those last three yards for the two points.

Tracy carried the ball 17 times for 129 yards and threw it 21 times, completing 10 of them for 142 yards. That was another 200-yard game for him. By the way, a lot of Ham's running, folks, is like a Fred Astaire dance ... tapping around a bunch of big guys who would like nothing more than to grab one of his legs and take it home for a trophy.

There were those two Harris guys and Melvin Bell blocking or taking the ball and churning out 70, 80 or sometimes even a 100 yards a game. That was some kind of backfield. How could we have been so lucky as to get guys like those at Southern so early? It was just that — we were lucky. They were good.

We got revenge the fourth game of the season. Remember that 44-6 shellacking by Gardner-Webb? We beat them, 25-11. It was a good victory for us in that Gardner-Webb was still a pretty good club. The most disappointing thing about that game was Gardner-Webb had a new head coach. Maybe I should have been glad, but I surely would have enjoyed some small measure of revenge.

That season I don't think too many opponents shoved Gardner-Webb around. But Tracy did his thing again by putting another 200 yards on the books, throwing the ball for 110 and running it for 92.

He'd given us 200 yards a game since we started the season. People were beginning to talk about number eight. Even with that we were just 2-2 for the season.

We played East Tennessee State in Johnson City the next week and were introduced to a couple of items worth mentioning: it was our first encounter with a Division I-AA team and they played on Astroturf. Remember that stuff we flew to see in the Twin Cities, back at the University of Georgia? This was a similar surface. This time we couldn't worry too much about the kind of shoes we'd wear on the artificial surface. We didn't have much of a choice. We borrowed basketball shoes from our "hoops" team and some players used their regular football shoes.

We played inside. It was is like playing inside an airplane hanger. The field was just as flat and as hard as a landing strip.

Tracy hurt his shoulder in the second quarter while the game was still in doubt. He wouldn't return to action during that game.

Steve Lamostro came in for Tracy. We lost, 24-7. It was a whole new experience playing a team of that caliber on that carpet. East Tennessee was a good representative I-AA team. We were in a little over our heads. We needed time to compete at this level with any consistent success. But our guys continued to play hard and we could see some light at the end of the tunnel.

Throughout those early years, our offense was clearly ahead of our defense. This is not said with Tracy Ham in mind especially, although there is no doubt Ham made the difference in what our ball club could get done offensively when he was in. Because he was a player who took the snap and followed the pattern until things in front of him started falling apart. Then something took over within him that didn't come from coaching, and it was his instinct that found the right step and made good things happen.

When I talk about the offense being ahead of the defense, I'm speaking of consistency and effectiveness. Some thought our defense might gear up pretty good because of my background as a defensive coach through the years.

It didn't work out that way at Southern. We were blessed with fine skilled players: running backs, a quarterback and wide receivers. That wasn't really true of our defense. We filled in around some pretty fair defensive players with those who were available. I'll say this about our defense though, they gave effort. What more can you ask? I've never been around people who tried any harder than some of those guys. Jenkins, Ward, Rossignol, Douglas, Durham and Richardson. I loved their attitudes.

Keep in mind we'd be playing a Division I-AA schedule. Though we might have been outsized in those early years, that never was a major concern on my part. In order to play football, a person has to be able to run. We tried to recruit people who could run. That was our first requirement. Speed wins. If you can't run, it's hard to play effectively.

There we were coming up against Newberry, a team we had beaten in '82. We played in Augusta on a drizzly night. We lost, 27-24, with just less than a minute to play. Tracy's shoulder was still stinging from the East Tennessee game, and he didn't play. But we had a great game out of Melvin Bell, who ran 144 yards.

Again, we were taking GSC football to different places and people, trying to gain that following and support that would be so necessary for success down the road.

For the first time in my coaching career, I decided to give up a safety to our opponent in exchange for good field position. "Boomer" Barker, our punter, delivered the best kick of his entire career — a 70-yarder that sailed over the safety man's head. And there we were, having them backed up with 70 yards to go for a touchdown, with just two minutes left to play.

They scored when a pass interference call gave them the ball at our 1-yard line. I wasn't coaching so well with Ham on the bench.

The next week we went to Catawba and led, 3-0, at the half. They were getting stronger and threatened to take the game away from us. Tracy wanted to play. I let him.

He made all the difference in the world. Though we only won, 10-7, it became obvious to everyone on the coaching staff, he was the difference-maker.

One thing I always liked about Tracy — he always gave credit to his teammates for his success. Throughout the remainder of his time at Southern, when he did something verging on the unbelievable, trotting to the sidelines he'd point to the offensive linemen and the others who had paved the way or kept the opposition occupied while he spotted a receiver.

He's still that way. When he stops by my office and we talk about the early days, he shares the success with every team member. Actually, he did have a fine supporting cast, but Ham was one of a kind.

Let me wrap up this season. Like the Catawba contest, we went on the road again the next weekend to Wofford, who had beaten us the year before. Wofford had a fine football program. Ham had a great game rushing for 132 yards and passing for 92. Another 200-plus outing!

We were then 4-4.

We won at home in our eighth game of the season, beating Mars Hill, 35-9. Hugo Rossignol, our outstanding linebacker, intercepted a pass and ran it back 95 yards. It was a beautiful day for football in Statesboro and the Eagles played super.

But then one of the most bitter losses came our way when Valdosta State whipped us with the "hideout play," which they used twice in the same game. To have it happen once is bad coaching. To have it happen twice is terrible coaching. They did it to us and I felt awful because I could have prevented it through better preparation. Our team deserved more effort from me.

In our final game against Savannah State College, we called off the contest with 5:40 left on the clock when the game turned into a free-for-all. I swear, I should have had my old bald head examined for running out there and trying to stop a whole bunch of young guys trying to find somebody to hit.

I finished off my old left elbow, which was just halfway hanging there anyway as a result of my having shown a freshman how to separate from a blocker. My participation in that fight led to surgery a few weeks later.

This reminds me of another story which took place in 1981. It was in early fall and the president of a Georgia Southern fraternity called and proposed a great way for the football team to make a lot of money. He asked if a couple of my assistant coaches and I would come to the county fair and sit in their dunking booth. That's where you get to throw three baseballs for a quarter and if the target is hit, the sucker falls into the water.

The fraternity president told me he would give me half of the proceeds.

That seemed like a good deal to me, so Hugh Nall, Ben Griffith, Mike Healey and I served as targets for the dunking booth. A young lefthander who had an unending supply of quarters knocked me off the board several times, each time to the roar of the crowd. The water was only about waist-deep. Then I fell in at a peculiar angle with all my weight on my left leg. That old leg wasn't too good anyhow. But that finished it off.

Net proceeds for the evening: $24. That's a dozen jocks.

The surgery was about $5,000.

We finished 6-5. Our second full season was behind us. I didn't feel too good about taking a step backwards as far as our record was concerned. But I felt we had made some progress. All our losses were by five points or less. We were always close and we would get better.

34 | *DIVISION I-AA– READY OR NOT!*

As our new staff gathered in our office, the trailer, back in late August and early September of 1981, I had a pretty good idea of what I wanted to do on offense. I knew exactly what we would do on defense. We'd use the "Spilt 60" package I had used for so long at Georgia. There was no doubt about that.

On offense I wanted to do the things that had been most troublesome for me to defend over the years. Specifically, we would use the sprint-out passing game, as opposed to the drop-back passing game. And I wanted to be able to run a good option play of some type. I wanted the option to be the strong part of our scheme.

For years, as we prepared for any opponent, I found that those teams which carried a good option game in their package were much more difficult to prepare for. It takes a lot of practice to successfully defend a good option. I wanted our opponents to have that problem.

We would "feature" these two plays from the "I" formation and, of course, complement them with standard, basic stuff. My objective was to keep things simple. We would apply the K.I.S.S. philosophy — "Keep It Simple, Stupid."

Ben Griffith was an excellent option teacher, having used the wishbone in high school for a long time. He got us off to a good start with his knowledge of the triple option.

With this brief background of how we started back in 1981, you can see what I wanted to do offensively. Our players and coaches were making it work. We were in the "I" featuring the triple option and the sprint-out pass.

As we gathered around the film projector and watched a hundred prospective quarterbacks on the window shade which served as our screen in the trailer, we evaluated them on their ability to handle this kind of offense. A little guy from Santa Fe High School in Alachua, Florida, looked like he might he able to do these things, so I said, "Let's take him." To make a long story short, that little quarterback was Tracy Ham. No college wanted him to play quarterback, except Southern. How lucky can you be?

There we were with two full seasons of club football under our belts. We had four full-time coaches. We had scholarship money for only about 20 players. We divided most of the money into partial scholarships and helped about 35 players. Contributions for our new stadium were moving right along, and we had a Division I-AA schedule coming up ... fast.

I felt that playing in Division I-AA after such a short time was professional suicide. We had gone against only one opponent from I-AA and had gotten beat. I feared the worst was coming. The reason I agreed to a giant step up in competition was I thought it would be an excellent avenue for our entrance into the Southern Conference. I thought this conference affiliation was what we needed for the future.

But then again, I reminded myself it was this potential situation that had attracted me to this job. Starting from scratch. Taking hand-me-down shirts, old equipment, a high school stadium and starting a football program. And as I looked at our squad that August of '84 and the schedule we faced, I said, "Russell, here it is. What are we going to do about it?"

In order to qualify as a Division I-AA team, we had to play a combination of at least six I-AA and Division I-A teams. Our '84 schedule did have six of those teams waiting. Our remaining five games were with Division II and NAIA teams. This would be extremely tough for our two-year-old football program.

During the summer of '84, Ben had stopped by the Houston Gamblers football offices while he was on vacation. After discussions with the Houston coaches and after watching their films, Ben became excited about their "Run and Shoot" offense. When he returned to Statesboro he put on a very good sales talk with me and our staff with the idea that this offense would be suited for our personnel.

I don't mind telling you it sounded pretty good, but it meant getting away from some of the things that had been good for us. It was also a 90 percent passing offense. I certainly wasn't ready for that. Not too many pure passing teams win a lot of games.

The possibilities presented by the "Run and Shoot" were good enough to be investigated further, and I sent Ben and Hugh Nall, our offensive line coach, back to Houston to learn more about the offense.

Both Ben and Hugh were ready to go all the way with the "Run and Shoot," but I wouldn't agree to do that. Not right then anyhow.

To make another long story short, we gradually worked some of the "Run and Shoot" into our repertoire. By the end of the '84 season, we were using it about 50 percent of the time. What we had done, however, was to make it a running offense as much as a passing game. We were doing the same things with the "Run and Shoot" that we did with the "I" formation.

I'll be the first to admit that our adapting the "Run and Shoot" and revising it into the "Hambone" was one of the best moves we ever made. It was tailor-made for our personnel, especially Ham. It spread the defense and forced them to defend the entire field. It was a personnel equalizer as we began our NCAA Division I-AA career.

The "Hambone" offense was most instrumental in the success we enjoyed.

Paulson Stadium was supposed to have been ready for our first game in '84. But like most things that require cement, nails and that other stuff used "to construct" as they call it, the stadium wasn't complete. So we rode to Savannah, got off that rickety "Eagle Special," took a deep breath and opened our season against Florida A&M.

Florida A&M was a perennial I-AA powerhouse. They had one of the finest football traditions in America. I'm sure they've sent as many players to the NFL as any college team ever has.

When you lined up against the Rattlers, you'd better tighten your chin strap. Our guys had been told that repeatedly.

The day was one of the hottest I had ever encountered. I was scared to death. When I say I was scared, I mean I was scared to the point I knew we would be fighting for our lives. This is a good kind of scared. It makes you compete harder. Our players were scared to death too.

Our fright was supported by the confidence and knowledge that Florida A&M could beat the fire out of us if we didn't play better than we were capable of playing. That's the kind of attitude I liked for my teams to have going into every game.

We won, 14-0 and I consider it to be one of the most important victories Georgia Southern ever earned. It was against a good I-AA opponent. We played extremely hard and it seemed to me we were a little bit stronger at the end of the game. Their big guys died in the fourth quarter and we were still coming.

It was a great victory.

But remember, the sweet taste of victory doesn't, or shouldn't, last long. As soon as we get together the next day and review the film, all that stuff is filed away and becomes a chapter in the history of Eagle football.

Next Saturday always looms large.

But I will admit, coming back to Statesboro that night the thought did occur to me that, based on this first game and the way our guys played, maybe, just maybe, we weren't as in-over-our-heads as I might have thought. But then this had just been one game. There were 10 more of those Saturdays. Each to be taken one at a time. Each the most important game of our lives.

We stayed on the road for the next two Saturdays. We played Presbyterian and had an easier time with them than I had anticipated. The score was, 41-6, our way. This was followed by a trip to the Citrus Bowl in Orlando, where we matched ourselves against Central Florida, winning that one, 42-28. This wasn't as easy as the score indicated. We scored two late touchdowns to ice the game.

All this time, Ham was healthy and our offense was moving the ball well. Our defense was playing pretty good. And it was becoming more and more apparent Ham was becoming something special. He would stay that way for most of his remaining career, after which he would head to the Canadian Football League, and in his second year, win the Most Valuable Player trophy.

There was an ability being developed, especially among our skilled people. At this early stage, they seemed to be showing they could compete with the talent we would face on this level.

With those thoughts crossing my mind about how we might be able to "hang in there" in Division I-AA, up came a Division I opponent, our first experience with a team of this caliber. We climbed on that old bus and traveled to East Carolina, a team that finished 8-3 the year before, only losing to Florida, Florida State and Miami in close games.

So there we came, three wins under our belts, headed for our first-ever Division I opponent. That Saturday in Greenville, North Carolina, was the game of our lives.

Our guys ran into the stadium in front of the largest crowd they'd played for — over 35,000 fans. You can be sure it was a new and different experience for the Eagles.

The score was, 34-27, and they won.

But we had two touchdowns called back and felt like we could have won that game with the kind of show our sophomore quarterback, Tracy Ham, had put on for all those fans. He had over 400 yards passing and rushed for 55 more. Those are great numbers against anybody, anywhere, anytime.

Robert Baker caught nine balls for 122 yards. Monty Sharpe had seven catches for 117 yards. What a great day for our receivers.

We came home feeling good about how hard we played. Yet, I never felt good about finishing second. I have to say the team had given its best effort, and in the long run, this outing was a confidence-builder.

By the way, the night before the East Carolina game I had to run Tracy and some of his friends out of the hot tub at the hotel ... reminding them this would sap their energy and make them weak for the game the next day. Tracy later reminded me the East Carolina game was the best he ever played. If I had been just half as smart as I'm supposed to be, I would have made them soak in the hot tub every Friday night.

They finished "Our House" and "Coach" Jerry Falwell, president of Liberty Baptist, brought his squad to Statesboro. The first game ever played in Paulson Stadium ended with Georgia Southern defeating Liberty Baptist,

48-11, on September 19. As it turned out, "Coach" Falwell wasn't with his team, and I always wanted to meet that good man.

We scored the first time we had the ball with Ham running an option keeper 34 yards.

It was good to be home. It was great to have a home. To have a friendly crowd. To baptize our new stadium in such fine style against Liberty Baptist. They were immersed that day, Southern style.

It was always helpful to a team's success to keep its best players in the game, or at least have them available to play when needed. We were always lucky not to have players injured for an extended period of time. We were also lucky that we didn't lose players through academic difficulties. We expected to have problems like this. We just didn't have many.

Sometimes students didn't "do right" and they had to be disciplined. Sometimes we had to suspend them for a game, sometimes for a season or sometimes, forever. Thank goodness we didn't have disciplinary problems on any large scale.

I attribute this to our having good people, good communication and a lot of luck.

There were unexpected ways to lose a good player, ways you couldn't anticipate. I'll never forget an incident which occurred right in the middle of the 1984 season. One of our best players came to my office and said, "Coach, I've got to quit the team. My girlfriend is pregnant and I've got to go home and get a job so I can take care of her."

I didn't know what to say. I could tell he was really serious. No matter what the problem, I sure didn't want this guy to quit, so I asked a basic question, "How for along is she?" The player thought for a few seconds and said, "About 70 miles from here, Coach."

In spite of our "mis-communication," he married the girl, finished the season and I believe things worked out well for everybody involved.

I walked into my office the next Monday morning and looked up and we were 4-1. But I was still scared to death. That's the way I was and always will be. And while looking up I saw we had to go on the road again. This time to Jacksonville's Gator Bowl to play 18th-ranked Bethune-Cookman. They had a quarterback by the name of Bernard Hawk. And he was going to drive me crazy for the next two years.

We won, 42-33, and were lucky to get out of there alive.

Hawk set a passing record, throwing 66 times and completing 40 of them for 527 yards. He threw to an end by the name of Gonzalez. Of course, his first name had to be "Speedy." Gonzalez is in the pros now. And I don't know why Hawk isn't.

By the way, "Speedy" caught 15 for 202 yards. I got sick of looking at him and hearing his name on the P.A.

Ham threw for 190 yards and ran for 135. Thanks to me, we were in the wrong defense the entire game, rushing three and defending with eight. I should have known better.

Coaches are human. But in my mind if we're gonna be that way, we need to be as right as we can. Putting our guys out there in a wrong defense, giving the other side another advantage: that's not good.

I tried to keep that in mind as we took on the University of Tennessee-Chattanooga in our house. This team had a long tradition of being pretty good.

Somehow we managed to win the game, 24-17.

It was, 10-10, at halftime. In the third quarter, we scored 14 points within a minute, and then our guys put on two of the finest goal-line stands I've ever seen. We held them four downs within our 5-yard line on two occasions.

But our joy was short-lived. The very first snap from our center to our quarterback following that second great stand ended in a fumble and they recovered for a score. A great goal-line wall. They still scored. But it wasn't enough.

Ham passed for 222 yards. We used the "Hambone" formation to good advantage in this game. We were beginning to use it more and more.

The next week was homecoming and we had a crowd of around 12,000, which made us feel good. We beat Newberry, 41-16, with Gerald Harris scoring three touchdowns and beginning a fine career as our touchdown-maker. He would continue doing the same thing for us for two more seasons and become one of the all-time scoring leaders in I-AA football.

It was a good victory for us and a crowd-pleaser. As a coach I had one thing really on my mind every game — a victory. If it happened to be a crowd-pleaser, that was fine with me.

Valdosta State came to our house and we worked the score, 38-8, our way. We rushed for over 500 yards with the two Harrises having over a 100 each and Tracy doing the same. I felt we were beginning to pull away from our cross-state rival. Remember, we started our programs the same year.

We were 8-1. We were playing in Division I-AA. But remember, I went on the field every Saturday scared. Scared because I knew if we didn't play the very best we could, we were going to get beat. And that's exactly what happened in games 10 and 11.

We went on the road and came home from Johnson City with a loss to East Tennessee, 20-17, and a week later from Middle Tennessee, 42-7, in the worst rainstorm I've played in until a couple of years ago when Hurricane Hugo came to Statesboro.

We were 8-3. We missed the play-offs. We wouldn't do that again.

1984 turned out much better than I thought it might. I was encouraged as we looked forward to our second year of Division I-AA football.

ERK

This had been a special year for me in many ways. I had a young team and a young coaching staff. The Southern Boosters were working hard to get us the money we badly needed. Everybody was working hard to help the program. Good things happen when people come together in a common cause and are willing to work for that cause.

And this was the season we had dedicated to Terry Woodard, a young man we lost on March 19, 1984, in a car accident.

He was an Eagle. His number was 92. Terry wasn't a starter, but he was one of those kind of young men who was going to be because he was a good player who tried hard and was respected by his teammates and the coaches.

He was out for a Sunday afternoon drive. Terry, a young black, in a truck with two of his white teammates, were on their way to the annual Rattlesnake Roundup in Claxton, about 20 miles down the road. A car ran a stop sign. It hit them broadside and Terry was killed.

Talking to our team, attending Terry's memorial service, driving to Dade City, Florida, and hugging his folks — all that was tough for me. Jean and I knew what his people were going through.

I made a little talk at Terry's funeral. That was one of the toughest things I've ever done. What can one say at a time like that? I think I knew how his mama felt, but there was little consolation. This was so final.

The team wore the number 92 on the sleeves of their jerseys. That was Terry's number. We dedicated the season to the memory of our teammate. Somehow, I feel Terry Woodard was proud of his team's effort.

35 | THE "FEATS" OF HAM

Our schedule had been upgraded again. We had replaced three Division II teams with Division I-AA squads. That meant we had nine of that kind waiting for us. And the element of surprise about, "Who are the Eagles?" was beginning to fade.

Our schedule was 40 percent tougher than the previous year. We weren't to the point in our football program where we could slide by anybody. Is there ever that time? Never in the 40 years I coached.

And we were going to play it one game at a time. One at a time. No other way. That is, I hoped I could convince our guys that was the way to do it.

I said in 1984 that Tracy Ham was the best quarterback in the state at any level. He had great ability to read the option and could turn a nothing-play into something good for our side. Quick hands and quick feet. And he was going to have to do all that because each Saturday was a challenge.

As usual, I was scared to death. Ben Griffith left our staff to become offensive coordinator at New Mexico. Paul Johnson took Ben's job with the offense. Now wasn't that a heck of a move — asking your defensive line coach to come over and coach the quarterbacks and coordinate the offense!

From the beginning, Paul gave every indication he was a fine football coach. It has always been my contention that a good coach can coach any phase of the game. In this case, that theory was right on the money. Tim Stowers came from Jacksonville State as our offensive line coach. And my son, Jay came from Barnesville Academy to coach our receivers.

We had five full-time coaches now in a league which allowed seven. I wanted more coaches, but frankly, we didn't have the money. The five we had were coaching because they loved to coach, not for the salary we paid. Our football budget was about half that of many Division I-AA teams.

I don't mean to keep crying about our lack of funds ... our budget compared with teams we were competing against. But let's face it, that's the way it was. We still didn't have the best of everything, but we were trying to make the best of everything we had.

When I ordered our first "game uniforms" back in 1982, the cost factor was the major consideration as we chose our attire. Our players and coaches would have loved to have had a blue stripe on our white pants, but a single stripe on the britches would add about $4 to the price of each pair. Likewise, our players suggested to me repeatedly that we put a white circle around the sleeve or neck of those plain navy blue jerseys. Any such addition to those shirts would add another couple of dollars to the cost of each. We just didn't have the money, so we settled for plain white pants and plain navy blue jerseys (white jerseys for the road games).

We got a little more money each year. So our guys still asked for stripes and rings and decals and other uniform decorations. I was the guy who made the final decision about things like that, but we were doing so well I saw no reason to change. As Coach "Shug" Jordan used to say, (and this has really stuck with me over the years), "If it is not necessary to change, it is necessary not to change." This is just another way of saying, "If it ain't broke, don't fix it."

I loved our "plain" uniforms. I loved to refer to Southern as a "generic" team. No frills. No additives. No extras except effort. Just a plain old GATA team.

I haven't had a coach or player suggest a uniform change in years. Nobody wants to change our generic image. Stripes and frills don't win games. Good people do.

Folks have accused me of trying to look like Penn State. Well, they dress out fancy compared to us. We didn't try to copy anybody. We just tried to get dressed. I loved the way our Eagles suited up.

Finally, as our group took the field, I believed those uniforms fairly cried out, "GEORGIA SOUTHERN TEAM."

We had Vance Pike on the offensive line. He was a quality player. He graded out high every game. He led by doing. He was not your "rah-rah" guy. He just went out there and pushed the defense all over the field. I'm glad we opened the season with him on our side.

And then we had Jesse Jenkins, Pike's high school teammate at Warner Robins, on the other side of the ball. He was the leader. He was the last of the original Eagles of 1981! He wasn't big enough to play, but he was our best defensive lineman. I told Jesse every day he was too little to play. He didn't believe me and neither did I. His attitude made the difference. His attitude was awesome, and it was contagious.

Here's a kid who, like Vance, was a great citizen off the field, studying and making those kind of grades that were good enough for the dean's list.

We opened with Florida A&M in Jacksonville. We were really fortunate to come out of there alive, 27-21.

Ricky Harris rushed for 117 yards. Tracy fumbled four out of the first five snaps from the center, and we lost three of them. I was thinking seriously of replacing him with "Snake" Burnette. Paul Johnson asked me to give Tracy one more chance. So did Tracy.

I did. And I'm glad. Things got better. We won.

We came home to play Middle Tennessee and we lost, 35-10, the first and last of that kind of outcome at home until 1990.

They had a little guy at quarterback that could make you miss him. And we missed him a lot. In the third quarter, while we still had a chance, he made two or three plays that put it out of reach.

Middle Tennessee would see us again later. They didn't know that. Neither did we. When we saw them again, they would be undefeated and number one in the country. But on this day, they whipped us good.

My thoughts at that time were, "We aren't a very good football team."

The third game in, the Eagles went to Troy State in Alabama, and although they are a Division II school, they are a perennial powerhouse in their league. They would win the National Championship of Division II that very year. We were fortunate to win, 17-10.

Tracy had a good day running and passing. He accounted for 252 yards of the final 314 we had for the day. But a Hugo Rossignol interception of a pass late in the fourth quarter stopped that Troy State group and really saved our hides.

Any time you go to their place on Saturday night and win, you've done a good night's work.

Speaking of night games, we had the same situation the next weekend against U.T. Chattanooga. The dressing rooms were about a block from the stadium. If we didn't start that walk early enough we'd miss the opening or the second half kickoff.

I can remember one end of the field sort of sloping up, while at the other end zone there were tree branches decorating the place. Funny what a coach remembers besides the score, which was, 19-14, and we won.

Ham fired a 20-yard pass in the third quarter to Monty Sharpe to put us ahead for good and Tim Foley kicked a 54-yard field goal. It was a terrific win.

Buddy Nix, the Chattanooga coach and a long-time SEC assistant, told me after the game that Ham was the best quarterback he had ever seen. I told him I knew he had seen some good ones over the years and I agreed. We got dressed, hopped on those buses and headed home. I saw the sun come up from my front seat as we approached Statesboro about 7 a.m. Why go to bed? Might as well start looking at next week's opponent.

ERK

I did my share of complaining about those long bus trips we had to make, but I never bitched about it to our squad. No reason to do that. We didn't have a choice of transportation. That was simply something that came with the territory at our level.

It is particularly tough on a team to have to play a night game seven or more hours away from home. We were lucky if we could get away from the stadium before midnight. And that meant we got home around 7 or 8 a.m. Sometimes I think the reason we played so good at home was we were so glad not to have to get on those buses and ride four states over.

Like most everything else that seemed negative, those bus rides had their positives. They weren't all bad. I felt I got to know something about our players in those close quarters that I might otherwise not have known.

Among other things, you can identify those who use a deodorant and those who don't. You learn who reads school books and who reads comic books. You get to the point you can identify a player by the way he snores. Some guys stay up all night and chatter. Others get up in the baggage rack and sleep. Dr. Swint used that tiny flashlight of his to read Tolstoy. He and I never slept.

You get to know who can play cards and who can sing and who can't carry a tune in a bucket.

A certain togetherness was developed on that bus. I got to know another side of our players. We had an opportunity to talk about things other than football.

Tennessee Tech came to our house the following Saturday and we whipped them, 34-0. We started a new winning streak at home that wouldn't quit for the next five years.

But I still wasn't happy with the turnout of our folks who said back in the early 1980s they'd come see the Eagles play. I didn't think we were getting the fan response we should have been getting in accordance to what we were doing on the field. We were winning. We had won in 1984 and by hard work and luck, we were giving those who said, "Bring us football," a 5-1 season when Bethune-Cookman came to Statesboro and we beat them, 46-26. Ham threw for 130 yards, Ricky Harris ran for 154 and Foley put it in the air and between the uprights for three field goals.

Why weren't the patrons at the game? I realize now that attracting new fans simply takes time. It would come. I was just impatient. We needed the money.

Newberry came to our house seven days later and we jumped on them in a big way.

We had 540 yards of offense and won, 38-17, and everybody got to play. Our guys were playing good now.

The next week we took that 10-hour bus trip north to James Madison University. It was 20 degrees, and it was their homecoming. We were playing to practically an empty stadium because all their fans are outside standing around bonfires on the hill overlooking the stadium, keeping warm.

We lost, 21-6.

We also lost Ham in the first quarter and Ernest Thompson, a true freshman quarterback, came in and directed the team.

What do I recall about that contest? The weather! Losing! My wearing a t-shirt during warm-ups, and during the first half trying to prove to our kids it wasn't really cold. And right after the game the motel manager came up to me and said he was missing 21 blankets.

So we had a "return the blanket special." And those who had felt so inclined as to want to take a souvenir home to their girlfriend, met our coaches for a long time in what we call "Sunrise Service."

Don't let Easter come to mind when I mention our "Sunrise Services." There are no hymns sung. There is no sitting down. There is no sermon. No. There is getting up at 6 in the morning and running until you are just short of a good hurt. I believe the "blanket" episode called for about two weeks of those "Sunrise Services." There were no further incidents like that as long as I coached at Southern. Not that I knew of, anyhow.

So then we were 6-2.

The Knights of Central Florida come to our house and right away jumped out to an 18-6 halftime lead. We couldn't get cranked.

Enter Tracy Ham, the second half. In the third quarter, we scored 22 unanswered points and seven in the fourth. We won, 35-18, with Gerald Harris running for 115 yards, Ham throwing for 111 yards and interestingly enough, the defense getting fired up and shutting down the Knights for the rest of the game.

During the first half of the game our offense was not very productive. When this happens, the people and especially the TV "color" men, always cry, "Poor old defense — they've been on the field so long."

It has always been my belief that if the "poor old defense" is getting tired, they can start fulfilling their responsibility — which is to give the opponent three downs and make them punt, or recover a fumble or intercept a pass. Then they can go to the sidelines and get some rest. You ever heard anybody say, "Poor old offense, they had to stay on the field too long?"

In our 10th contest, which was at home, we beat East Tennessee State, 46-7, with Monty Sharpe catching two touchdown passes from Ham, who threw for 171 yards. It was a sweet victory for us. We had gotten whipped two straight years by this club at their place. It was time to return the favor.

We were 8-2. Everybody was thinking play-offs. That 8-3 might not get us in, but 9-2 would make it a certainty. We barely missed the previous year and it boiled down to Saturday's game with South Carolina State. It was pretty much cut and dried. Win and play some more, or lose and the season could possibly end.

So in Orangeburg, we put the number 43 up there on the scoreboard to their 30.

It was a marathon. I swear it was whoever had the ball last ... would win. Gerald Harris and Tracy Ham helped by totaling over 400 yards between them.

Now we could offer a good record for those folks who made up the play-off selection committee. There was no way they were going to keep us out.

It was November 30, 1985. We were invited to the play-offs for the first time and we would host Jackson State.

36 THE POWER OF EAGLE CREEK

Pat Spurgeon had seen Jackson State play. They were impressive. Their record was 9-2 with a tough schedule. And they often sent their alumni to the National Football League. To recognize the quality players of Jackson State, check the NFL roster for names like Walter Payton.

Listening to what Pat had to say and looking at the films of Jackson State, we knew we would be going against the biggest team we had ever faced. And a program with a great football tradition, something we did not yet have.

Now in our second year of Division I-AA competition, we were one of 12 teams left out of the 88 who began the season.

We always emphasized "just one more time" in every practice.

Anybody can do anything just one more time if he really wants to. Run one more sprint. Play one more play. Get off the ground after being knocked down and GATA, just one more time.

When I learned we had made the play-offs, I ordered the second batch of "Just One More Time" t-shirts to distribute to the Eagles. The first batch I gave to the Dogs prior to the Notre Dame game. If that message helped us then, maybe it would help us again. Just ... one more time.

There was a press conference. Jesse Jenkins, sort of small at 210 pounds, and Vance Pike represented us. They wore their "Just One More Time" shirts to the media meeting. I can remember to this day, Jackson State's big old linebacker, who later went high in the NFL draft, looking over there at Jesse and Vance and in a deep bass voice saying, "Just one more time, huh?" And with that he let out the kind of laugh that you'd expect to hear from a 6'5",

250-pounder. "Huh! Huh! Huh!" Like he didn't believe there would be a one more time for our guys.

They were physically intimidating. But our guys weren't particularly intimidated, because we won the game, 27-0.

We scored in every quarter. We kept them out of the end zone. That's a tough combination to beat, isn't it?

Ham threw to Tony Belser twice for touchdowns, and Gerald Harris scored. Foley kicked two field goals for us. We had four interceptions and two fumbles recovered. Our defense played as good as they could play.

Thus, the first of our play-off experiences. But as I have said many times, victories are short-lived. We talk about the game and watch the films, point out the good and bad things and file it away and it becomes a chapter in the history of Georgia Southern football. That game is over — gone. Now let's get on with the next Saturday. By beating Jackson State we had given ourselves the greatest opportunity possible. Middle Tennessee was next.

They were undefeated and ranked number one in the country. They had beaten us, 35-10, at our house. They had beaten us by a total of 77 points to 17 during the past two seasons.

It was December 7 when the official raised his hand in Murfreesboro and things began.

This was the last game in the world.

Gerald Harris took the ball, tucked that head, squared his shoulders and ran for 148 yards. Ham moved those feet and kept his eyes open and passed for 125 yards. Our defense wanted to get off the field so they intercepted twice and recovered two fumbles.

We led at halftime, 21-0.

But that wasn't good enough. Not against these folks. They came back and things got tight. It was the fourth quarter and we were ahead, 28-21. We were on their 40-yard line and it was fourth-and-two. We had to ensure this victory. I made the decision not to punt. There were two minutes to play. We had to keep the ball. Middle Tennessee had the momentum, scoring 21 points in the second half. They couldn't have the ball.

We called for a sprint-out pass and told Ham if he could, to run it. He started sprinting to his left. And there was Middle Tennessee all over him. Now this was the guy whom I have said can take nothing and make something out of it. I stood on the sidelines watching. That's all a coach can do with seconds ticking away and with it, your very life, and the lives of your players.

Ham couldn't run it so he pushed, like a shot put, a 2-yard pass to Herman Barron. First down, Eagles! We ran out the clock — beating the number one team in the nation at their place. Suddenly, we had another Saturday to play. Our fans who traveled with us made that joyful noise.

By the way, we flew the team to that game. For two-thirds of our team it was their first time on an airplane. What an experience! I'm not too certain which was the stronger of the two highs on the trip back — those big engines as we headed homeward or the spirit of our boys who had just beaten the undefeated, number one team in the country.

I looked out the window of the plane as we circled Savannah to land. Already my thoughts were, "Thirteen games ago there were 88 teams playing in Division I-AA. Now there were just four. And the Eagles were one of them."

What did I say to the Eagles when I told them we were going to play Northern Iowa, 1,500 miles away in Cedar Falls, next week?

"Let's just do it one more time." I didn't care where we had to play. We had another of the greatest opportunities in the world. We had another chance to play.

Pat got us going with the scout report on Monday. We practiced well and I felt as good as I ever did in this kind of situation. I was scared.

The Friday morning we were to leave, I was having coffee at Snooky's, letting my mind run across what had happened and what was about to happen. It was raining outside as I looked out over our practice fields where our team had been going at it for the past 16 weeks. I thought about our boarding the buses shortly for the trip to the Savannah airport and the long flight to Iowa.

Then it came to me. Why not take something "Georgia Southern" with us?

I asked my good friend, Bruce Yawn, if he had an old milk jug. I took that jug and walked across the practice fields to that stream of water which was Beautiful Eagle Creek. I filled up that jug and put a cap on it.

Our team made the trip to Cedar Falls, where the temperature was 13 degrees with a wind chill factor of 20 below. Thank God we played indoors. Snow and ice were all over the place. I lived in fear that our boys would get into some kind of snowball fight and slip and break something.

That night we took our players to the field to let them run around and loosen up. It was at that time I broke out that first jug of Beautiful Eagle Creek water. There we were — coaches and players starting at one end zone and sprinkling it good with the murky water, chanting something like, "Let the Eagles in and keep those other guys out."

Then we moved up the field to the 25-yard line, stopped and sprinkled more water and said, "This is the spot where we are going to get a 75-yard touchdown run." We moved further downfield and sprinkled more water in that area in which we would recover a fumble. We continued baptizing their field with the spirited message, "This is to let the Eagles in and keep Northern Iowa out."

Our guys had no idea what was forthcoming. And I didn't either.

I did explain the purpose of this water to our men. I told them as night passed in this enclosure, the gnat and mosquito larvae contained in this magic water would hatch and the next night would harass the enemy, while making us feel right at home.

Hey, we had come a long way. We wanted to bring something with us which would be "home" to our guys, or be a part of where we came from. We had nothing to lose. I'm certain half the team thought a mosquito had already bitten this bald-headed old man and I was raging with fever.

The game was one of those "whoever had the ball last" engagements. We had a hard time stopping them and they had the same difficulty.

I can remember reading in the local newspaper out there, Northern Iowa had employed the services of a high school quarterback to run the option in practice like Tracy Ham.

They never saw much option play in that part of the country. And to think they had a high school quarterback who could impersonate Ham gave me at least a measure of optimism — 'cause there wasn't anyone anywhere who could run the option like him — much less a high school kid.

We only punted the ball twice in the game and had no turnovers.

Again, it was our getting and going with it and then scoring with it. It took awhile, but we did. Then they'd get it and go and go and finally score. They had a total of 552 yards offensively. We had 505. Of that, 415 came by rushing, with Gerald Harris running 179 yards and Ham with 157 yards on the run. He threw just four passes but completed two for 90 yards. But one of them was for a 75-yard touchdown to Sharpe.

Back and forth, back and forth we went, inside that dome sittin' on turf. People back home were watching on TV. Of all people, Larry Munson was calling the game and he had a great one to call.

It was a nail-biter. Not a place for the weak of heart. Nobody sat down. The fans were screaming. The place was alive and their dome echoed with the roars. Where were the gnats and mosquitos? We needed their help!

We had some fans in those stands, 1,500 miles from home. They were clustered together and they were yelling.

Time was running out. In fact, time seemed to be that player both teams wanted to stop. In its hands lay the destiny of one of those groups: Georgia Southern or Northern Iowa. Which would it be? To win and go to the finals and have another chance, "Just one more time?" Or to go home and wait for 1986?

We were driving. The score was tied, 33-33. The ball was on their 20 with 34 seconds remaining when we called that "safe" play to use a little more clock. Foley could kick the winning field goal.

But what was happening? Ham checked off. That was not what we wanted to do.

Ham was under the center and it was his team. He stepped back with the ball and ran a trap option to his left ... 20 yards untouched into the end zone where we had emptied that last bit of Beautiful Eagle Creek water.

Foley added the point after and we led, 40-33, with 25 seconds left. Brad Bowen intercepted a desperation pass, and the game was over.

Eighty-eight teams started the season. Now there were two. Georgia Southern was one of them.

It was still 10 degrees outside, but nobody cared.

37 A BULLET FOR FURMAN

Back home in Statesboro we had good practice sessions. Remember, we had already played 14 games in 1985. Our guys were excited about their opportunity, and we had to work to keep our sessions from becoming too intense.

Furman University, the Paladins, were the most important opponent the Eagles would ever face. This was for the National Championship. Pat had told us everything we needed to know about Furman.

They were good, no question about that. They had our utmost respect and they were waiting for us in Tacoma, Washington, 3,000 miles to the northwest.

Can you imagine that? Furman and Southern going at it on the other side of America? We lived only four hours from each other but we had to make that long trip in order to get at each other.

We had been lucky throughout the season in many ways. In particular, we had no injuries really to speak of. And thank goodness, we were in good physical condition for the championship game that Saturday, December 21.

We pulled into the Savannah air terminal and there were folks waiting for us — friends and alumni from the Savannah area wishing us well. Tradition was beginning to build. We had gained followers and it was good for our team to know there were those who cared.

On every trip, there was anticipation. Whether it was riding the "Eagle Special" to Harrisonburg, Virginia, or to Murfreesboro, Tennessee, there was a sense of duty that always stayed with the team and coaches. But after awhile, there was usually horseplay, a card game, somebody would write a letter. There would be loud music.

But for a long time as we moved from one corner of America to the other on this trip, the team was quiet.

I understood. Because I have to say, heading for the Diamond Bowl, as the NCAA called this Division I-AA championship game in Tacoma, filled me with excitement. The same I felt when flying to a game with the Dogs that would decide the Southeastern Conference title, and then on to the Cotton or Sugar or Gator Bowl. My excitement at this moment was greater than any of those. Who would have ever thought this would be happening? I wouldn't have.

I looked around. My crowd was seated where we always sat. The coaches to my right, me in the first seat behind where the bus driver sits, Doc Swint, our team physician, behind me. I had my briefcase, which carried the real necessities like Red Man and cigars and a good supply of matches. And yes, down between my left foot and the wall of the plane, was that milk jug of Beautiful Eagle Creek water.

As our plane approached Tacoma, there was nothing but fog. Fog everywhere. All aircraft were being diverted to Portland. But our guy in the pilot's seat looking out into that sea of white stuff, spotted a tiny opening, and said, "Hold on, we're going for it."

He got down through that soup and found some military base. The Eagles had landed! To me that was a good omen. An indication of what might take place. I'm always looking for a sign — like the following year, '86, when we flew to Reno and our flight number was 711. Can you believe it? We went to Reno on flight 711! Talk about a good omen.

We were 12-2.

Entering the stadium against Furman University would be our 15th game. Little did I know how long and exciting the season would be when we boarded those buses to go to Jacksonville to play Florida A&M back in September.

The highlight of the pre-game festivities was a nice, formal banquet put on by the bowl committee for the benefit of both teams and the official parties. The players were introduced. The presidents were asked to make a few remarks, as were the head coaches.

Now you must use your imagination to really appreciate the setting. There was Furman University, rich in football tradition, their color purple, a symbol of royalty. And there was Georgia Southern, in just its second year as a Division I-AA team. No tradition. An unknown. Our color, blue, like in "blue collar."

When my turn came to say a few words, I alluded to those obvious differences. How privileged we were to have the opportunity to compete against their great university.

Then I couldn't help it. It just came out. I told them the story of "Timbuktu." And it goes like this: These two men met St. Peter at the pearly gates at the same time. St. Peter asked each what he had done on earth as an occupation. The first guy stepped forward and proudly stated he was a poet. And he really was. He had published several important works. (This was Furman.)

The second man timidly said he was a poet too. But then he began to wonder, "Why in the hell did I say I was a poet?" He had done a few lymerics in his time, but that was all. (This was Georgia Southern.)

Old St. Pete said, "Before I let you in, each of you must recite a short poem using the word Timbuktu."

Without hesitation, the first man came forth with ...

"As I walked along the shore
And heard the mighty breakers roar,
A sailing ship came passing through
It's destination ... Timbuktu!"

St. Peter stood in awe. "That was great." Then St. Pete turned to the other guy. "Now, it is your turn." Again the second man was asking himself, "Why did I say I was a poet?" There he was calling on all resources available. Help me!

And then it came to him and he blurted out ...

"As Tim and I a walking went,
We saw three maidens in a tent.
Since they were three and we were two,
I buck one and Timbuktu."

The point of this story is that if one wants to get the job done badly enough, he will always find a way. Hopefully, we could find a way to beat Furman. Hopefully, we had a "bad case of the wants."

Our locker room was not usually noisy. There was taping to be done. Stretching. A few conversations went on here and there. Then we went out, and loosened up and broke a good sweat before returning for the final few minutes together.

Nothing was different for the Furman game. This is what took place. Except everybody in the dressing room knew out there somewhere was the biggest trophy of them all.

This was the final game. With a victory, the Eagles would return home the number one team in the country in our division.

We won the toss and elected to defer!

During the first half, both teams moved the ball pretty consistently. But whereas Furman's drives ended in touchdowns, ours were resulting in field goals. That wasn't good.

Furman scored three times. Their total points were 21. We kicked two field goals. Our total was six. Six from 21 is a long way. That's how the first half ended.

I can clearly remember my remarks to the team just before we took the field to begin the second half and we were behind, 21-6. "Furman has scored touchdowns. We have settled for field goals. They really haven't stopped us yet. We stopped ourselves with mistakes. Now this is the second half game plan. We'll receive the kickoff. Drive for a touchdown. Go for two and make it. The score will be 21-14. We're right back in the game. That's all we have to do. Let's GATA!"

We took the second half kickoff and were penalized for clipping on the return. On third down and five we were penalized again, this time for holding, which put us back at third down and 15.

We had to punt the ball. And here they came again and didn't stop until they reached glory land. The score was 28-6. Our second-half game plan wasn't working.

While Furman was scoring that touchdown making it, 28-6, we told Ham we were just going to have to let it all hang out. A week ago we had thrown the ball only four times against Northern Iowa.

We had to go ahead and throw the ball. And throw it he did! Mixed in with our regular option game.

We scored 22 unanswered points and the numbers at the end of those 15 minutes read, Eagles 28, Furman 28.

Our defense stopped Furman on three straight possessions, and our offense put it in the end zone each time they got it. That was about as good a "stretch" of football as I have ever seen.

But the Paladins didn't roll over and it started up again — we'd score, they'd score.

With 12:21 to go, Ham passed to Herman Barron for 12 yards and a touchdown. The score was 35-28, Eagles. But wait, with 7:51 left, Furman found pay dirt and the score was 35-35.

Only 3:37 was left on the clock when Foley kicked a field goal from 39 yards out. It was 38-35, our way.

There was 1:32 on the clock when Furman scored a touchdown and they led again, 42-38. Thank goodness we let them score in a hurry. We still had some time left.

A minute can be a lifetime, that is, if you are ahead. We were in Tacoma, Washington, and there was no more than a minute and a few seconds left in the season. Time flies. We were behind by four and the crowd was going crazy. What a football game!

We took the kickoff and moved it pretty good until we hit a dry spell and it was fourth and 12. The clock was down to 30 seconds.

Ham took the snap, retreated, pulled up and looked. Nobody open. He moved around back there as his receiver began to improvise. We couldn't block 'em all day. The dam broke. Ham scrambled. They had him. No, he got away. He spotted Tony Belser 14 yards downfield, right on the sideline. Ham turned it loose and Belser caught it.

We had a first down. We were still alive, but time wasn't on our side. We had to hurry.

Then we dropped back and threw it twice. Once on a throw-away because every receiver was covered. The second attempt was incomplete. Remember, a field goal wouldn't help us — we had to score a touchdown.

Paul Johnson called the play and Jay Russell passed it to Ham.

In the huddle, someone said, "Frankie (Johnson) is open." It was probably Frankie who offered that remark.

It was "third and forever."

Ham took the snap, rolled left and fired a 13-yard bullet between the outstretched hands of the Furman defenders to Frankie in the end zone. Frankie wasn't open like somebody had said, but somehow the ball got there and he caught it.

The play: "370 A-middle!" The greatest call of all time.

The score then read, Georgia Southern 44, Furman 42.

We missed the extra point. That was rare for Foley. The way things were happening that night, we needed that three-point margin. I was scared again.

The clock read 10 seconds when Ham found Frankie. That one-sixth of a minute in football action will forever remain in the minds and hearts of so many.

Victory was ours. The trophy was ours.

We were the National Champions.

Can you believe that shortly after the game, a man had the audacity to ask, "Mr. Russell, as an old defensive coach, isn't it rather embarrassing to win a game, 44-42?" I told him, "Hell no. I've cried too many times when we lost, 10-7."

Two hours later, the Georgia Southern Eagle football team boarded the plane and flew home to Southeast Georgia. In Hanner Fieldhouse back on campus, several thousand fans stood and cheered and cheered and cheered as we moved across the gym floor ... tired, but happy.

I thanked the folks for coming out and meeting us. I told them how proud I was of, and for, the team and for the community and Georgia Southern College.

I also told them since we were the National Champions, I'd like to see all those Georgia and Georgia Tech bumper stickers and window decals around town replaced by the Georgia Southern kind.

Some of the players were invited to the microphone. And while they cut up with the crowd and held up the trophy, I eased my way toward the back of the fieldhouse, found Pat Spurgeon leaned against the wall and looked around.

This was the place I had stood five years earlier, with a borrowed football, and made a commitment.

There were tears in my eyes as I lit up a cigar.

38 | *DEFENDING THE TITLE*

Winning a National Championship is great. But you can't enjoy one very long — because you've got to defend it. And it's a lot harder to defend than it is to win in the first place. It gives every team on your schedule an added incentive to beat the champion. Besides that, as we looked at our '86 schedule, there was the University of Florida ... our opening opponent.

Can you imagine a four-year-old playing a perennial power like Florida? People asked over and over, "Why do y'all want to play Florida?" The answer was simple. We needed the money.

As we approached spring practice that April, I had the Florida game on my mind. We couldn't afford to go to Gainesville and be embarrassed.

I began trying to think of something that would stimulate our team to greater heights of performance against the Gators. Something that would stoke their fires and get them ready for the game of their lives.

I had played against them four years while at Auburn, and had coached against them five years at Auburn, one year at Vanderbilt and 17 while at Georgia. So I had a natural, built-in dislike for the Gators. But my players had no such experience and I was looking for something we could hang our hats on ... to go to war with.

I wanted to feature the Gators the very first day of our spring practice. Honestly, that very day the headlines carried the story of how "Coach" Ronald Reagan had ordered Libya bombed and strafed in an effort to get rid of that idiot, Khadafy, who was screwing things up over there. I saw that incident as my opportunity to stimulate the squad's dislike for the Gators.

That afternoon as we met for our first practice session, I called them together and said, "Men, we are all aware that we open with Florida in a few months. I'd just like for y'all to know that S.O.B. Khadafy went to the University of Florida."

Then I had to spend the next 10 minutes explaining who Khadafy was.

We had a good spring practice though, and when our guys left school in June, we were all set to begin the '86 campaign.

Sitting around the table at Snooky's during the summer, the topic of Lynn Bias and Don Rogers, two great athletes who had recently died from overdoses of cocaine, came up. During the discussion, Jimmy Redding, a retired businessman, remarked, "Messin' with that stuff (cocaine) is just like sticking your hand in a rattlesnake's mouth."

That statement really impressed me. It was simple, therefore I could relate to it.

Georgia Southern was instituting a new drug testing program and an explanation of the new program would be given to the players at one of our meetings in August.

When the time came for that explanation to our team, Redding's remark came back to me, "Messin' with that stuff is like sticking your hand in a rattlesnake's mouth."

At Snooky's I asked if anybody knew where I could find a live rattlesnake.

Every spring in nearby Claxton, the annual Rattlesnake Roundup is held and I thought somebody over there might have a hold-over from the last event.

If you mention it at Snooky's, the job gets done. By the time I got back to my office, I had a call from a Mr. Norwood, one of those rattlesnake collectors from Claxton.

He would be glad to provide me with a fine live specimen. He would have it at the fieldhouse at the designated time.

When Bucky Wagner, our athletic director, finished his drug policy talk to the team, I ushered the players to an adjoining classroom. No furniture. Just one table in the middle of the room. The team came in and sat around the wall as I proceeded to give them the usual drug lecture.

Sue Colson, my secretary, had provided the baking soda which represented the cocaine. She also provided sugar cubes to represent the "crack." I took a straw and pretended to sniff that white stuff up my nose, like I had seen on TV. As you would expect, there was some snickering and a lot of yawning at this "ho hum" drug lecture.

We talked about these killers, the kind that had recently destroyed the two great athletes, Bias and Rogers. "Now I want you to meet another killer," I stated. And with that I motioned to Mr. Norwood to bring the rattlesnake into the room. He had the biggest, ugliest, meanest looking snake I have ever seen in a mesh wire cage, and that baby was singing. I mean, he was using every rattle as Mr. Norwood entered the room.

Fully one-half of our squad exited the room through the other door. We got the strays back into the classroom. I asked for the snake to be put on the table. When Mr. Norwood did, many players again left the room. My point was made! I didn't have to say anything. Mr. Norwood took his snake and went back to Claxton.

We got the players settled in the classroom once again. Then I made my final comment, "Men, if you're ever in a room and anybody brings that white stuff in, promise me you'll leave, just as you did when we brought that other killer in — the rattlesnake who had never killed anybody."

I doubt if anyone present that evening will ever forget the association of the two killers — cocaine and the rattlesnake.

I won't.

Three weeks later, we went to Gainesville to play Florida.

My Khadafy strategy didn't work too well, because Florida waxed us pretty good, 38-14. We played them better than the score indicated, but we had some problems turning the ball over and it took us 30 minutes to get our feet on the ground in the midst of all those people. This was a terrific experience for our team.

Ham threw an interception right at the end of the first half when we were going in. Scoring at that point would have been a real morale boost, but it didn't happen.

According to somebody, the 74,221 in attendance marked the third largest crowd ever to attend a Florida game. That didn't mean a lot to me as we got on the bus and came home.

All I know is, we got whipped and we had another 10 games to play. For the most part, our effort was good. Florida was simply better than we were. We did bring home about $125,000 for our aches and pains. Maybe we could add that blue stripe to out britches.

The next week we were back in Florida, this time it was Jacksonville for our annual face-off with Florida A&M. We whipped them, 35-12. Our senior backfield did its thing. Ham ran for two touchdowns, as did Gerald Harris. Belser caught one from Ham on a 36-yard pass play.

Then it was a return match with Middle Tennessee, and we had to go to their place. Do you suppose they were ready for us after what had happened in '85?

We won the game, 34-31, on a 33-yard field goal by Foley with less than three minutes left in the game. And it was a tug of war all the way. Things got off to a terrible start when Middle Tennessee scored on its first play. The numbers read, Georgia Southern 14, Middle Tennessee 14, at the end of the first half.

But we won with determination and that foot of Foley's. Then we had a seven-hour bus trip home to Statesboro. It was a night contest to begin with, and we left right after the game with those box lunches. Later, the players went to sleep. I looked over notes of the game and tried to sleep, but I never could. I had to help the bus driver drive. I also tried to whistle so he'd stay awake.

While we're talking about buses, we got on that "Eagle Special" early one morning in March of that year, 1986. The Georgia legislature had invited our seniors to the capitol so they could be honored for having won a National Championship, and for representing the great state of Georgia so well in all endeavors.

So Roger Inman, or Mr. Fix-It (also known as one of the most dependable members of our staff), cranked the bus and we headed out about 6:30 that morning for a long drive to Atlanta. We're 40 miles up the road when the "Eagle Special" gave up right at the Soperton exit. Just stopped. Roger and the "Eagle Special" had been friends for a long time by then. So Roger began tapping around and looking under the hood. That might have been the first time I had seen Roger stumped. He couldn't make it work, but he did crank it up so we could limp into Soperton and catch a ride back to Statesboro.

I called our representatives in Atlanta and told them what had happened and asked for a rain check for the event. By then, the governor, lieutenant governor and his staff, and all the other state politicians had given up and gone back to work ... or whatever they do up there.

They did give us another appointment and we were saluted and hailed and told how great we were. What a terrific opportunity that was for me to stand before that august body and tell them how much we needed an appropriation for a new bus at Georgia Southern. I didn't have the guts. We still had the "Eagle Special."

But back to the season. The University of Tennessee-Chattanooga came to our house the next week following that Middle Tennessee game and we put another win in the good column, 53-14. Our team was simply ready. We played well. We intercepted seven passes that day and seven different players did it.

Everybody was feeling pretty good about the Eagles and the way we were executing. The crowds at Paulson were getting better also.

We were still working on a good home winning streak. We knew everyone was after us. The more you win, the more people want to beat you.

I met with the players every day and constantly reminded them the only game folks remember is the last one we played. The one that matters to us is the next one. The next game is the only game.

There is no other way.

Throughout my nine years at Southern and in every coaching position I held, I always told our men we would never be good enough to whip anybody without maximum effort on our part. I'm certain at times they thought I wasn't giving them proper credit. There were times I knew for sure we were better than an opponent. That certainly didn't mean we would win. That other team might not realize how good we were. I'd rather not give my team proper credit than let them feel they were better than they actually were, then lose!

The point I am making comes with this illustration. We'd go to the stadium and stand on the sideline and I'd have one of our players roll his pretty blue helmet out on the field where the sunshine made it sparkle. It looked good. That blue hat represented Georgia Southern football.

We all stood there watching to see what that helmet would do. It just sat there. Didn't do anything. Do you realize some teams think they're so good that they only have to roll their helmets out on the field and they'll win? That's when they get beat.

No matter how good something looks, unless we made it happen, it wasn't going to happen. In other words, those helmets weren't worth anything until we put them on and made them work.

I recruited Chip Wisdom to the University of Georgia and he became one of the best linebackers we ever had there. I can remember his telling me that he thought all he had to do was put on one of those red helmets and good things would happen. He found out real quick how wrong he was — that putting the helmet on only meant that his head was protected. The player makes it happen, not the helmet.

So we took those helmets and made a seven-hour trip to Cookeville, where we whipped Tennessee Tech, 59-13, and everybody got a chance to play.

Bethune-Cookman came to Statesboro the following Saturday and we put another win in the correct column, 52-31. This was the game when Ham threw the longest pass of his career, hitting Belser on a 77-yard bomb. Another thing he did was change a coaching call at the line of scrimmage and, catching their defense totally off guard, kept it on a "quarterback sneak" that turned into a 50-yard touchdown run.

We were 5-1. And things were looking pretty good. It was my job as coach to keep my players' minds settled every week. Remembering that the next game is the only game of their lives. Right at that moment my philosophy of what was going on with the team based on their behavior was challenged a bit.

It worried me, quite frankly, about this group — especially during practice. They were loose. I was concerned about what they would do come game time. Across my years as a coach I always tried to figure out what my squad was going to do based on how they acted during those bus rides to the stadium or those few moments in the dressing room just before the kickoff.

But Saturday after Saturday, those seniors really got with it and punished the visitors or hosts, whichever. They clicked.

I learned two things that 1986 year with those seniors: first, a coach will never really be able to figure out a team based on how noisy or quiet they are before a game; second, I learned about myself, that trees which bend with the wind last longer. I told them how I felt, and they told me how they felt. We communicated. Things were okay.

I realized this was a loose team and they should be given some leeway as long as they performed and as long as they didn't step out of bounds.

The personality of this team was different. Not bad, just different! I understood that.

We went back to East Carolina, where we had suffered a bitter defeat in '84. The same service was held for us again. We lost, 35-33. It was a "back and forth" game after they had jumped out to a 15-point lead.

We went ahead by one in the fourth quarter. With just 12 seconds left on the clock, their kicker put up a 47-yard field goal that just barely ticked the crossbar and fell good onto the other side. Once again, victory slipped from our grasp.

Our two losses were to Division I teams. But like I've said, that still didn't make me feel any better. A defeat is a defeat. But gosh, I respected our guys for their effort.

We made our first trip to Bowling Green, to play Western Kentucky. It was during that game Ham put on the most sensational show I ever witnessed by a football player. Ham, I can remember on one play, started out on an option to the left, completely reversed his field and it seemed like every Kentucky player had a shot at him on a busted play. He ran 45 yards for a touchdown. That was Ham's specialty, the busted play.

It scared everybody, the opponents especially. And his coaches too.

The final score was, 49-32.

I wasn't very good at staying where I was supposed to during a game. If someone didn't watch me, I'd be a few yards onto the field. That wasn't a good example to set for the players or coaches. Many times I had been warned about keeping myself in the proper place. Well, things sort of fell apart up there in Kentucky and I wandered out too far and the official threw a yellow flag.

After that experience of getting penalized, I started a new saying and termed it KYAOOTA, which meant, "Keep Your Ass Out Of This Area," (and is pronounced Kie-ah-oo-tah). From that moment on, anytime someone yelled out "KYAOOTA," our team and coaches responded and backed off the field.

The next week we traveled to Central Florida and won, 33-23. Beating this team was never easy. Each squad seemed to have the ability to score on the other. This game was no exception.

We won and headed home to get ready for James Madison, a team which was never a picnic. They always "dressed out" good.

Keep in mind now, as we prepared for this club, we were fighting for our lives. We had lost two games. If we lost another, there was no assurance we'd make the play-offs.

James Madison came to town with a real good football team. It was Georgia Southern's homecoming. Everyone was standing and cheering, expecting the Eagles to take off and fly. But the fan who didn't know a whole lot about the game might have overlooked that strong hand of James Madison's that wanted to grab just one foot of the Eagles' and hold on for dear life. They had play-off aspirations too.

This was the only game of my coaching life I can remember in which there were no punts.

They led, 24-21, at halftime. We led, 35-32, at the beginning of the fourth quarter. We outscored them, 10-3, in the fourth quarter and won, 45-35. What an effort by our players! James Madison was good and we had to play well to beat them.

Now we were 8-2 and proud of it. But we had one more to go, South Carolina State.

At the end of the first half it was, 7-7, and we weren't doing very well. But at halftime we had a great attitude adjustment session, with the emphasis on, "Do you want an opportunity to defend your National Championship?" South Carolina State's band won the halftime show. We won the game, 28-7. And our regular season ended at 9-2.

Our first play-off game was at our house against North Carolina A&T. Gerald Harris set an NCAA record, running for 181 yards, scoring five touchdowns. We led, 31-0, at the half and coasted home, 52-21, with everybody playing.

Nicholls State came to town and we jumped out to a 28-0 lead and won, 55-31, in our second play-off game. Ham ran the ball 191 yards and threw it 167 yards. Again, it was a matter of coasting on in. It was during this game I made one of the dumbest calls of my life.

We were fourth-and-one at our 45-yard line. We sent in our "Power I" team and faked our one-yard power play and Ham kept the ball. He went 55 yards for a touchdown. This was a dumb call, particularly since it was our first possession of the game, but the gut feeling said, "Do it".

For some reason I felt we needed a first down. Instead, we got a touchdown.

Our record improved to 11-2.

The offense was really in motion. The up-front guys, those in the trenches who are seldom noticed, were making the machine go. So was the defense. Everybody was playing well. Everybody felt good.

And now we were in the semi-finals. There were four teams left. We went from Statesboro to Nevada, where we met the University of Nevada at Reno.

With the cooperation of the NCAA, Nevada had selected one of the big downtown casino hotels as our headquarters. It was the Golden Nugget. I preferred our team not to be in that extreme environment the day and night before such an important game. So I chose a quiet Holiday Inn on the edge of town.

By the way, this was another trip for that jug of Beautiful Eagle Creek water. On Friday afternoon during our warm up, we went through our ritual of making certain that water was sprinkled in all the right places. By this time, the water from Beautiful Eagle Creek had received enough exposure that Nevada knew we were bringing it. They tried to counter our magic with some water from their Truckee River. But it wasn't even close.

Beautiful Eagle Creek prevailed, 48-38.

Nevada had not seen the option very much. We jumped out with 10 points right at the start and led at halftime, 24-10. Then we matched them pretty much point-for-point in the second half. They had a fine football team. A great offense.

They were ranked number one. They had a long home winning streak going and they were confident. But don't forget, folks, our flight number to Reno was 711. How 'bout that omen? They had already chartered a big jet and had made room reservations for the finals in Tacoma. Plus they had those "zonies."

"Zonies" were the folks who sat in their end zone and hollered and threw things at opposing team. But they were friendly, which meant while they were cussin' you and throwing bottles at you, they smiled.

When we were down that way trying to move the ball into their end zone, it was difficult to hear the quarterback. They even threw ham sandwiches at Tracy Ham.

Yet, we wanted our players to stay calm, no matter what. The "zonies" weren't wearing the uniforms we were after. Nevada was. And as bad as some of our guys might have wanted to climb up there in that end zone, we told them to save their energy for the Nevada players. The best way to quiet a group like that was to get out in front and stay there. We did.

We had to go right by the "zonies" coming from our dressing room. But we put a quiet on them with the victory. There wasn't too much anybody could say about that.

I do remember at halftime, our guys were headed for the dressing room and I was the last one in our group to file by. As I walked by the "zonies" one of them leaned way over into my face and shouted, "Hey, you old bald-headed fart, we're going to get you in the next half."

I told him we'd be back.

After the game, some of our players had some of the "zonie" towels. I didn't ask any questions. We just spent the night and let them go into Reno to have a look around.

While we were enjoying ourselves the next day, a representative for Nevada-Reno was calling an airplane company and a hotel in Tacoma ... cancelling.

39

CHAMPS – JUST ONE MORE TIME

e had played hard. We had been lucky. And our guys had done a good job with our two basic rules: GATA and Do Right.

We were headed for Tacoma. Our opponent was Arkansas State and all of our coaches agreed, they were the toughest team in Division I-AA. In spite of the first place position previously held by Nevada-Reno, that year the people in Arkansas played better football than those in Nevada.

Now we really had the media on the sidelines during our practices. Every day, someone had a tape recorder or a microphone or a camera and they'd ask questions like, "Did you ever think the Eagles would come this far so soon?" "Are they aware they could make history if they win?" "Nobody has ever won back-to-back titles." "Are you nervous?" "Is the team nervous?" "Is Ham ready?"

I always tried to be patient with the press if they would leave me alone until my job was done. I didn't mind them talking to the players. I had complete confidence in our guys' ability to handle the media. We tried to coach that too.

Three years earlier, we were lucky to get the local newspaper to drop by. This was a great experience for Georgia Southern College and it was free.

I looked up and television crews from Augusta, Atlanta, Savannah, Macon and other places were stringing wires everywhere. They were even taking pictures of Beautiful Eagle Creek. But, then again, that was alright. The more they wrote about us, the more folks would come out to watch us play. And the more people would know about Statesboro and Georgia Southern.

ERK

Spurgeon got us off right and we had a good week of practice. Our players were looking forward to a return trip to Tacoma. No one was hurt. We were at full speed.

During our meetings that week, the coaches agreed that Arkansas State would be in a better position to stop our offense than most anybody we had ever played. They were a wishbone team. And a good one. Their coach admitted later they felt like they could put on our picture for themselves simply by running their own offense.

However, what they could not underline was there was no way they really could get that picture on us truly. We had Ham and his supporting cast. They had a picture all their own they were going to present.

We felt like Arkansas State, through their comments in the paper and being with them at the banquet, was extremely confident. And well they should have been because they had a fine football team. They had a great quarterback.

One thing in our favor, their fullback wasn't at top speed.

And here we were again, and I reemphasize this, with no players injured for an extended period of time during the season. We were extremely fortunate.

But now it was time to play. The teams had been cordially received, well fed and made to feel welcome. We had run through some drills and sprinkled that Beautiful Eagle Creek water over the field.

Our guys had been together — some for four or five seasons. Many would be playing their final game for Southern. Those seniors may have been loose, but they were ready to play.

During the introduction and the singing of the National Anthem, I was scared to death. That is all I can say.

So what else is new? I always was. The fear of losing was my motivation.

We jumped out to a 10-0 lead, and came on strong in the second quarter and led 26-7, a far cry from the Furman halftime score when they led, 21-6. I still wasn't all that comfortable. We did it to Furman in the second half. Arkansas State could do it to us that night.

We were just as strong in the second half as we were in the first. My worst fears never materialized. This might have been Georgia Southern's finest performance of all time.

The game ended, 48-21. We were National Champions for 1986. We had just done something never before accomplished in NCAA Division I-AA history — we had won back-to-back championships. We did it by running and passing for over 600 yards against the number one defense in America.

Through this exposure people heard about us. They came to see us. They liked what they saw, and a lot of them stayed. Georgia Southern was growing like crazy, and Statesboro wasn't doing bad either. We got a new Wal-Mart. Arby's moved to town. We got three new filling stations. And a new motel. Good things were happening.

Here was a bunch of guys led by a group of coaches who just wouldn't be out-worked by anybody. And they had made decisions that had led us to two National Championships. It's really unfortunate! The head man gets all the credit and the guys who do all the work get so little.

That cold churn of ice water got dumped on me and then I was on my players' shoulders and I really didn't know what to do.

There wasn't much time to think about this being the last time number eight, Tracy Ham, and his running partners, Ricky and Gerald Harris, would be around.

The fans who flew out to be with us were yelling and crying. Even though I was a long way from Statesboro, looking into their faces brought a great chunk of home to me.

I saw Jake Scott do crazy things on punt returns at Georgia. I saw Herschel Walker run through four Tennessee Volunteers in his freshman debut. I was in the Sugar Bowl when Georgia claimed the National Championship.

All of those things were great, but you can't beat what this bunch in the generic uniforms had just done.

Erk Russell did none of this by himself. This was accomplished by a great coaching staff and a group of young men who wouldn't be beat.

We flew home to 3,000 fans in Hanner Fieldhouse.

I thanked them again for waiting for us and turned the mic over to the players.

I moved to that back wall again, found Spurgeon and listened to the seniors saying goodbye, telling everyone how much they would miss playing football for Southern.

I reached in my jacket pocket and pulled out that long cigar and crammed it in my mouth as the crowd started the chant, "One more time, one more time."

Everything was just great ...

40 | *THE SUPPORTING CAST DEPARTS*

Everybody expected Georgia Southern to fall back in 1987. Ham and his supporting cast had departed. But so had a lot of other fine players, like those up there in the trenches who had opened holes for those runners or held off would-be-tacklers, so our quarterback could find a receiver.

Our offensive linemen took pride in their work. They called themselves the "Hawgs," a name their coach, Tim Stowers, developed with them. They were a tightly-knit group and for the most part, they were overachievers.

Fred Stokes, now a Washington Redskin, had as much ability as any-body could want, even though he did play in Vidalia's band until his senior year. But as a group, our offensive line depended upon their "wants" to excel. They were proud of the fact we led the nation in rushing offense.

Each year the offensive line would come up with a slogan. The one I liked best was in 1986. They had t-shirts printed that said, "Without hawgs there would be no Ham." Ham knew that so he let his linemen know he appreciated them.

Anyway, football fans have a tendency to follow the ball, which is only natural. Heck, who's interested in two guys beating each other to death at the line of scrimmage? That's no fun to watch! So my hat's off to those front line players who get the job done for the heroes we read so much about. To reinforce our feelings about the importance of our offensive linemen, we always gave a copy of the following poem to each of them. A revision of Grantland Rice's "The Cry of the Blocking Back" says it all. An offensive lineman can relate to this.

I'm no hero to the mob that shouts its loud acclaim.
I'm no dashing, darting ghost who gathers in the fame.
I'm the one they rarely see on any touchdown play
'Cause when the hero takes the ball I merely clear the way.

No one has a crown around to place upon my brow.
No one gives me olive sprigs, none the laurel bough.
Headlines rarely know my name who takes the heavy load.
'Cause when the hero gets the ball I merely clear the road.

Harris runs for fifty yards, the headlines swing across.
I only knocked two tacklers down who had him for a loss.
Ham's dashing, darting feet explain why we have won.
Nobody saw the avenue I opened for his run.

I'm no hero to the mob but that won't bother me.
Someone has to clear the way to set the hero free.
It seems to be the way of life no matter what we do.
Some hawg up front must clear the way,
To let the hero through.

Sitting down with the coaches in the spring of 1987, or really earlier than that, the question was, who would be our quarterback? The two candidates were Kenny Bullock, who had played very little for us, and "Snake" Burnette, who had seen limited action as a back-up quarterback to Ham for a couple of years. We had recruited a kid from Hinesville, Georgia, who was a good prospect. But he was just out of high school and I couldn't see him playing quarterback as a true freshman. We didn't even give that a great deal of thought — until later.

As I said, we were missing a lot of those big guys on that offensive line, too. We were graduated down to the nub.

Tim Foley was back for one more year. We'd need his foot, for sure. Pat Douglas, who had coached our secondary for three years, left to go into business. He was replaced by Tommy Spangler, who became an exceptional addition to our staff.

And we had another championship to defend. Everybody was going to be gunning for the Eagles each of the 11 games we were about to play. Knock us off, and that would make somebody a good year. National champs two consecutive years? I could hear the wheels turning in the minds of every coach we were gonna face. I could see them licking their chops in their eagerness to get to these young, green Eagles.

I didn't blame them. Had the trophy been somewhere else, I'd be doing the same thing, like I did against Florida. Nothing could please me more than to sneak up and knock off one of those big boys.

ERK

During a hot summer afternoon in July of that year, offensive tackle Ronnie Warnock, one of our few returning lettermen from Eastman, Georgia, and a good one, was riding his motorcycle. It seemed, according to Ronnie, that he and the bike parted company and both of them skidded a long way down the pavement, with him getting the worst end of the deal.

When the ambulance delivered him to the Dublin hospital emergency room, doctors said he wouldn't be playing football for the Eagles that year. Seventy-five percent of Ronnie's skin had been removed as he skidded down that street. And there were a few broken bones, as well.

The doctors were right about their physical assessment of this young man's wounds. But they came up short on his mental attitude and his ability to heal. Because when we opened that first Saturday in '87, Ronnie had on that "generic" uniform and was ready to play.

He went on to do a fine job for us, as he had in the past. Here is a kid from middle Georgia, too small at 5'10" and 220 pounds to really play offensive tackle. But play he did for the Eagles, overcoming what he lacked in size with a heap of desire. And out of that story about how hard Ronnie worked to get back with us and play, was a perfect example of that attitude which is, "A bad case of the wants."

By the way, Ronnie had a broken hand that never really got well the entire season. Can you imagine wanting to put on a uniform every day for a long fall quarter with a broken hand and going out there to find some big guy who wanted to break the other one?

We told all of our guys if each one of them could catch Warnock's "wants," we could beat anybody.

Catawba, a fine NAIA school, came to our house for the first game and we whipped them, 27-0. It was the kind of game we needed to open with because it gave our new players some much-needed playing time.

We then went to Jacksonville to meet Florida A&M and came out on the short end, 17-14. We started Bullock and replaced him with Burnette. We had beaten these guys in '84, '85 and '86, and now we lost. We couldn't put anything together. I felt we were in trouble. In fact, I knew we were in trouble if we didn't play any better against our future opponents.

We decided to give the ball to "Snake" so we could see what he could do with it the next Saturday at home against Middle Tennessee. We had a terrific defensive game going, but they led at halftime, 6-3.

In the waning minutes of the game, "Snake" put together a fine drive, almost the length of field, and we were down there with less than a minute to play. "Snake" checked off and pitched it to a young freshman by the name of Joe Ross, who ran it in. We won, 17-13.

Ross was a freshman playing with a broken hand, which he picked up in the Georgia All-Star Game just prior to joining Georgia Southern. He was a good runner and we felt with time and a lot of repetitions, he might fill

Gerald Harris' shoes with one added talent. When Ross got through that line, he had the speed of a sprinter. He could just plain put on those afterburners.

We visited East Carolina for the third time and lost to them for the third time, 16-13. I lost it for us. I'll tell you how in a minute.

Whereas the other two contests against East Carolina were scoring marathons, this game was a defensive outing. On paper the stats had us winning. In fact, we were leading in the fourth quarter and were trying to stop their last-minute drive. They had it third-and-four and we held them. But a flag was thrown and I found myself halfway out on the field trying to discuss with the official what face masking really was. I wasn't too certain he understood. But he made certain I understood, by taking that yellow thing hanging from his back pocket and dropping it right at my feet. I should have kept on going to the dressing room.

That flag was the opening East Carolina needed. A 15-yard freebie and a first down. They kept going and took it in with just over two minutes to play. If one of my players had done that, I would have fired him. I thought about firing myself. Self-control in football is essential. I lost mine and I lost the game for my team.

Central Florida came to our house the next week. In the fourth quarter we fought back and scored a touchdown and added a field goal to win, 34-32. We also set a penalty record in that game with 140 yards.

There comes a moment in everybody's life when he has a chance to do something which makes all the difference in the world. This person may not have been heard of before his special moment, nor afterwards. But one of our defensive backs, by the name of "Jo Jo" Robinson, intercepted a ball deep in the fourth quarter and preserved that victory over Central Florida.

It's the only big play he made for us. But it came at a great time and it gave him a story to tell his children and his grandchildren. I'm glad "Jo Jo" was there to get this story under his belt.

So then I looked at our record. The narrow margins of our victories or our defeats let me know we were struggling. After our win over Catawba, we lost by three points the next week. Then we won by four points, lost by three points and now we had won by two points. The hair on my chest was beginning to fall out.

The next week was no different. We played Bethune-Cookman and came away with a 14-13 win. It was in the Gator Bowl and Ross, our freshman fullback, ran for 130 yards. Ross was going to be good. In the second quarter, we gave the ball to another freshman, Raymond Gross, a kid out of Midway, Georgia, below Hinesville. Remember, he was the quarterback who I thought was too young to run our offense. He was too skinny, also.

Seven days later we went to Monroe, Louisiana, and played Northeast Louisiana, a team which would eventually win the National Championship in '87. Gross had become our starting quarterback. His debut was not sensational. He had 13 carries for 36 yards, and completed nine of 29 for a touchdown and threw three interceptions. We lost, 26-17.

Even with those numbers, Raymond did enough good things to let us know he was our quarterback of the future. At this point our future didn't look too bright. We were 4-3.

The turnaround game for us was a week later against Western Carolina. Playing at their place, we knew we had to win. If we lost, any chance to defend our championship was gone.

Our guys responded, leading, 14-3, at halftime and, 17-9, after three quarters. We scored 20 points in the fourth quarter to win it, 37-16.

Gross, our new quarterback ran for 115 yards, including touchdowns of 37, 22 and 20 yards. We had a total of 358 yards rushing with Ross right in the middle of it all. Our defense did an outstanding job, playing extremely well as they held the opponents to 13 yards rushing.

This game showed our players they could be a good team by putting forth maximum effort. And our skinny freshman quarterback was helping too.

Western Kentucky came to Statesboro a week later and we got by them, 23-20, based on pure desire brought on when they messed with Beautiful Eagle Creek. It seems as they arrived in town, one of their buses stopped long enough for a couple of WKU players to get off and dump red dye into the creek.

Two of our guys just happened to be right behind the buses when all this took place. They checked the water where the red dye had been dumped. They got a bottle, scooped up a sample of the pinkish stuff and gave it to our defensive line coach, John Pate, telling him what they had witnessed.

The next morning at our pre-game meal, Coach Pate gave me the bottle and told me the story. I held the bottle high for our players to see what it was and explained to them what those Kentucky guys had done. It infuriated our men.

As Coach Pate so aptly put it, there are three things you just don't do: You don't say anything bad about somebody's mama; you don't move around during the National Anthem; and you don't f__k with Beautiful Eagle Creek.

Our guys took that seriously against a fine Western Kentucky team and won by three. Western Kentucky was big and talented and we had to really play hard. Late in the fourth quarter, we had an outstanding goal-line stand. A real lifesaver. Charlie Waller, a tough kid at 6'3" and 240 pounds, made a great submarine charge to keep their ball carrier out of the end zone. If you're going to be a good team, somebody has to step forward and "make the play" when the game is on the line. We were beginning to find some play-makers and our team was getting better.

Ross ran for 143 yards and Gross passed for 102. Good work for a couple of true freshmen. Then we headed into our homecoming game with a record of 6-3. It was James Madison time again, and that was never good news. In that game Foley set an NCAA record by kicking a 63-yard field goal which stood for only about an hour until a kid from Arkansas State kicked one the same distance later in the day.

By the way, having Foley kick that long ball was one of the worst calls I ever made, but it somehow turned out to be a good one. It was really too long to be a good percentage shot, and we had only a three-point lead at the time. I gambled and it worked. You could see the visiting team wilt when Foley hit it.

We made our homecoming fans happy with a 26-7 victory. Everybody was playing hard and we were getting better.

We headed on to Orangeburg to play South Carolina State. They'd always given us a good run. But we prevailed, winning it by a 30-13 score. Gross had a total of 125 yards; Ross, 98 yards; and Frankie Johnson, who had to work his way back from a broken ankle, took it three times in the game for a total of 75 yards. It was "hurry back Frankie," because we needed him.

Every time I see that kid, I want to hug him for making me look like a decent coach.

So we had an 8-3 season, which was well beyond my highest expectations. We won several close games and we lost some close ones. When I look back at the Florida A&M game, I feel as if we could have won that one. I know we should have beaten East Carolina and would have, had I not "dumbed us out of it."

That 8-3 got us another play-off berth. And guess who was coming to town? The University of Maine, now led by President Dale Lick. What a coincidence. Dale accepted that new presidency just a year earlier.

Being the diplomat he was, Dale stayed home. His son, Ron, came down for the contest and did a nice job for his dad.

Kidding aside, Dale would have been right there in Paulson Stadium had it not been for a prior commitment. But I did have a funny feeling when we came on the field that afternoon. But not that funny. Dale or no Dale, I wanted to win. So I told our guys to show "Coach" Lick how well his football program had done since he moved. This would mean ending Maine's season during the next two and a half hours.

Maine had a fine football team, featuring a solid passing game. Buck, their quarterback, put it in the air for 229 yards that day. I'd say that was impressive, particularly when the scoreboard showed them leading us, 28-10, at halftime.

I asked our defense in the dressing room if they wanted to rest up some during the next 30 minutes. They said, "Yes." So I told them to go out there, give Maine three downs and make them punt. Give our offense a chance. They did. And our offense responded by scoring 18 second half points. Maine didn't scratch.

We had a chance to clinch it with a few seconds left in regulation play by kicking a field goal. It was unlike Foley to miss it but he did and that sent us to overtime.

The game ended, 28-28, in regulation.

In Division I-AA overtime, the officials place the ball at the 25-yard line going in. They flip a coin and the winner has a choice of offense or defense. We won the toss and chose defense. We held them three downs and they missed a field goal. Then it was our turn. We had rehearsed what we were going to do in that very situation — and that would be on first down we'd send in the field goal team and kick a field goal.

But I got chicken and called for a run. We gained one yard. Then I came to my senses and sent the field goal team in and Foley won the game for us, 31-28.

In Boone, North Carolina, spring lasts exactly two weeks. Long enough for every living soul up there to get out and buy groceries and gas and get a physical checkup and other things most normal folks do. Then winter comes again bringing snow, sleet and ice.

Seriously, for some strange reason the NCAA sent Georgia Southern from Statesboro, Georgia, where the temperature was 70 degrees, to play Appalachian State in Boone, North Carolina, where it was about 10 degrees, snowing and sleeting.

At 10 o'clock the day of the game, Bucky Wagner and I walked out on the field, which was artificial turf. It was a solid sheet of ice. I thought there was no way we could play football under those conditions.

They had a couple of backhoes pushing the ice around, trying to find the field. But they weren't making much progress. It was bone-chilling cold, and snowing. I was hoping to find a way to call it off. I suggested we go to Statesboro and play the game. They didn't buy my idea.

Without making any excuses, Appalachian beat us, 19-0, and ended our season. For the first time in over two years, we were not National Champions.

We had some opportunities but we couldn't cash in on them. Our success depended on our quickness, and we weren't too quick on ice. Running the option means running east and west, especially with our quarterback and pitch man. We never could find that sure footing to turn the ball upfield.

Don't get me wrong, Appalachian had a good football team. They were better than we were that day.

It was the first shutout for our Eagles since we started the new era in 1981. It was also our first play-off loss in 10 attempts.

I want to add, however, our coaches may have done a better job with this group finishing the season 9-4 than with any previous team. This group came further with perhaps less ability, less experience and more determination, than any of their predecessors.

41 FOUR YARDS SHORT

We were coming out of 1987, which had been Dr. Nick Henry's first year as president of GSC.

Dale Lick had won a National Championship in 1985. Dr. Harry Carter, Southern's academic vice president who had served as acting president during 1986, had also won the big title. So I told Nick at the first Boosters' luncheon in August of 1987, the pressure was really on him to keep the quality of coaching going.

Nick smiled and said, "Being a freshman such as I am with this new title, I will do my best." He went on to remind me that when he was a visiting professor at the University of Georgia, the football program was on NCAA probation. And when he returned to his position at Arizona State, they were on probation as well.

I told Dr. Henry, "You don't have to worry about Southern being on probation. It takes money to cheat. And we ain't got no money."

Even though Nick didn't win a National Championship the past year, he might have done a better coaching job than Dale or Harry. To go 9-4 with the Eagles losing as many players as we did was a great accomplishment.

But here was 1988.

We opened with Newberry and beat them with ease, 55-7, at our house.

Game number two — we went down to Jacksonville, struck hard and came away with a victory over Florida A&M, 42-14. Gross had 120 yards and a sophomore by the name of Karl Miller, who was going to start doing some fine things for us, had 79 yards on just three rushes.

We went to U-T Chattanooga for game three and with Raymond throwing for 125 yards and rushing for another 125 yards, we won that one,

13-3. Giff Smith, a young defensive lineman from Mableton, Georgia, kept his arms around the Chattanooga quarterback like they were going steady. Smith had five sacks that day. He was going to get better. In his junior and senior years, he terrorized a lot of people and made All-American.

The next week we got on that "Eagle Special" and headed to Murfreesboro to play Middle Tennessee. Gross was about half hurt with a bad ankle and I was not feeling too good about that. When we arrived at the stadium, we found ourselves in the middle of a full-fledged electrical storm. We stood around for an hour wishing the officials would just call it off. I don't have a good feeling about lightning anyway.

But we played.

They got to Gross' ankle in the second quarter and he was gone. "Snake" came in and did his best, but that wasn't good enough. Between him and Raymond, we threw four interceptions and came up short, 26-10.

So, we were 3-1 and headed for Tallahassee, Florida, for a date with Florida State. That, by the way, was when I had to leave a really good offensive lineman at home, which was tough because we needed him. But not that bad. He was from nearby Jacksonville, and this was going to be "his" game. I had to leave him at home because he didn't, "do right."

We billed this game as the opportunity of a lifetime. I guess we could have told our guys Noriega had gone to Florida State. But Khadafy didn't help us on the University of Florida trip, so I just told them this was the greatest opportunity they would ever experience.

The Seminoles were everybody's choice to become the number one team in the country. Though they had just lost a tough opener to Miami, they were ranked number five nationally. And there we were, with our sophomores, headed down there to take them on.

Florida State was the kind of team that could beat you, 65-0, and smile about it. That's how good they were.

We knew we had two hopes. One, our guys would play completely out of their minds and over their heads. And two, that Florida State would be looking forward to the homecoming dance. Both things happened.

Our guys played like crazy. Those 'Noles weren't very inspired by playing Georgia Southern and the first play of the fourth quarter, Gary Miller scored and the numbers read for everyone in the stadium: Georgia Southern 10, Florida State 7. What an experience! With nine minutes left, the Eagles were leading a great ball club. We had a legitimate chance for one of the greatest upsets in modern day football.

Florida State eventually won the battle, 28-10, with two touchdowns in the final five minutes.

What happened? They wore us down with their depth. They started completing some passes, those high jumping kind that were just out of the reach of our secondary.

You know how it is on Saturday afternoons throughout this great land of ours. CBS, NBC, ABC, ESPN, TBS and all the networks giving out the scores of the top 10 teams. "And here's a fourth quarter score from Tallahassee, Florida. Georgia Southern College 10, Florida State 7," an announcer reported.

One guy said to the other, "Who in the hell is Georgia Southern?" This actually happened on one of the networks. His partner replied he didn't know. So they put their research team to work and came back and a few minutes later with, "Georgia Southern is in Statesboro, and they won the Division I-AA Championships in 1985 and 1986." They gave us 30 seconds of prime-time air.

We didn't have enough money at our place to buy exposure like that. And I'll say it again — people heard about us, came to see us, liked what they saw and a lot of them stayed. Georgia Southern was booming. The enrollment had almost doubled in four years. Football was the vehicle through which folks found out about Georgia Southern.

We stayed in the ball game by playing strong defense. We held Heisman Trophy candidate Sammy Smith, who now runs for the Miami Dolphins, to 30 yards on eight carries. They rushed for only 115 yards. We had the ball nearly 35 minutes of the game.

Florida State's coach, Bobby Bowden, said in the papers the next day, "The Eagles whipped us in every phase of the game except the score. They beat us on the line of scrimmage on both sides of the ball."

This game took me back to 1981 and our battle against the Florida State Junior Varsity. There we were in the same dressing room. Similar circumstances. I remember telling our guys in '81 I didn't want anyone feeling proud of themselves for playing well and almost winning. Then seven years later I tell them the same thing. "Don't ever be proud of yourselves for almost winning."

However, as I looked into those faces after the game with a lump in my throat, I added, "But I appreciate the effort." And our players did give one hell of an effort.

By the way, before the game, these two guys dressed like SWAT team members walked up to me. They introduced themselves and said although it had never happened, in case anybody should call a bomb threat into the stadium, they had no choice but to clear the place out and stop the game right there.

I thought that was most unusual, because I had never heard of such a thing. But as scared as I was before the game, I really kind of let what they said slip my mind.

If I was half the coach some of my good friends thought I was — if I had been half the coach I thought I was — right after Miller scored and we were ahead, 10-7, I would have given Roger Inman a dime and told him to go make that phone call and we would have won.

I knew Raymond Gross was ready for our next game against Northeast Louisiana. Because it was playing this very team the year before that he had become our number one quarterback. With a second chance to play them, he knew much more about what he was supposed to do. We turned a close game into a one-sided affair by scoring 21 unanswered points in the fourth quarter.

Gross had a good day passing. He was only five for nine, but it included a touchdown and total air travel of 166 yards. Sixty-seven of those were on a touchdown pass to Karl Miller.

The score ended Eagles 43, Northeast Louisiana 11.

After the game, the players gave me a ball with "60th" on it and told me it was for my 60th win at Georgia Southern. I accepted and told them how much I appreciated them thinking about me. I said this only left me some 250 victories behind Coach "Bear" Bryant, but we were getting there ...

We sent Bethune-Cookman home the next Saturday by a score of 38-14. Karl Miller was playing a lot more as a true sophomore, scoring two touchdowns. With him were those two other sophomores, Gross and Ross.

We had experienced offensive linemen in Dennis Franklin, Sean Gainey, Brad Bernard and Sammy Twiggs. They helped our young backs do well. They were going to assist them in becoming the best rushing group in the United States as far as Division I-AA was concerned.

We went on to Orlando and beat Central Florida, 31-17. It was a competitive game until the fourth quarter with the score, 17-10. But then the Eagles turned it up a notch and wrapped up the victory.

We had to make that long trip to James Madison a week later. It seemed those guys always dressed out better than anybody else. We couldn't stand to lose another game. And we didn't.

We won, 27-13, with Ross taking off for 139 yards.

David Cool kicked a 60-yard field goal (shades of Foley's record field goal against James Madison earlier), which set a new NCAA record for a freshman kicker. James Madison sagged after that, and we had our way.

We were 6-2 and headed home to our house.

Samford came to town and we won, with Ross running again for 111 yards, only to be outdone by Frankie "The Catch" Johnson, all healed up, who rushed four times for 150 yards. Frankie was coming on then and we really needed him.

The Samford game was our homecoming in 1988. We gave the fans a treat, 49-21. They gave us one back by filling Paulson with a crowd of 20,340. We only seated 16,000.

South Carolina State visited us to finish the season. At the end of the first quarter it was 7-0. We won the game, 53-0. A good time was had by all. And we were in the play-offs, "Just one more time."

The Citadel was our first round foe.

They're a tough team to play against with their wishbone offense and their band playing "Dixie." But my love for that great song stopped when the ref blew the whistle. We were behind, 20-14, at halftime. Our guys got going and we won, 38-20, and then we had a home winning streak of 24 straight.

Ross had 149 yards and Frankie did his thing again on four rushes for 103. Looked to me like we weren't giving Frankie the ball enough. Funny story about The Citadel. They wear those military uniforms everywhere they go. Straight, good posture, snappy salutes ... all that stuff.

At the banquet that Friday night I was sort of moving the program along. This was a chance for our guys and their guys to "eyeball" each other without the face masks. The food was served buffet style.

Being good hosts, we allowed the visiting team to go through the chow line first. They did. About the first 20 or so of these soldiers went through the line, then stood by their chairs waiting for someone to tell them to be seated. I was impressed. I like that kind of stuff.

I was the "commander" that night, so I went over and told them to sit down and eat — not to wait for the other 75 or 100 of us.

As usual I tried to put some humor in the evening. Part of the program was introducing two or three of their top players and ours — their outstanding receivers, their strong linemen or runners.

So I called on their offensive guard — a mammoth kid — God he was big. And then I introduced our guy he would be facing the next day. When this big Citadel guard stood up, I called on one of our student trainers, but used my player's right name, of course. And there was our little guy, 5'6" and about 116 pounds. I let that go on for awhile and we all had good fun with it. By the way, a coach from a team, which would visit later when we used this same "fun format," accused me of intimidation.

The Citadel contest allowed a Southern Conference team to see our facilities and look at our program. I guarantee you this had a lot to do with our eventual invitation into the Southern Conference.

So the next week, Stephen F. Austin came to Statesboro. They had a fine football team and one of the best defensive squads in the country. At halftime they led, 6-3. But in the second half here came that sophomore backfield behind that experienced offensive line. We shut them out and won, 27-6. The defense was outstanding that day.

We gained 280 yards on the ground. Gross moved over the 1,000-yard mark in passing and 1,000 in rushing. Pretty good for a sophomore.

The third play-off contest was one of the best games ever played in Paulson, against Eastern Kentucky.

We won, 21-17. What a battle!

They had the ball at our 2-yard line going in and their quarterback fumbled. We recovered. We had 340 yards rushing. They had 318.

Let me say this about Darren Alford, our defensive end who got the ball from Eastern Kentucky when their quarterback fumbled "going in" late in the fourth quarter. It was the play of that young man's life for us, and it kept us in the play-offs. A great example of "making the play" when we had to have it.

By the way, in the third quarter Randell Boone, our "boney" safety, went up in our end zone and intercepted a pass. He "made the play." Mark Giles, a freshman who was going to become a specialist in blocking punts, got one in this game. He didn't know it yet, but he'd do it a second time in the Furman game ... just around the bend.

With the win, we moved on to the finals out in Pocatello, Idaho! This time the NCAA sent two schools just four hours apart some 2,000 miles to play for the National Championship.

The word had gotten out as we prepared for the championship game that I had been contacted about the head coaching job at the University of Georgia. That news supposedly bothered our players. I don't feel it did. In the team meetings, I told them our game against Furman was the the most important thing in the world to me.

We looked up and there came the Purple Paladins of Furman ... again. And they had business on their minds. We lost this one, 17-12. A heart-breaker.

Had it not been for the winning tradition of our football team, Furman could have really whipped up on us. Because we played poorly. Of course, Furman had a lot to do with that.

Remember Giles, the freshman? He blocked two kicks — a field goal and a punt. This was just about our only bright spots of the game.

The numbers read, 17-12, Furman's way. There we were inside their 5-yard line late, late in the game, still with a chance. We had made our only real drive of the contest.

Gross got hit from the side. He fumbled four yards short of the goal line. They recovered, and that was the game.

Do you have any idea how much difference there is between being champion and being runner-up? It's a million miles. Actually, it's immeasurable. It ain't even close. Especially when you've been there before.

I remember Raymond Gross' mama standing outside the dressing room. We cried together. I told her there'd be a time we would laugh together. And it happened in 1989.

42

GEORGIA DID CALL

Bob Bishop, the chairman of the search committee to find a head coach for the University of Georgia, called me for the first time in Pocatello, Idaho. He said he didn't want to bother me, because of the National Championship game my team was facing. But he did want me to know he really needed to talk to me once I got home.

That Sunday, Jean and I walked in the door of our home. We had just lost to Furman. We had been through a 15-game season and I was tired. I only had a few hours to pack everything again and head for Montgomery, Alabama, where I was going to coach the Gray squad in the Blue-Gray All-Star Game.

The phone rang.

True to his word, it was Bob Bishop. Jean handed me the phone and Mr. Bishop said, "Erk, the committee wants you to come to Athens and run the football program for the University of Georgia." He told me his committee felt my background and reputation at the University made me a natural for the position. I thanked him for the call.

Thirty minutes later, I called him back and told him to scratch my name from the list. I was not interested ... to go to the next name. I just wasn't willing to make a long-term commitment to anybody.

He said, "Erk, I just can't go back and tell my committee that. We want you to be our football coach. You are breaking my heart." Ten minutes later Vince called. He told me I was the one who could make their transition easy. Vince could really relate to my situation. Having been a coach, he said, "I know you are tired. Just sleep on it."

I thanked him for calling and told him I'd sleep on it. But I didn't think

I would change my mind.

I took off for Montgomery, but that didn't slow things down. Over there the press was waiting. They wanted to know how I stood on the Georgia situation. I told them I really didn't have a comment. They wanted to know if I had been contacted by Georgia, and I said, "Yes."

While in Montgomery I talked to several people from Athens, including Mr. Bishop. I talked to him two or three times. Each time he made it clear that the committee wanted me to be the head football coach at Georgia. It was that plain and simple. Telegrams poured in. I had to stop taking phone calls.

Shortly after I told Mr. Bishop for the last time that I wasn't interested, I held a press conference. The question was asked, "Has Georgia offered you the job?" I told them, "Yes." What would you have thought?

So when the University president, Dr. Charles Knapp, made the statement I had never been offered the job, I was really hurt. That's the story, folks. That's exactly how it happened.

What nobody knew was that back in 1988, I had started thinking about "hanging it up" come the end of the '89 season. And I realized too, that in my 39th year as a coach, as I said earlier, I was turning more and more of the duties over to my assistants. And though I always enjoyed sharing the responsibilities of football with my staff, I did it because that's the way I coached. Now, I found myself doing it because I was weary.

A year later, Dr. Knapp was being considered for the presidency of the University of Virginia. When it got down to serious selection, he reportedly withdrew his name, which is what I had done just a year before at Georgia.

At the 1989 Georgia Sports Hall of Fame banquet, the news about Dr. Knapp and the University of Virginia was still fresh. And with my having an opportunity to say a few words to those attending the banquet, I told that crowd, "Dr. Knapp couldn't turn down the Virginia job, I didn't offer it to him.

Would I have accepted the Athens job if I had been 55 instead of 62? Yes.

43 | ADIOS, IT'S BEEN FUN!

As we started the 1989 season, I had made up my mind this would be my last year to coach. I had promised Bucky and Dr. Henry that I would coach one more year and hang it up. We had the understanding that when I retired, I would have a voice in the selection of my successor. I let it be known to them that I preferred for the next head coach to come from my present staff, provided a strong candidate could be found there. Actually, we had four or five guys who could have taken my place. Bucky and Dr. Henry agreed to my request.

I was determined that our assistant coaches would continue to have coaching jobs at Georgia Southern when I stepped down. In so many cases, when a new man comes in, the assistants have to leave. That just ain't right, and I wanted to make certain it didn't happen here.

Another thing that was important to me was when I quit, the cupboard wouldn't be bare. When I turned it over to another coach, I wanted him to have a chance to win.

My energy level was not as high as it needed to be in order for me to coach the way I liked to coach. It was a little tougher to get down in a stance and show a freshman how to separate from a block. When I butted them it was beginning to hurt instead of feeling good, like it was supposed to. As a result, I was turning over all the coaching responsibilities to my assistants.

Did I plan a grand finale such as the 15 straight wins and a National Championship in Paulson Stadium televised across America? No. Remember, I coached from fright. My main motivation came from, and always has come from, my fear of losing. We had a tough season coming at us. My backfield was a group of juniors who knew the game pretty well. Barring injuries, I felt like we were in good shape to meet the 1989 challenge.

But for certain, I was going to hang it up after that last game, no matter what the record might be, 15-0 or 3-8.

I have never regretted making that decision. I miss the daily association with my players and coaches. I think how long this was such a strong part of my life. That's what I miss most.

I don't miss those "two-a-days" when it was a 100 degrees during both sessions and my back was hurting and I was blowing the gnats out there on the banks of Beautiful Eagle Creek.

Two other things about my state of mind at that time. When my seniors came to me before the 1989 season and told me their plans to win it all that year, it brought back to me that the difference in being number one and number two is a million miles. That's the way it is in football and in life. Being number one is the highest of highs. But being number two brings on a low that is a lot lower than the highest high.

There's no other place but number one.

Secondly, I was about to kick off season number "40" against 11 teams. And whoever ended up in the finals would play in our house. Can you imagine that?

Bucky Wagner, one of the most capable athletic administrators I've ever been associated with, brought the National Championship game to Statesboro for the next three years. At the time I thought this was one of the most ridiculous decisions I had ever heard of.

What if Maine and Idaho played in our house for the championship? I could see us losing thousands of dollars when nobody showed up to watch the game. Of course, large numbers of people had made the pledge to buy those tickets regardless of who was playing. But I wasn't too sure how those pledges would hold up with Maine and Idaho. I'm still not sure.

They weren't going to bring too many followers.

Well, that's how I felt about the deal. I was wrong, or I should say, Bucky has done the equivalent of hitting the Florida lottery two years in a row. The Eagles have been there twice with one year to go. I will say one thing about bringing the National Championship game to Statesboro. From the beginning, the very thought of another team occupying the home team dressing room has been a great incentive for the Eagles to be there. Honestly, those guys in '89 couldn't bear the thought of two strange teams playing at our house.

We opened with Valdosta State and beat them, 31-10, on one of the hottest days I've ever seen. That game was a renewal of an old rivalry.

Next, West Georgia came to town and we won, 48-7.

We moved on and played Florida A&M in Jacksonville. Ross ran the ball for 160 yards. Our defense played well and we shut them out, 28-0.

Then came that "Hurricane Hugo Bowl" and Middle Tennessee. We would be on ESPN ... national television ... Thursday night. We were the only football game "in town" for the entire country to see. We were ranked first in the polls. They were number three.

I wasn't too sure I wanted this to happen on Thursday. We would be giving up a couple of our good edges — a Saturday afternoon with a possible 100-degree temperature and gnats swarming around our opponent. Those were advantages for us when we played at home on a Saturday afternoon.

We also would play at night and I don't like night games. It meant only three days of practice in getting ready for a good football team. Then we had to rent those portable lights and there went our profit.

When the weather turned bad and those edges were gone, I really felt we had screwed up. So there we were. Thursday, Hurricane Hugo was bearing down on Savannah, and we're just 50 miles to the left with a football game scheduled to begin in a few hours. Already the winds were whipping it up pretty good at the field and it was raining like crazy.

ESPN was watching the weather report. So were Dr. Henry and Bucky Wagner. So was I, hoping they'd postpone the game until Saturday.

At 3 o'clock that afternoon they said, "The contest is on." At game time, the eye of Hugo would be only 160 miles offshore in the Atlantic. I could just see us involved with Mother Nature and those guys from Middle Tennessee, trying to keep us from running the option, pitching it or throwing it.

Middle Tennessee had the type of offense that could play in that mess. I'll tell you the truth, I really didn't think it was to our advantage to play the game under those conditions.

I couldn't have been more wrong. I've never seen our guys more ready to play. They wanted to be on national television. They welcomed the opportunity to play in the rain. It was inspirational for us to see those crazy fans show up in the stadium during a hurricane to watch us play ... all 16,449 of them.

Middle Tennessee never had a chance.

I think our guys could have beaten Notre Dame that night. They fired off the ball and took it to Middle Tennessee. Instead of Middle Tennessee having the type of offense I thought would really show up in that weather, we intercepted them twice and gathered in five fumbles for seven turnovers. Our players had reached that ideal state of mind I like to refer to as "Intelligent Fanaticism." That rain came down so hard against my face and old bald head that it might have hurt (under different circumstances). That night it felt wonderful.

The score ended, 26-0.

Then for sure we had a pretty good rivalry going with Middle Tennessee. I'm not certain of this, but I wouldn't be a bit surprised that as our seniors graduated year to year, they'd pass on the word about Middle Tennessee being the only club to have whipped us at our house and they'd make certain the freshmen kept that in mind.

I don't know that for certain. But it's a good thought.

Seventeen days later we played a Savannah State team that had great ability. As I feared, we were due for a letdown. And 17 days is a long time to wait for the next game. We led, 21-14, at halftime. They proved to be a tough team. However, we won, 35-14.

We then went to Thibodaux, Louisiana, the next week to play Nicholls State. We were behind, 13-7, at halftime. Nicholls State didn't have a very good record. I think this was one of those times when our guys thought they might just roll their blue helmets out there on the field and good things would happen.

Fortunately they found out that wasn't going to work and what they did was get out there and put it in gear in the second half. Even with that, we had to play extra hard to win the game, 21-13, and to get out of bayou country alive.

Randell Boone intercepted a ball at our 16 to preserve the victory. That's how close it was. And that still proves my point: On any given day, you're never good enough to beat anybody unless you're playing as good as you can play. I think our guys realized this now. Or maybe, at least they would remember for a week or two.

At home the next week we faced Central Florida and won again, but it wasn't easy. We were behind going into the fourth quarter, 14-13. But we scored 18 points in that last period. Our total rushing for the game was 420 yards, yet we had a hard time pushing it in. The score ended, 31-14, our way.

As I looked across the field to the Central Florida bench, there was my number one son, Rusty, calling the defense for our opponent. It's pretty tough to play against your son. I'd rather it hadn't been that way, however, somebody had to lose. Better him than me and Jay.

We went to Birmingham the next week and beat Samford, 52-7. Everybody played.

After a week of some good hard practicing, still keeping in mind that we might not be all that good if we didn't play up to our potential, we climbed on that "Eagle Special" and went on the road to meet James Madison.

They led us at halftime, 21-19. Nobody scored in the third quarter. But we jumped in there and put 17 points on the board in the last period and won, 36-21. Everybody in the world was playing us tough. Everybody.

David Cool kicked a 54-yard field goal, just six yards shorter than the one a year earlier. Ross and Gross had over 200 yards together. And Rodney Oglesby returned a punt in the fourth quarter for a touchdown, which iced it and sent us home still undefeated ... but nervous. This was the game when Everett Sharpe and Michael Berry, two starters, missed the team bus going to the stadium. They sat out the first half because they couldn't tell time. They later learned when 6 a.m. rolled around, as we provided them with a series of those "Sunrise Services."

U.T. Chattanooga came to our house and there we went again. They led us, 10-0, the first quarter. We tied it up and it was, 10-10, at halftime. In the dressing room, maybe the seniors got together and talked. In the second half, we scored 23 points to their three and won the game, 34-13.

Ross ran for 121 yards. Gross put it in the air for 151 yards.

Records indicate we had 24,578 in the stadium that day. For a long time our attendance wasn't keeping pace with the development of our program. Now that had come full circle. We were winning and lots of people were watching. In 1981 I asked for a place to play and for a whole bunch of fans to watch us. I'm not sure 24,000 people saw us the entire season back in '82.

A lot of good folks worked on that part of the Southern story. I will always be grateful for them giving me that 12th player, the fans, at our house.

We were living now with 10 straight wins. That was something new. Another first.

Marshall University, with a fine ball club, came to Statesboro for the last game of the season. They had a great passing team. Their quarterback, John Gregory, threw for 311 yards that day. I'd say they had that part of the game down pat.

The first half was one of those games, "Okay, you score, then we'll score." We were leading, 28-24, at halftime. In the second half, we turned it up a notch and put up 35 more points to their seven. We won, 63-31, behind Joe Ross' 280 yards running and three touchdowns.

Sixty-three points — what a day offensively!

We extended our winning streak at Paulson to 33 straight and finished the season 11-0. Folks, undefeated seasons are hard to come by. I had one at Grady High School, one at Auburn, one at Georgia and then, one at Georgia Southern. That's only four in 40 years. They are precious and enjoyable.

I was hoping those seniors were still talking and reminding themselves and everyone that the next game was the most important two and a half hours of their lives.

Villanova came to town for the first play-off game. We were losing at halftime, 21-13.

In the third quarter, we hit pay dirt for 25 points. For the game, Ross ran for 190 yards. Gross threw for 129. We beat them, 52-36.

Their coach was a quality guy. I know because he sent me a box of really nice cigars the following week.

Then we looked up and those buses from Middle Tennessee were pulling in and they were still full of revenge over the "Hugo Bowl." I don't like to play a good team twice in one season. That second shot is always a tough one.

But we seemed to pick up right where we left off. We were ahead, 31-3, at halftime and went on to win, 45-3. Raymond came to play, running the ball 100 yards and throwing it for two touchdowns and 117 yards. Our defense was super.

We had a kid, by the name of Lester Efford. He played behind Ross. Lester stood about 5'7" and had a butt that stuck out so far you could sit a glass of iced tea on it. And attached to that rear end were a pair of legs that reminded me of oak stumps. We put Lester in that game and all he did was run the ball 123 yards. Look out Joe Ross ... way to go Lester.

I like those types of stories. There was Lester, unselfish in every way. He practiced hard, and walked the sidelines as Joe Ross did his thing. Now and then, Lester would go in.

And a coach never knows ... because when Joe was hurt, Lester would come on and do good things. He did them because he had some ability and loved to play. He and Joe were the best of friends. When Joe came off the field after doing something really good, Lester was there to congratulate him.

For the period of time Joe had that bad knee and Lester was in there, you might have thought Joe was the daddy watching a son play ball. He pulled for Lester. And hugged him when that big butt bulled its way for an Eagle score.

The semifinals came and the Grizzlies of Montana were here. We welcomed them with a cold, overcast day, offering sleet and 30-degree weather. Come to think of it, Montana brought that stuff with them. Where were our gnats and the heat?

We had them, 31-7, at halftime ... and won, 45-15, with Raymond Gross throwing two touchdown passes. We blocked another punt for a touchdown just as we had the week before against Middle Tennessee. The greatest "thud" in the world was the sound of a blocked punt when we were doing it to them. Of course, it was absolutely the worst sound when it happened to us.

On many occasions, I have been called the oratorical equivalent of a blocked punt.

So there I was that next Saturday, the final game of my life as an active coach. What a day.

The Stephen F. Austin coach had called the NCAA headquarters and told them he and his team would not be attending any pre-game socials. He had been at our banquet the year before and thought my humor had intimidated his team. God, I wish I was that smart.

It was sunny and crisp ... perfect weather. We had 25,725 in the stadium, a record for Paulson, plus a national TV audience. As our guys warmed up, I thought back to those early years at Womack Field and a crowd of maybe 2,500. I recalled the Fort Benning Doughboys and our old jerseys and that trailer with that lovely bathroom. I took my sweater off to show the boys an old, tattered t-shirt from 1980 when the Bulldogs won it all. Maybe, just maybe, that old t-shirt with "Just One More Time" on it would come to life and help us when we needed it the most.

Southern in the first quarter was, 14-0, and we were on our way to their end zone again when Ernest Thompson fumbled the ball. S.F. Austin got new life and started coming back. The score at halftime was, 20-17, our way. They had the momentum.

S.F. Austin seized the moment in the third quarter and went up, 27-20. At one time we led, 14-0, and were driving for another score. We could have made it a rout, but we didn't. Then, we were behind. Fourth quarter ... the last quarter of football left in my life as a coach.

Suddenly, right out there in front of all those crazy people in the stadium and for all those watching on television, we came alive and scored 17 points to their seven in the fourth quarter.

We won, 37-34.

Joe Ross was hurt, but still totaled 150 yards. After the game, he would go to the hospital to have that knee fixed, allowing him a fine senior year. Gross ran for 103 yards and threw for another 113. But let's look at our defense.

In the fourth quarter, it was 34-34. Their quarterback was suddenly harassed by an Eagle named Darrell Hendrix. With nothing left to do, the Austin thrower tried to toss it out of bounds. But another Eagle, Taz Dixon, intercepted at their 30.

Nine plays later, Mike Dowis kicked a field goal for us with 1:42 left. It was, 37-34.

I watched the clock run down. S.F. Austin tried a desperation pass. We intercepted it to close the game.

Suddenly, my 40 years as a coach were over. This football team had just extended its winning streak at home to 37 straight. They had finished a perfect 15-0 season. No college football team during the 20th century had ever won 15 games in one season. And we were National Champions again.

What were my thoughts right then and there? I just stood back and watched our fans pull down the goal posts. The seniors were hugging each other and crying and shouting.

It was bedlam right there in our house. Our fans had waited a long time for this moment and no one was going to take it from them. They pounded our guys and thanked them for doing just about the finest job of winning they had ever seen.

I can remember so many coming up to me, players and friends, shaking my hand. It was all a blur. But a beautiful blur — full of those great colors, blue and white.

We were National Champions for the third time in five years. What a moment for the players. What a moment for their parents. And for our alumni. For everybody.

It was late and the stadium was empty. I was sitting there, puffing away on my cigar. By the way, I presented a cigar to each senior for a job well done. I looked up and there came Raymond Gross and his mother. My mind went back to the previous year and the fumble ... and the heartache and the tears.

I stood up and moved toward them. Get it. The stadium was quiet except for the wind moving hotdog wrappers around. And there I was hugging a player and his mom.

We didn't speak. We couldn't. The emotion was really there. I looked into Raymond's face and said, "You did what you had to do. You came back ... came back from that tough moment of '88. Now look around. This is yours and your teammates. This is the greatest victory of your life, so far."

His mama kept her arm tight around me. It was a good feeling. The kind a coach never forgets.

They moved on.

Then I turned toward the car. Jean would be home waiting. My back was killing me. So was this left knee. I felt as if I'd been in my khaki pants and blue sweater for a week. I wanted a shower and a cold beer. I decided I'd go by Sammy Johnson's and get that "one for the day" he'd always offered me.

In the distance, I heard a roar moving across the Georgia Southern campus. It was the one and only sound of victory.

I got in my truck. The local radio station was replaying parts of the championship game. I turned it up, and enjoyed every minute of it.

I stopped by Sammy's. And the Bud was never better.

MY PHILOSOPHY

One of the highest honors I ever received was being asked to be the keynote speaker and kick off the 1990 meeting of the American Football Coaches Association in San Diego, California.

Since I really haven't spoken about anything which has to do with any knowledge or wisdom gleaned over a 40-year coaching career, I'm going to share some of my remarks from that occasion. In a nutshell, what follows is my feeling about football and about teamwork:

The fact that I have been coaching football for 40 years does not qualify me to make this presentation (nor does it qualify me to write this book). There are probably some out there in the audience who have coached even longer than I have. We have had a great success at Georgia Southern, but so have many of you at your respective schools. The one thing that does qualify me to stand before you today is that the program chairman asked me to do it (just like I was asked to do this book).

I asked him how long I should take and he said 50 minutes. I said, "How about 20?" He said, "Whatever." So I'm going to tell you the same thing Henry VIII told each of his wives, "I won't be keeping you long."

I don't have a topic for this presentation but it could be, "Survival: 40 years of coaching football." My greatest claim to fame is that I have coached 40 years without getting fired and that is survival.

I'm sure you've read that Coach Bobby Bowden of Florida State University was recently given a lifetime contract by his people. That's a great way to survive, but be careful. I can remember several head coaches ago at the University of Georgia there was a very fine coach by the name of Harry Mehre. He dedicated beautiful Sanford Stadium with a great victory over Yale and went on to win 10 games that year. The Georgia people wanted to show their appreciation and gave Coach Mehre a lifetime contract. The very next year, Georgia was 5-5. They declared him legally dead and fired him.

I was asked not to make this an "X's" and "O's" presentation. That bothered me a little because it is easy for me to talk plays and defenses up here on the screen. That way I could just talk off the top of my head. As you can see, I have obviously talked from the top of my head far too much.

Coaching is a "people thing" and when you think about it, all those "X's" and "O's" that we draw up and talk about simply represent people. It's a helluva lot easier to get those symbols to play great offense and defense than to get people to do the job right.

Look at it this way. We usually carry about 100 people on our squad. They come from many different backgrounds. Most have different problems. Most have different interests. There are 100 different personalities represented here and 100 different egos with which to deal.

ERK

Then you throw in your managers, trainers and coaching staff. The cast soon totals 150. That's 150 different people, 150 different personalities. Somehow, we must squeeze all of these into the framework of TEAM before we even have chance to win.

Since "F" words are so popular nowadays and our players can relate to them, I have developed a philosophy (another "F" word), of squeezing people into the framework of TEAM using four key "F" words as a base.

1. The first "F" word is FIRM. Be firm with your people. Don't be unreasonable. FIRM means different things to different people. To me it means there are things that must be done in an effort to achieve our goal of TEAM. Every person must be aware of the expectations we have for him. All must comply. To be FIRM does not necessarily imply stern discipline. It is simply a standard, a guideline for all to go by.

2. The second "F" word is FAIR. Be fair with your people. "Fair" means different things to different folks. To me, it means basically, treat people with respect, as long as they deserve to be treated that way. Let your standards of fair play be known and stick to them.

3. The third "F" word is FUNDAMENTAL. Fundamental means basic, sound, simple. I have always been an advocate of the K.I.S.S. philosophy of coaching. This means, Keep It Simple Stupid. If I keep things on my mental level, I know my players can understand what's going on.

I have seen coaches hand out page after page of training rules, long lists of things one cannot do. Not very effective. They don't read or remember. At Georgia Southern, in trying to keep things simple, we have two basic rules. One guides our actions on the field. We hammer these on a daily basis. We talk about them all the time. While we're on the field it's G.A.T.A (get after their ass). Off the field, it's DO RIGHT. We don't have anybody in our program who doesn't fully understand these two fundamental rules. I have to do some interpretation for some of our guys occasionally. Then we go back to "F" words FIRM and FAIR.

Many coaches, when experiencing difficulty on offense or defense, tend to add more and more to the game plan. I have done the same thing. Shoot, we can show our opponent 14 different defensive fronts and 57 different pass coverages. That's not the answer. "Simplify" is the solution. Stick to basics. Stick with those things you know will work. Give your people fewer responsibilities. I'll guarantee things will get better if you keep it simple. It is not fair to your people to give them more than they can handle.

I don't know who said this, but it has stuck with me and I have used it for years. "The best way to win a game is not to lose it. The best way not to lose is to not make mistakes. The best way to not make mistakes, is to keep it simple."

The best solution to a problem is often the simplest one. Sometimes we coaches go to the extreme to make things worse.

228

4. The fourth "F" word is FUN. We're talking about people and people like to have fun. But Coach, this is football. Football is blood and sweat and drudgery and being tired and sacrifice and all those things. Football is all those things and more. That is why, somewhere during that necessary drudgery, some fun has got to be injected.

Sometimes we have to make fun of ourselves about how hot it is during two-a-days when it's 100 degrees. Sometimes we just call 'em together and tell a story that's supposed to get their minds off their misery, then send them back to the pits. My guys have heard the story about "Timbuktu" over and over. They still laugh. The story still makes a point. They have a little fun and so do I.

We're trying to squeeze 150 people into the framework of TEAM and the "FUN" word makes it easier to do.

Be FIRM with your people. Be FAIR with your people. FUNDAMENTAL things are most important. Keep it simple. Have FUN!

The thing I miss most, as a head coach, is not having my own group of players to work with on a daily basis. I miss coaching them in the techniques of their labor and I miss not knowing all about each one, personally. Folks, that's what coaching is all about. Most head coaches have to give up the "real coaching" and the entire squad becomes his group and ultimately his responsibility.

Every day that we practiced, I spent a few minutes with my squad and mostly we talked about the ABCs of football. The assistants, the working coaches, drill the team on the physical aspects of the game. I tried to emphasize the intangibles of football and their importance. I did so by using the alphabet as an outline. Can't get much simpler than that. Everybody knows his ABCs by the time he gets to college. That is, they did at Georgia Southern.

I'll ask the squad for a football word beginning with the letter "A." Words like agility and ability will come forth. I'm looking for an intangible, a non-physical word. Somebody says "attitude" and that is what I want to talk about.

Attitude is a state of mind. It is the way we feel about things. During the time our team is together on football business, I want the attitude to be that this is the most important thing going on in the whole world, right now. When we go to class, that becomes the most important. On a date, maybe, that's most important.

Just about any time you get 100 people together, you'll have three types of attitudes: 1. Awesome 2. Average 3. Awful. (We also use a word that refers to the lowest extremity of the alimentary canal to describe this group.) Note that these three types of attitudes also begin with the letter "A."

An "awesome" attitude is best described as a "bad case of the wants." We have a few, but not enough of these when we begin. An "average" attitude can be described as inconsistent, good some days, not so good on others. This is always the largest group. The "awful" group is usually fewest in number.

Our objective is to have a room full of "Awesome Attitudes." We think this is the epitome of TEAM. This is where it begins. The "awfuls" will change or be gone, so it is those "average" attitudes that we've got to really work on. I used "The Obituary of John Averageman" to point out how dangerous an average attitude can be.

THE OBITUARY OF JOHN AVERAGEMAN

To whom it may concern: John Averageman was buried today. Born: 1924 into an average family.

Schooling:	attended grade and high school and managed to graduate without distinction. Voted most likely to remain average.
Married:	1945 to Mary Mediocre.
Children:	John Averageman Jr. and Mary Mediocre Averageman.
Employment:	42 years of undistinguished service to the Mediocre Products Co. John held several unimportant positions and managed to turn out mediocre products which brought him an average livelihood.
Biography:	John Averageman never took a chance. He managed to develop practically none of his talents or abilities. He never became involved in anything or with anyone. His favorite book was "Non-Involvement: The Story of Playing it Safe."
Achievement:	Lived 65 years without Goals, Plans, Desires, Confidence or Determination.
Burial Arrangements:	John's remains will rest undisturbed by the visits of friends in the Ordinary Man's Cemetery.

HERE LIES
Mr. John Averageman
Born: 1924
Died: 1945
Buried: 1989
"He tried never to try."
"He asked little of life."
"Life paid his price."

I want to emphasize that "Average" is a state of mind, not a measure of one's ability. Those who try to be good are not average. Those who don't care to get better will remain average. Our players could relate to John. I could, too. Sometimes, I got into that average attitude rut and I would break out the story and think, "How's your attitude, coach?"

The letter "B" is a tough one to relate to football. One of our guys suggested "break," because this was his favorite period in the practice schedule. We did emphasize that each player must strive to get "better" every time he practiced or played. The one I liked was "B" is for balls. It takes 'em to play the game and it takes 'em to coach the game if you do it right. Enough said.

There are so many good football words that begin with "C." Courage, confidence, consistency, concentration. We would talk about all of those. All are important, but the word we spent the most time discussing was "communication." Communication is the most important coaching technique in football. Without communication there can be no teaching and teaching is coaching.

That's you, coach, conveying your message to your players. You let them know what you expected of them and what they can expect of you. Let there be no misunderstanding. If there was, a mistake might occur and if we made a mistake, we might lose.

You must communicate eyeball-to-eyeball with your players. Give them a picture, an example. I brought a live rattlesnake into the meeting room to show the players a killer other than cocaine. That was communication. I got their attention.

A lack of communication leads to problems. I know this man who recently visited a proctologist. The nurse showed him in an told him the doctor would be along in a minute. While he was waiting, his eyes drifted to the doctor's instrument table and he saw a fanny spreader, a rubber glove, a big jar of lubricant and a bottle of beer. When the doctor came in, the patient said, "Doc, I can understand the spreader, the rubber glove and the lubricant, but I can't figure out that bottle of beer." The doctor said, "Damn that nurse, I told her I wanted a butt light."

Don't worry coaches, I don't have time to cover the entire alphabet but I do want to point out two or three important letters of the alphabet.

"D" is for "determination" and "desire" and "D" is for "dead" and that's what you'll be if your players don't have those first two.

"E" is for "effort." This one really excites me, because all you can possibly ask of a player is to give his best effort. It doesn't take an expert to recognize effort and when it is present, success is just waiting to happen.

"M" is for "motivation" and I have been accused of being a motivator. That is a great compliment, but I'm not sure what motivation is. I think motivation is creating an atmosphere or an environment in which motivation can take place. This can be accomplished, but it takes time and hard work and love. Motivation is not standing before a group and in two minutes, inspiring them to greater heights of performance. Motivation is the four "F" words and the ABCs and the prettiest little stadium in America and the feeling that nobody will come to our house and beat us. At Georgia Southern, we have an environment in which motivation can take place. It took time, hard work and a lot of love, but we've got it.

Gentlemen, I see my time is almost up. Before I go, I want to give you just a little more information about Georgia Southern. We haven't been playing football too long and I know you haven't heard much about us. I'll tell you just like I told the student-athletes we were recruiting, the ones we wanted to come and live with us for the next four or five years.

"We're Georgia Southern. Our colors are blue and white. They call us the bald eagles and we call our offense the Georgia Power Company. (Our snap count is "rate-hike.") We practice on the banks of "Beautiful Eagle Creek" and that's in Statesboro, Georgia, the gnat capitol of America. Our weekends begin on Thursday. The coeds outnumber the men, three-to-two. They're all good lookin' and they're all rich." Y'all come to see us."

FROM THE SIDELINES

Erk Russell touched many lives during his 50 years in sports. Without a doubt another book could be published offering stories from "those many" reflecting that special time with Erk.

"From The Sidelines" is the one section of the book the coach did not see as we went to press.

I was sure he would have looked at me and said "no way." And he would have meant it. But this book would have been incomplete, had not there been a place for a few to share a story about this man: the son, the coach, the dad, the husband.

R.M.

"In the beginning — a bundle of joy, to be followed by more joy than a mother could ever wish for.

"Early childhood — big blue eyes, curly blonde hair and a smile that charmed everyone. Pre-high school — good student, well behaved and teachers' favorite. Regular attendant at Sunday school. One Sunday when asked what the class would like to sing, his response, 'Let's sing, 'Sweethearts on Parade.'

"Summer Camp — when his suitcase remained unopened and a bar of soap unwrapped, but a good camper and outstanding leader. Participated in all sports in season, including marbles and flying kites, as well as football, baseball, tennis and basketball. He did them all, and well. Fishing with his dad created a lasting friendship of mutual love and respect. They were friends.

"High school — 'Happy days are here again.' Good student, popular, aggressive. Took part in all activities, plays, operettas, etc. Voted most popular and crowned "King." All this and time for football.

"Handsome in his R.O.T.C. uniform, shoes kept shinning as they are today. Our house was always open house. I never knew how many biscuits to cook for breakfast. High school graduation and offers of football and scholarships to many colleges including Auburn and Alabama.

"To complete his term of service during World War II before entering Auburn, he joined the Naval Air Corps and served for two years. At one time he was stationed at San Clemente Island, California. He visited Hollywood and met many movie stars. His term of duty was one grand ball, but he regretted not having seen active service. Writing home regularly, each letter a masterpiece.

"Back home and off to college (Auburn), breaking home ties because trips back home were few and far between.

ERK

"College . . . marriage . . . graduation . . . launching a coaching career. The years following brought happiness, honor and many blessing with dignity always present.

"Of life's abundant blessings, the nicest one by far is the joy of having a son as special as he is."

Mama
Mrs. Rybie Russell

***

"When I get ready to compete in anything today, I always remember a little speech Coach Russell gave before every game. No matter what the weather, he would say, 'This is a great day the Lord has given us. Let's go out and take advantage of it.' Those words have been a great inspiration in my approach to competition."

Herschel Walker
Tailback 1980-82 University
of Georgia, Heisman Recipient '82
Running Back, Minnesota Vikings

***

"It is December of 1985 and we're thousands of miles from home, playing for the National Championship in of all places, Tacoma, Washington. We're losing to Furman in a game which they're dominating, 21-6, at halftime. In only our second year in Division I-AA, we're all starting to wonder what's happened to our miracle season.

"As I'm walking down to the dressing room, many thoughts are going through my mind. I almost reach the door and there's Coach Russell. He looks me square in the eye and says, 'Tracy,' then as he pauses, I start wondering what is coming next. His was not a voice of fear because Coach Russell always gave me confidence and inspiration. In fact, he gave me a chance to play quarterback when everyone else said no.

"Coach Russell put his hand on my shoulder and said, 'We've got Furman right where we want them.' He walked off and I couldn't figure for the life of me if he was serious or not. The more I thought about it, the more confident I got.

"Shortly after the second half began, we went down by another touchdown and I think most people wrote us off. Then things started to happen for the Eagles and 25 minutes later, I found Frankie Johnson crossing the end zone and his outstretched hands pulled in the pass and we left with a miracle, 44-42. "Coach Russell's confidence in me when everything appeared hopeless will live with me forever. No matter what I've done since or what I may do in the future.

"As a team, we never gave in ... never. Simply because of that bald-headed man on the sidelines."

Tracy Ham
All-American Quarterback
Georgia Southern University
Canadian Football League MVP
Edmonton Eskimos

* * *

"I met Erk Russell in 1964 and from that date to the present I have considered him a close, personal friend. Biographies are usually written in the past tense, made up mostly of recollections of long ago times and deeds. However, a book about Erk can't be the history of a life remembered; it is the story of a life that is a work in progress. I say this because Erk doesn't quit; he is one of the greatest competitors and the greatest motivator I have ever known. I was president at the University of Georgia in the years that Erk became a legend as Bulldog defensive coach. He is not acquainted with losing, on the football field or anywhere else. We were often bumper pool partners at postgame gatherings at Vince Dooley's home and (as I selectively remember it) defeated all comers, particularly our consistent victim, Coach Jim Pyburn. Winning is Erk's creed and victory is his goal; Erk is the one you want in the foxhole with you under any circumstance. I admire his accomplishments so far, and I know there are more to come."

Dr. Fred C. Davison
Former President
The University of Georgia

* * *

"When you talk about southern football coaches, Erk Russell has to be one of the people you are talking about.

"He's coached at a lot of places, including Auburn, Vanderbilt and my alma mater, Georgia. But what he has done at Georgia Southern is tremendous.

"To start a program from scratch and build it to a national champion is one heck of an accomplishment.

"It's a credit to Coach Russell as a coach, an organizer, a leader, a motivator and as a man."

Pat Dye
Auburn University
Head Football Coach
and Athletic Director

* * *

ERK

"I have known and followed Erk Russell since he was in high school, right through his days at Auburn and then in his coaching career. He is an excellent fundamentalist. His teams always featured great defense. I would have loved to have had him on my staff just to build morale. His teams played with as much spirit, desire and courage as any I can remember."

Bobby Bowden
Head Football Coach
Florida State University

* * *

"Erk never forgot what it was like to be a player. That was what made him a tremendous coach and a greater human being. Erk truly cares about people."

Jake Scott
Former Defensive Safety
and All-American
University of Georgia
NFL Miami Dolphins
All-Pro

* * *

"Erk Russell is absolutely the master of motivators. He could inspire a group of ragtag players into performing like All-Americans."

Bill Stanfill
Former Defensive Tackle &
All-American
University of Georgia
NFL Miami Dolphins
All-Pro

* * *

"At the first National Championship, I discovered one of the secrets of Erk's success. As I watched the team go into the huddle, they held hands around the circle. This reflected the close unity that the team had. Erk, through his uplifting leadership and motivational approach, such as "Big Team and Little Me," had inspired an intimate unity in his team. This same unity permeated all aspects of Erk's football program, from the initial support group to the total community involvement. Three National Championships during his final five years nicely highlight the strength and depth of the tremendously positive unity Erk inspired in his team and everyone who was touched by his efforts. And what a personal pleasure it has been for me to be a part of this unity and a member of Erk's team."

Dr. Dale Lick
Former GSU President 1978-86
President, Florida State University

✳ ✳ ✳

"When I speak of Coach Russell I speak with almost fatherly affection. I vividly recall the quietness of the dressing room immediately prior to going out and doing battle with the opposing team. Coach Russell would always walk around to each player at his locker and very quietly in his own simple way voice his encouragement to the task ahead. No 'rah-rah' type speeches were necessary as the look in his eyes and the few words spoken always provided the comfort and confidence needed to go out and play one's hardest and get the job done.

"I recall one humorous incident involving Coach Russell, Kirby Moore, Ronnie Jenkins, Hardy King, Edgar Chandler and myself. After practice one day, we had driven several miles out into the country to consume a cold beer at a place known as the Rockwood Inn. We had only been there long enough to order a beer and have a few sips when the door opened and Coach Russell walked in. And we had a team rule against drinking beer so we were all obviously quite concerned about his presence. Coach Russell with his cigar in his mouth swaggered over to the table and looked down at us and I will never forget what he said.

"'Men this is my place, you are going to have to find your own damn place. Now get out of here.'

"We immediately jumped up and departed the premises and never returned. Each of us fully expected that he would report the situation to Coach Dooley and were prepared to face our punishment the next day at practice. However, it apparently was never reported to Coach Dooley as we were not punished and Coach Russell never mentioned the incident again. You can be assured that Coach Russell never had to again worry about our presence at the Rockwood Inn."

Kent Lawrence
Tailback 1966, '67, '68
University of Georgia
State Court Judge
Clarke County, GA

✳ ✳ ✳

ERK

"My most memorable moment of Erk Russell takes me back one dismal night in December, 1985. To most GSU fans that night brought us our first National Championship, but for me, it changed the rest of my life. The game was in the middle of the second half and we were down by 21 points. Coach Russell made one of the many decisions that made him a great coach. He chose to put a freshman in the game that had very little playing time that year. Somehow he felt that a skinny freshman could make a difference. Well he did put me in and the rest is history as I caught the winning touchdown pass on our last play. That night Coach Russell won his first National Championship as a head coach, and for me, it opened up doors that have changed the course of my life."

Frankie Johnson
Former Slotback
Georgia Southern University

* * *

"When I think of Coach Russell, the one thing that comes to mind most often is respect. The great amount of respect that I have for him, not only as a coach, but as a person also. In Coach Russell, you have a man who genuinely cares for his players and treats them with respect and as young men, which is reflected by his one rule: 'Do Right.' This rule puts responsibility on the individual players and as a result I think that it instills an awful lot of self respect in his players as well."

Vance Pike
Former Offensive Lineman
and All-American
Georgia Southern University

* * *

"Coach Russell is a player's coach and a parent's dream. A man who is your friend as well as your coach. I feel that every college football player should have the opportunity to play under him and be a part of this unique experience."

Raymond Gross
Former Quarterback
Georgia Southern University

* * *

238

"It was December 29, 1989, and six seconds were left in the first half of the Montana game. We had the ball at mid-field and the clock was running. I signaled for Raymond Gross to call time out. From my left the intimidating bald-headed figure came rushing at me shouting, 'What are you doing?' I thought to myself, OK, now I've really screwed up. It was obvious the man just wanted to let the clock run out and go in at halftime leading, 24-7. I looked at him and said, 'We might as well take a shot at it.' He said, 'Well, do it then.'

"We lined up in the Big Ben formation. Raymond rolled out to the right and threw the ball to the end zone. There were three Montana guys and three Eagles. The ball was tipped by Karl Miller right into the hands of Donnie Allen. Touchdown!!

"There was a mad celebration. Dad calmly walked over, put his hand on my shoulder and said, 'Great call Jay.' To me that was the ultimate compliment."

Jay Russell
Son and
Assistant Coach
Georgia Southern University

* * *

"The first time I remember meeting Erk was at Auburn when he was coaching Grady High School and had come down for a visit. He was sitting in my apartment. My first impressions were he was a gregarious person and you couldn't help but notice his bald head and the fact that he had a can of beer and a cigar and he appeared to be thoroughly enjoying himself.

"That first impression has characterized Erk more than anything else during the 30-plus years I have had the privilege of knowing him. He was generally always happy, offering a great sense of humor. He loved to tell and listen to a good joke. He thoroughly enjoyed a can of beer and a big cigar. He even got me to the point that after a good meal or as part of a celebration, there was nothing that tasted better than a big, first-class cigar!

"We coached at Auburn together and I recall we were going out to San Francisco for the national coaches convention. While we were waiting for the plane in Atlanta, Erk received a call from Vanderbilt. At which time, he left to join Jack Green's staff as defensive coordinator. I knew he was serious about leaving when he passed up a wonderful opportunity to stop by Las Vegas on the way back from the clinic.

"Erk loved to gamble. Perhaps it was part of his competitive instinct. He loved the horses, the dogs, the cards and perhaps most of all 'rolling the bones.' He was a sight to see at a crap table. His adrenaline was flowing and he was fun to watch and to listen to as he talked to the dice.

"The next time I heard from Erk was when I had accepted the head coaching job at Georgia. He called me while he was in Atlanta recruiting for Vanderbilt. He said, as only Erk could say it, 'Hey Vince, how about a job?'

"I remember responding, 'Hey Erk, let's talk about it.' It ended up of course being one of the best decisions I ever made in my life. He was such a tremendous asset to me especially during the early days at Georgia.

"I was a young coach who was a hard driver. Erk was a great complement to me since he was older, had much more experience and related much better to the players. I was more of a disciplinarian during those early years which Georgia defiantly needed. It was complemented by Erk and his understanding and compassion.

"Erk started out as the defensive coordinator and the defensive end coach. After our first ball game, I really felt like he would be more valuable to us by getting down in the trenches on all fours and coaching the defensive line. I always referred to Erk as an 'in the trenches on all fours' type coach. A player's coach.

"Many people remember Erk in pre-game warm ups actually butting with the players. As he butted with that bald head he would scratch himself and start to bleed. His blood would really flow particularly on a hot Saturday afternoon when his adrenaline was pumping. Of course, our players always loved to see a coach bleed. It was a tremendous morale boost that got them ready to play.

"Erk was great on sayings. He would constantly have little notes to himself in the locker room: 'If you do they will.' OR 'If life deals you a lemon turn it into lemonade.'

'I remember one of the most embarrassing times of Erk's career at Georgia. In 1974, our defensive team was absolutely the worst defensive team we ever had. We had gotten away from some of the basics. We all admitted we didn't do a very good job at coaching. It was a situation that once we got into it and tried to make adjustments, every decision we made would be wrong. We ended up at the bottom of the league at every imaginable category in defense known to man.

"Total defense, scoring defense, rushing defense, pass defense — it didn't make any difference, we were at the bottom.

"In fact, David Davidson, still with the Atlanta Journal-Constitution, wrote that Georgia would need next year a three-digit score board in order to keep up with the scoring against the Bulldogs. I remember Erk cut out that headline and posted it next to his desk so he would have to look at it all winter, all spring and all summer in preparation for the 1975 season.

"There is no question this was a great motivating factor. In our Bulldog years those great defenses, 1975 and 1976, were known as the "Junkyard Dog" defense.

"Erk and I basically had the same philosophy about football: If you play good defense, you could run the football, minimize your mistakes, have a sound kicking game and play hard for 60 minutes you would be tough to beat. In fact, if you were able to do that you had a chance in every game despite how much you might be physically mismatched.

"Because we both believed in the same philosophy and had mutual respect for each other, during those 17 years Erk and I had very few disagreements and maintained a good working relationship.

"Erk of course was extremely popular with the Georgia people. He had his own radio show. I had many coaches tell me that this would become a difficult situation. To be a head coach and to have an assistant coach with that many prerogatives and that much popularity. Fortunately, I didn't take their advice.

"I felt comfortable with Erk. I respected him. I knew if I was loyal to him, he in turn would be loyal to me. I never felt threatened by Erk.

"Erk was the master of the underdog. I enjoyed being in the underdog position. People used to accuse me of always overstating the opponents and understanding our ability. I suppose in the final analysis that was true. But, it was done in all sincerity because I always felt like if you prepared for their best, that is prepared for your opponent to be at their very best, then the rest would take care of itself. I also wanted to make sure that our team was constantly challenged. When they did not play up to their expectations then I didn't mind saying so and was trying to prepare our team when they didn't play good. In any event we both loved the underdog role and Erk was a master of it with his defense.

"Sometimes Erk would complain he didn't get the best athletes, which was of course an exaggeration. I recall players like Bill Stanfill, Jake Scott, Jimmy Payne, Freddy Gilbert, Steve Greer, Billy Payne and Eddie 'Meat Cleaver' Weaver, and several others. But, on the other hand, maybe I did short-change Erk from time to time as I reenforced our offensive line.

"He always liked for the offense to have the first-class meeting room. He would take the second class meeting room or any other example that would put his defense in an underdog position. He loved that saying, "If life deals you a lemon turn it into lemonade." He carried that philosophy to Georgia Southern where it was extremely effective as he began building a program from scratch.

"Erk was the life of the party. He would traditionally play Santa Claus starting with the first one in the Sun Bowl out in El Paso, Texas. Every Christmas Erk was Santa Claus with his big, "Ho-ho-ho." John Kasey, who has been our Santa Claus since Erk left, was his helper.

"It was tough losing Erk after 17 years. I sensed it was time for him to have a new challenge. I will have to say as I have many times before that Dale Lick, then GSC president, did the finest job of recruiting that has ever been done in this state. Much better than even Herschel Walker. Erk really loved Georgia, and the people. He had perhaps the greatest of all jobs as an assistant coach.

"But there was definitely something missing. He wanted a team of his own. Going to Georgia Southern was an opportunity for him to start from scratch and build his own team as an underdog. Of course the rest is history. What an incredible job he did at Georgia Southern by taking a couple of exceptional athletes, and a bunch of average athletes who were over achievers, and played sound football. What an absolute amazing record they compiled.

"Erk and I used to always talk about one day when we retired we would go back to the Georgia-Florida game together and sit and enjoy it. We had some unbelievable moments in the Gator Bowl. We haven't done that yet. I rather suspect that somewhere down the road we will be sitting in the stands watching the Bulldogs battle the Gators.

"Speaking of the Georgia-Florida game, I always kidded Erk because the very year he left, about two weeks before the G-F game he called me and said, 'Hey Vince, how about four tickets to the game?'

"I let him have them each and every year."

> **Vince Dooley**
> Athletic Director and
> Former Head Football Coach
> University of Georgia

∗ ∗ ∗

"There are so many stories about Erk both personal and professional.

"I can still remember the day he introduced his thoughts to me about moving to Georgia Southern. I know this man well. And I knew when he began talking about the idea, he had put in a lot of time, considering all the possibilities.

"He explained to me why he was interested in the Georgia Southern job. 'It is a chance very few coaches have,' he said. 'To start from scratch.'

"We drove to Statesboro for my first visit. I looked around and liked the town. But when I saw a high school stadium and very few facilities for a college level football program, no team, no coaches, and thought about Athens and the University of Georgia and what Erk had to work with there ... you can imagine my reaction: 'My husband has gone completely crazy.'

"Of course I didn't tell Erk that. As I have in every instance of his discussing with me a possible professional move, we would talk it over and I would always say! 'Erk, I'm with you all the way. If you want to do this, let's do it.'

"But Georgia Southern was a real challenge in my thinking about what Erk was considering doing.

"There were just the two of us. Rusty and Jay, our sons, had finished school and were doing fine.

"I remember the day we packed and left our home of 17 years in Athens. It was emotional, of course.

"But we moved to Statesboro and Erk started football at Georgia Southern . . . 'Just One More Time.'

"I am proud of all the things he has accomplished across his career as a coach, especially what he did at Georgia Southern. It was a special experience for Erk. Starting something from scratch as he described it.

"Those nine years in Statesboro gave my husband one other opportunity, I feel down deep he really had wanted for a long time. A program of his own.

"He was and still is a fine husband and a good father. Football has been our life and I've enjoyed every minute of it and have been proud to see him walking those sidelines all those years."

Jean Russell
Wife & Head Coach of
the Russell Huddle

* * *

"One day in June, 1981, I was having lunch with a friend who told me that Erk Russell was quoted in a local paper as having everything in his office to get his new football program started but a good looking secretary. So I picked up the phone and called him and told him what I had heard and let him know I would like to be his secretary (he couldn't see what I looked like over the phone). He told me to call back the next day and he would find out when one was going to be hired. The school went through the employment procedures and seven people were called in to interview for the position.

"When I went in for my interview all, Coach Russell said was, 'Well, when you gonna get started?' Two weeks later, I walked into the office for my first day and he was sitting at my desk. I waited and waited for him to get up and he never did. So I asked him when he wanted me to start work? Erk came back with, 'Well Sue, it's the only desk we have in here so you've got to share.'

"Nine years later when Erk announced his retirement I was still running him out of my desk, although he had a very nice office. Erk Russell was the best boss I ever had, 'Big Team, Little Me' was truly his belief."

Sue Colson
Eagle Football Secretary
1981-Present

* * *

ERK

"After my first staff meeting with Coach Russell in 1985, I knew I was at the right place. Coach took a ball of chew out of his mouth, sat it on the table for later use, lit a cigar and said, 'Men what I want our team to do this spring is just run into each other.' We proceeded that spring with this three yard-and-a-cloud-of-dust approached referred to by Georgia Southern coaches past and present as 'Erk Ball.'

"Coach Russell had a great knack for simplicity. He could simplify complex situations in a manner that made everyone involved a believer. This simple hard-nosed, jaw-to-jaw, check-to-check philosophy laid the foundation for Georgia Southern's first National Championship in 1985, and for others to come."

> **Tim Stowers**
> Georgia Southern University
> Offensive Line Coach 1985-1987
> Offensive Coordinator 1987-1989
> Head Football Coach 1990-Present

✳ ✳ ✳

"Erk Russell, due to his unique appearance and his high visibility, is recognized by nearly everyone. In my 10-plus years of traveling with Erk, it never ceases to amaze me at the number of people who acknowledge his presence. Erk and I have never driven down I-16 in the daylight that some car hasn't pulled along the side and waved to Coach Russell. The most unusual and as you will read, the absolute funniest incident that ever happened in this regard took place on a day that Erk and I had taken the seniors of the 1989 National Championship team to the Georgia's Capitol to permit the State House of Representatives and Senate to honor them. Our good friend, Morris Lupton, met us there for the occasion. Morris, Erk and I were leaving the Capitol building after the ceremony. As we entered the elevator, a well-dressed businessman in his 50s noticed Erk and moved from the back of the elevator to the front where Erk, Morris and I stood. The man looked at Erk and said, 'Coach Russell, you probably don't remember me?'

"Morris and I really paid little attention because this was a common occurrence when you were with Erk. Erk, in his usual compassionate way, acknowledged that he didn't recall the man. The man said, 'I lived down the street from you in Athens.' Erk took a long look at this guy trying to place him.

"About that time the elevator stopped. The man then blurted out, 'Don't you remember? Your dog screwed mine.'

"As the door of the elevator opened, Morris and I just fell out laughing. As I turned around, Erk, straight-faced said, 'By golly, I do remember that.'

244

"Morris and I had to get out of the building. Once outside, Morris laughed so hard his face got completely red, I thought I was going to lose him. I laughed so hard my stomach hurt. Erk, upon getting outside and seeing us, completely broke down laughing to the degree that tears filled his eyes.

"Everybody knew Erk, some better than others. . ."

Bucky Wagner
Athletic Director
Georgia Southern University

* * *

"Erskine Russell was a wonderful teacher. His subject matter was college football and his classroom, the gridiron. His commitment was neither a job nor a profession; it was a way of life. His colleagues envied his broad knowledge of the game, but his genius was motivation. Erk inspired young men to overachieve, and he did this in typical Erk-fashion: tough but warm, confrontational yet cerebral, serious yet witty. Most importantly, Coach Russell conveyed to his players that he genuinely cared for them — even though he would work them to utter exhaustion. Yes, I loved that damn baldheaded fellow with the cigar, and always will."

Dr. Tommy Lawhorne, M.D.
Academic All-American
Linebacker 1965-67
University of Georgia

* * *

"As I staggered into the coffee shop at the Ramada Inn in Jacksonville that Saturday morning shortly before 7 a.m., I was haggard and drawn and felt terrible as I usually did on Georgia road trips. For many years I had been working Georgia football while living in Tennessee. Many Friday nights I sat in airports up north, trying to get the first possible plane out on Saturday mornings or the last possible plane out on Friday night.

"On this weekend in 1975, my two early morning coffee drinking companions were waiting for me: Erk Russell and Bill Pace. Pace smoked cigarettes as fast as he drank coffee, and Erk and I always exchanged big cigars on every road trip. We started our usual coffee drinking contest that morning and immediately Bill Pace got out in front. He always did. With the score something like 11 cups to eight cups to six, and with all the smoke pouring out of our booth, we finally got around to the game that day against the Gators. Erk said, 'Munts, we may do something today that you should watch for.' He then pulled a paper napkin out of the container and took out a pen. Bill Pace said that Florida didn't know that our tight end Appleby was an ex-high school quarterback. Together the two of them took that napkin and diagramed that end-around pass play they had come up with to use sometime during the game that day. The play worked.

"That is the only play I can ever remember being drawn up for me on a napkin in my whole life. Never had it been done by any team in any league in any city anywhere. Erk never had much to say on the morning of a game on the road, but if I told him I had just gotten in and hadn't even been in bed for 48 hours, he would answer everything that I threw at him. I suppose that exchanging cigars with Erk Russell for 20-odd years should be the main story. But the fact that just once, he showed me something that the Dawgs had worked on to throw at Florida and that play turned out to be such a stunning success. I think that the paper napkin down in Jacksonville will always stick in my mind. More than the cigars."

Larry Munson
"Voice" of the Georgia Bulldogs

* * *

"I had spent a week recruiting in Georgia for Southern Methodist University in the fall of 1990. It was dad's first season as a retired coach. Tim Stowers was the head Eagle.

"Before I flew back to Texas, I went on to Statesboro for the weekend. It was the Saturday Georgia Southern was into their second playoff game against Idaho. The contest was Idaho proceeding to beat the slop out of the Eagles, but with the Eagles continuing to come up with the play that kept them in the game. "There I was standing by my father in his spot in the end zone and here came that Idaho club down the field. They were getting closer to pay dirt when dad said, 'We got to have a turnover, right now.'

"Would you believe within the next three plays, one of those Idaho runners let the ball loose and the Eagles recovered?

"In the second half, we had gone up to the Boosters' booth and were looking down on the field where those Idaho guys were at it again. And it was getting late in the game and they were driving. Driving. Doing good!

"It was then dad said, 'We got to have a fumble,' sort of mumbling it. I asked him what he said. He repeated out loud, 'We got to have fumble.' And with that everybody around my father started sort of chanting, 'We got to have a fumble.' 'We got to have a fumble.'

"The Idaho quarterback dropped back and hit his receiver crossing into the Eagle secondary. The catch was made. But just about two seconds following the catch came the hit of the game when an Eagle just popped the hang out of that Idaho receiver and with that the Eagles recovered and stopped the drive.

"I turned to my father and said, 'That's the damnedest thing I've ever seen.'

"He looked at me and said, 'Son, down here, you got to just believe that sort of thing is going to happen.'

"It's been great having this man as my father and as my coach. He really keeps life interesting . . ."

> **Rusty Russell**
> Linebacker Coach
> Southern Methodist University
> Linebacker
> University of Georgia 1973-1975
> Honorable Mention
> All Southeastern Conference

* * *

"I have seen him standing on the sideline at Georgia, blood dripping from that head of skin from bashing heads with some of his Junkyard types. Always the macho man, muscles bulging, veins in his neck standing out like ropes and his strident voice carrying out over the field. He never asked anything of his men that he didn't ask of himself.

"I was particularly angered when the Georgia people denied that he had ever been offered Dooley's job, when I knew darn well he had been offered it. I was pleased when he made the point that he had indeed turned it down, and he wanted the record straight. Good for him.

"Then I think back to the Tacoma Dome, and something a little personal, for Furman is still the old school to me. I must admit it strained at my heart to see Georgia Southern come back and beat the old school from such a deficit. It was one of the most remarkable comebacks I ever have seen, an offensive surge pulled off by a team coached by a man whose stock in trade was defense.

"Just say that when I see an Erk Russell, I know that I am seeing a M-A-N."

> **Furman Bisher**
> Executive Sports Editor
> The Atlanta Journal

* * *

As a member of the original group attempting to bring football back to Georgia Southern College, I knew the excitement level was high, the area was willing to support it and that football would be a success at the Division II level. The decision was made to bring football back. The conversation then began to center around Erk Russell, the defensive coordinator for the University of Georgia, being the head coach of this new program.

Having doubts about such a rumor, I called Coach Russell to put my doubts to rest. From that conversation and the questions Coach Russell asked about the area, I knew he was giving serious consideration to moving to Georgia Southern. I also knew that Coach Russell would bring instant credibility and immediate success to any level of football at Southern.

As a former offensive lineman at the University of Georgia during the '60s, my association with Coach Russell was limited. But I knew his enthusiasm, knowledge and presence were the lifeblood of our team.

His daily presence at Snooky's has given me an opportunity to get to know him personally and observe others' reactions to his presence. He has a wit and an imagination that draws folks to him and attracks many individuals to be a part of his program and do things for him.

Many of the luxuries now present at Georgia Southern University are the result of needs expressed by Coach Russell in casual conversation at Snooky's.

Statesboro owes him a debt of gratitude that is impossible to repay. Any attempt at repayment would only bring embarrassment to the most unselfish man I know.

> **Bruce Yawn**
> Left Offensive Guard
> University of Georgia 1965-68
> Snooky's "cashier"

* * *

Erk was the most interesting person I've ever interviewed on a regular basis. He always came up with something different on each occasion. He set the tone for me as to what was to come, when I went down to speak with him in the Georgia Southern locker room. This was Georgia Southern's first game against an outside opponent and GSC had led most of the way before losing it late. I stopped by to tell him how well I thought we had played and to congratulate him on our efforts. He in turn, looked at me and said "Don't ever congratulate me after a loss. We had them by the gonads and let it slip away." After that, I sent someone else down to do the post game interview.

During each football season, I would go by each Monday to tape our weekly coaches show. He would give me a copy of the scouting report that was presented to the players. By the time I finished my work and listened to him talk about each week's opponent, I was worried about all the bad things that could happen to us on Saturday. I realize now, that he was testing me. He figured if I believed him, surely his team would also.

Nate Hirsch
"The Voice of the Eagles"

* * *

ACKNOWLEDGMENT

Like the game itself, putting together a book is a team effort all the way.

I begin by thanking the coach for taking time to sit in his office with me for hours and doing something he has always found uncomfortable — talking about himself.

Yet, on this occasion, because so many were ready to read what had gone on in that bald head, he, midst answering the phone, stuffing a "chaw" or pulling on one of those mighty cigars, took me back to a small town in Alabama and began sharing his story.

Erk is a patient man. I found this out on each occasion we met with "the box" as he unlovingly referred to the tape recorder.

Before we finished our time together, he actually would have risen from his chair and had shown me how a quarterback pivoted properly; would have stuck one of his massive arms into an ancient file cabinet and pulled out the very document needed at that time; and would have really given me every ounce of his scowl when I asked a dumb question.

I am proud to have had the privilege of sitting and listening to "the legend" as he talked about the good times and the tough times.

Often, midst trying to recall a play or a player or a detail of a game, he would look right at me and say, "for the life of me, I don't know why were doing all this."

I came away from this experience of being with Erk, knowing two things: he has no earthly idea the everlasting impression he has made on so many; and he, without a doubt is the best storyteller I have ever known.

Roy Akins, my long time friend and partner in this venture, and I had to really talk to "the coach" before he consented to this book. "I don't want folks to think I'm bragging," he said.

We assured him the readers wouldn't!

To Roy, a genuine thanks for believing in the project, for his suggestions and for his encouragement throughout the months. The name Roy Akins is synonymous with Eagle Sports in the south. I am grateful to Roy's Uncle Lewell who took time to read the script and add his touch. Lewell truly knows the context of being tough in the trenches.

To Claude Felton, Sports Information Director at the University of Georgia and his Administrative Assistant Karleen Lawrence, for details and caring, and to Frank Fortune, Director of Photography at Georgia Southern University for his pictorial offerings, all three of you are appreciated greatly.

To Chuck Perry and Jill Dible of Longstreet Press. I could not have made it without your support.

To the talent of Southeastern Marketing: Elizabeth and Robin for their creative help, to Peri, a special friend, for adding polish to the script and especially to Kim Rogers for her hours of hanging in their with the coach and me as she unscrambled our scribblings ... thank you all for devotion to the project.

And to Sue Colson, Erk's secretary for eight years, I do appreciate her sense of humor and calm during the hundreds of phone calls from a frustrated me; and the same for Jean Russell, Erk's bride. I was blessed with her love for this book by her man.

Finally, to my family: Rich and Jan and their son Micah, whose outlook on life lets me know how to keep things straight; to Joe and Deanne, for always "being there" so many times when it rained and to Mark for his charm and wit, and to the mother of this warm and wonderful gathering who once upon a time read one of my poems, thank you'all and I love you.

"Feelings" to the others with whom I share this moment... you know who you are.

Ric Mandes
1991